Praise for

The Farmers Market Cookbook

You know how you go to the farmers market,
you buy all sorts of amazing produce but never know what
to do with it all when you get home? Well, this book is what.
Its advice is clear and instructive, its recipes delicious and,
most importantly, manageable. Along with all those wonderful
fruits and vegetables, this book belongs in your market tote.

— Adam Rapoport, Editor in Chief, *Bon Appétit*

In this handy guide/cookbook, Shanks and Grohsgal
offer practical tips on how to store and prepare your
farmers market and CSA veggies.

— Mat Schaffer, *The Boston Herald*

A book of imaginative and simple recipes for
an abundance of vegetables and fruits.

— Omar Sacirby, *The Boston Globe*

Just leafing through will inspire you to head out to
your local farmers market and start cooking.

— Taryn Plumb, *Taste of the Seacoast*

[Shanks and Grosgahl's] collective wisdom on culinary
techniques and fresh produce has helped to create a highly
targeted guide with dozens of seasonal recipes that
maximize freshness and flavor.

— T.W. Barritt, author, *Long Island Food: A History from
Family Farms & Oysters to Craft Spirits*

Really, really, really fantastic! [*The Farmers Market Cookbook*]
offers cooking tips, how to store [the produce]
and how to use it right.

— Annie B. Copps, chef, writer and cooking teacher

More praise for
The Farmers Market Cookbook

I love farmers markets, and often pick up quantities of
fruit and vegetables just because they look so good—and then
am left wondering what to do with them. [This book] solves
this problem, with lots and lots of tempting recipes that
are creative without being overly complicated.
— Lisë Stern, author, *Culinary Tea*

The recipes are easy to follow and a great beginning for
the new cook or a great launching platform for the experienced
or adventurous cook. Great recipes enhance the fantastic quality
of the produce I receive from my CSA each week.
— Mary U., Lusby, MD

Even though I've been cooking all my life and have a
collection of literally hundreds of cookbooks, using this cookbook
has gotten our whole family even more invested in participating
in the CSA program…it's like a "how to" manual for being
a CSA member…what to do when it's just me and that
box in the kitchen at dinnertime.
— Ruth K.

I highly recommend this [cookbook] to help CSA members
make the best use of the seasonal vegetables available from their
farmers. Thanks for providing the cookbook for us!
— Kathryn P., Washington, DC

the Farmers Market Cookbook

THE ULTIMATE GUIDE to Enjoying Fresh, Local, Seasonal Produce

JULIA SHANKS and **BRETT GROHSGAL**

Illustrations by GENEVIEVE GOLDLEAF

new society
PUBLISHERS

Cover design by Diane McIntosh.
Cover photo © iStock. All illustrations © Genevieve Goldleaf.

Printed in Canada. First printing April 2016.

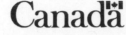

Inquiries regarding requests to reprint all or part of *The Farmers Market Cookbook*
should be addressed to New Society Publishers at the address below.
To order directly from the publishers, please call toll-free
(North America) 1–800–567–6772, or order online at www.newsociety.com

Any other inquiries can be directed by mail to:

New Society Publishers
P.O. Box 189, Gabriola Island, BC V0R 1X0, Canada
(250) 247–9737

LIBRARY AND ARCHIVES OF CANADA CATALOGUING IN PUBLICATION

Shanks, Julia, author
The farmers market cookbook : the ultimate guide to enjoying fresh,
local, seasonal produce / Julia Shanks and Brett Grohsgal

Includes index.
Issued in print and electronic formats.
ISBN 978-0-86571-822-7 (paperback).—ISBN 978-1-55092-615-6 (ebook)

1. Cooking (Natural foods).   2. Farmers markets.   3. Local foods.
4. Cookbooks.   I. Grohsgal, Brett, author   II. Title.

TX741.S52 2016   641.5'63   C2015-907549-1
                                                         C2015-907550-5

New Society Publishers' mission is to publish books that contribute in
fundamental ways to building an ecologically sustainable and just society, and
to do so with the least possible impact on the environment, in a manner that
models this vision. We are committed to doing this not just through education,
but through action. The interior pages of our bound books are printed on Forest
Stewardship Council®-registered acid-free paper that is 100% post-consumer
recycled (100% old growth forest-free), processed chlorine-free, and printed with
vegetable-based, low-VOC inks, with covers produced using FSC®-registered
stock. New Society also works to reduce its carbon footprint, and purchases
carbon offsets based on an annual audit to ensure a carbon neutral footprint.
For further information, or to browse our full list of books and purchase
securely, visit our website at: www.newsociety.com

To our mothers, Roberta and Judith,
who taught us how great food can be!

And to our fathers, Clifford and Hershel,
who taught us the beauty of the written word.

Contents

Introduction

We have written this cookbook to help farmers market customers and CSA subscribers easily enjoy the diverse bounty of local farmers' crops.

Brett worked in restaurants for over 18 years, being the chef, the executive chef, or a hustling line cook in over 14 establishments. Foods as fresh and intensely flavorful as what his farm (Even' Star Organic Farm in Lexington Park, MD) now grows were almost never available. Then, he and his kitchen staff instead had to make do with chemically intensive but flavor-deficient shipped produce. Now his farm customers eat infinitely better. It is glorious to be a seasonally oriented farmer, growing traditional and cutting-edge foods in all twelve months of the year. His family is happy to grow organic and real tomatoes, real strawberries, real everything.

Julia met Brett when they cooked together at Restaurant Nora in Washington, DC. She learned first-hand about the difference in organic produce and what it means to cook seasonally. She worked as a chef in three restaurants, and as a line cook in many more. As a culinary instructor, she helped countless students really learn the differences between local foods and insipid out-of-season tomatoes. In her backyard, she grows vegetables seven months of the year in her tiny urban garden.

We proudly disregard the absurd dogma that the market only cares about uniform and cheap foods and is concerned not a whit for safety or for flavor. We grow and eat artisanal foods, "slow foods" in European terms, and Even' Star will never farm for distant markets where looks are paramount and where safety and flavor are not even important.

The incredible number of people who buy locally make our farming possible. You actively and tangibly support local growers.

The passion of Even' Star customers for outstanding foods gives us long lines at farmers markets when our ripe heirloom tomatoes—ugly to see but oh, so wonderful to taste—are pouring out of the fields. It is refreshing to so often hear loyal patrons describe our petite but intensely aromatic and sweet strawberries to newcomers: "Yes, they're small. But these are real berries, and the big ones have no flavor! We only buy small strawberries now!" Your devotion and willingness to spread the word about great local foods empowers farmers to focus on farming. You advertise and market for us by spreading the word about the great flavors and economic benefits of locally grown produce. The gifts that loyal customers bestow on farms are immeasurable, and we deeply thank you.

We also know that you are busy. You don't often have the time to make complicated meals. We have hence kept the recipes in this book on the fast side, or at least straightforward enough that you are not chained to a stove. We follow the classic Italian tradition: a few outstanding foods simply prepared usually taste much better than a host of mediocre ingredients blended with secret seasonings and complexity.

But our busy schedules also mean that we advocate taking the time, when you have it, to prepare some of farm foods for long-term use and storage. Salad dressings come to mind: these take only minutes to fix, keep for months in the refrigerator, and let you reach for a convenient, flavor-packed aid to a fast meal in the future. Canning is great, but many of us lack the time for such projects. For a quicker solution, we advise freezing a few containers of stewed tomatoes (see recipe on page 237) or puréed basil for winter use. High summer does not really last very long, but we can store a few treats for the frosty nights of autumn or the howling winds of January.

CSA (Community Supported Agriculture) is an agricultural model built upon the relationship between farmer and consumer. CSA farms are partially or entirely supported by members who pay in advance for weekly distributions of fresh produce. By accepting the possibility that certain crops may do poorly or even fail, members share in the inherent risks of farming. This model demonstrates a commitment to the farmer, and it allows small farms to thrive in otherwise unfavorable market conditions. Given the alarming disappearance of farmland across the nation, more and more people are abandoning the supermarket and joining CSAs.

Farmers markets have become the new best place to find cutting-edge foods. From professional chefs to home cooks to food writers, farmers markets are now the destination to find the most high-quality, diverse, and exciting vegetables, fruits, meats, and cheeses. By contrast, supermarkets, even the high-end ones, can never offer truly ripe and superbly flavorful produce.

But the amazing diversity of foods from local farms can be confusing. This cookbook is designed to help you navigate through newly discovered foods. We want you to understand what produce is available, how to choose truly ripe vegetables and fruits, and how best to store them. Finally, a larder of great recipes is essential to best appreciate what the farmers have grown for us.

We thank all of our customers for supporting local farms. You are the people that will let progressive American farms thrive in the 21st century. You make possible our stewardship and environmental goals.

We acknowledge that recipes are in the public domain once printed. We encourage you to use and share these recipes most freely. We ask nonetheless that you credit the source, *The Farmers Market Cookbook*, when and if you copy or distribute any recipes from this cookbook.

Thank you for supporting local farmers!

— Julia Shanks and Brett Grohsgal
March 2016

Eating Seasonally 1

No matter where you live, eating seasonally and locally offers a different way of thinking about food. While some regions are relatively blessed to have locally grown fruits and vegetables for longer seasons, such as California and Florida, even these regions still have strong seasonality as to when each type of produce is at its best.

By contrast, other parts have exceedingly short seasons, where summers seem like spring by New England standards—places like Minnesota and the Dakotas, and Newfoundland. In these regions, consumers face much greater challenges when it comes to eating fresh produce seasonally and locally.

Eating seasonally can indeed be a challenge—especially now that we can have anything we want anytime by heading to the supermarket. But making the effort to rise to that challenge can be a source of great satisfaction. Eating locally engages our powers of creativity, learning, and experimentation. Who would have guessed that fresh kohlrabi and okra could please so many grown-ups, that greens and sliced turnips right out of the fields could

so easily draw kids away from packaged snacks?

Perhaps most important for us as food lovers, eating seasonally is glorious. Biting into the first ripe apple of the season, where the flavors perfectly match those of a crisp autumn evening, has made us stare at that apple in awe.

There are few joys greater than incredible tomatoes grown in your backyard or from a nearby farmer, brought to perfection by hot, sweltering sun. No shipped tomato, with their cardboard texture and insipid taste, can ever compare with the summer jewels. Cold-grown salad greens, traditionally the first crop harvested after the bleak winter, have exponentially more flavor, texture, and excitement than shipped generic salad mix.

Of course locally sourced and seasonally raised foods taste better. They spend more time in the fields ripening—developing sweetness and flavor—because they don't need to be picked underripe for shipping thousands of miles away. Picking underripe vegetables also reduces the nutritional value. Farmers can grow more diverse varieties, bred for quality and flavor rather than long shelf life. And though a region may experience a drought or unusually cold weather for a season, the fruits and vegetables still grow at their optimal time, ensuring the best possible taste. Picking underripe vegetables reduces the nutritional value.

Buying local also benefits the environment and economy. When we reduce our "food miles," the distance our foods travel from farm to table, we reduce our carbon footprint—the impact of transportation, refrigeration, and packaging needed to carry produce around the country. With each local food purchase, you ensure that more of your food dollars go to the farmer and local economy in the form of revenue and taxes. Buying local food keeps your dollars circulating in your own community. In Massachusetts alone (where Julia lives), if every household purchased just $12 worth of farm products for eight weeks (basically the summer season), over $200 million would be reinvested in our local farmland.

When you buy local, you help to ensure our farms survive for many years to come.

Produce Descriptions 2

These general descriptions are intended to help you understand the flavor profiles and culinary uses of many vegetables and fruits you will find in the farmers markets and CSA boxes. No single farm grows all of these foods, and there are thousands of varieties that, in the interest of space, we cannot list here.

Apples

A favorite fall fruit, ideal for cooking or snacking. They make a bright addition to a salad with dried cranberries, walnuts, and/or cheese. Refrigerator storage helps them maintain their texture, though they can handle a few days on the counter.

Crispin
Good eating apple, first-class cider and sauce. Green fruit ripens to yellow.

Empire
A cross between a Macintosh and Red Delicious, these are perfect eating apples with a crisp texture and white flesh, with a floral scent.

Fuji
Crisp, juicy, and slightly acidic. It has white flesh with outstanding texture.

Gala
A versatile apple, it's good for baking, in pies, and snacking. Gala apples have pinkish stripes on yellow skin. This variety is very sweet.

Ginger Gold
This variety has a sweet-tart flavor, good for pies, sauces, and eating. It is an early apple, available in August or September.

Golden Delicious
Mild sweet flavor, juicy, crisp, light yellow flesh. It's not as tart as other varieties and holds its shape well when baked.

Granny Smith
Tart with the best texture for baking and sauces. Across the globe, it's the #1 all-purpose apple for eating and baking.

Honey Crisp

This is a new variety of apple, which was introduced in the early '90s. The skin color is a combination of red and yellow. It is not well-suited to baking.

Jonagold

Available in September, this variety is perfect for making pies and sauces with its balanced sweet-tart flavor.

Melrose

Firm and quite coarse in texture, this apple's creamy white juicy flesh is slightly acidic in taste and actually improves with age.

Red Delicious

The skin color of this variety of apple is red and has a very sweet taste. Mostly just an eating apple, though you could bake with it.

Stayman/Winesap

Firm texture with a sweet-tart taste. It's a great all-purpose apple—for eating, baking, and sauces. It's available in October.

Asparagus

The woody ends of the asparagus naturally snap at the point where the stem becomes tender. Some people like to peel their asparagus, but if you've snapped off the woody part, this is not necessary. Asparagus can be steamed, boiled, sautéed, grilled, or roasted. It should only be cooked until it turns bright green to keep its crunch. The longer it cooks, the stringier it becomes. Simply steamed, it can be served with a sauce of mayonnaise and ketchup (see page 265) mixed together. Or toss the spears with olive oil, salt and pepper, lay them in a single layer on a sheet pan and cook it on the floor of a 375°F oven for 8 minutes.

Basil (all types)

One of the treats of high summer cooking and salads, with very unique flavors treasured by cultures around the world—from Italy to Vietnam. It's best not to cut basil until just before serving as the leaves will blacken quickly. If using in a curry or stew, add a few sprigs in the beginning of cooking and a few leaves at the end for a bright pop of flavor and color. On a hot summer day, a Basil Gimlet is a wonderful thing.

Thai Basil

Has a hint of anise and mint underneath the classic basil flavor.

Lemon Basil

Has a lemon scent and flavor. Outstanding for pesto sauces to be used for seafood. Also excellent in cocktails, such as a Basil Gimlet.

Genoa Basil

The classic Italian basil. Intense, pure flavor.

Beans (fava)

Unlike other shell beans, favas require a double peeling. First remove the beans from the pod, then the outer husk of the beans. To remove them from their husks, boil the beans for 1 minute, then drain and run under cold water to stop the cooking quickly. The beans will pop out of their husks. You will be rewarded with a firm, creamy bean that's both sweet and earthy.

Beans (pole, snap)

Pole beans are named for the trellises on which they grow. When young and tender, they can be eaten whole. As they grow larger, they should be shelled, and then only the beans eaten. Fresh young beans are so naturally sweet, they need minimal cooking. They can be steamed for a minute or two, just enough to turn them bright green.

fava beans: outer and inner husks removed

fava beans

Beans (yard-long)

An Asian green bean known for their length, though in reality they are only about ½ yard long. They taste similar to regular green beans, but their texture is best retained through stir-frying, rather than steaming or boiling.

Beets

Beets sadly receive a bad reputation from the olden days when they were always served mushy from a can. Fresh beets evoke a cult-like following because of their sweet, earthy flavors. Both the green tops and the roots are edible. The greens can be cooked similarly to Swiss chard or kale. Beetroots can be served raw if sliced thin like carpaccio. More often they're cooked until tender by roasting, boiling, or sautéing. They can be peeled before or after cooking, but waiting until after they're cooked provides a good indicator of when they are, in fact, cooked as the skins will peel off easily. Once cooked, peel them with a paring knife or peeler and cut. You can add them to salad, or season them simply with vinaigrettes.

Beets stain easily. To clean hands and cutting boards, wash them with baking soda and cold water.

Chioggia

Sometimes called "candy stripe" because of their white and red stripes and sweet flavor, these beets stain less than traditional red beets. While the stripes fade with cooking, they are tender enough to be eaten raw when sliced thin.

Golden Beets

Milder than red beets with a bright yellow color.

Blackberries

These fragile berries taste best at room temperature, but must be stored in the refrigerator. High in antioxidants, they are great for snacks, or cooked in a cobbler or pie.

Blueberries

They have a sweet taste when mature, though the smaller berries tend to be more tart. Ideal for snacking, for topping cereal, or mixed into pancakes or muffins. Mixed with cinnamon and lemon zest, they make an ideal summer dessert.

Broccoli

Often a favorite vegetable for kids because of the tree-like appearance. Fresh broccoli is sweeter than the commercial varieties. Wonderful steamed, sautéed, stir-fried, or just eaten raw as part of a crudité platter.

Brussels Sprouts

Brussels sprouts look like tiny green cabbages. They are best after the first frost when the flavor sweetens. Our favorite way to prepare them is simply roasted in a 400°F oven until golden brown, seasoned with olive oil and salt.

Cabbage

Green or Red

Often thought of as a low-brow vegetable, cabbage's stature has been elevated as chefs have taken to serving it with more refined ingredients like lobster and truffles. Classically served raw in slaws, green cabbage makes a great addition to Chinese stir-fries or fried rice. Simply braised or stewed in tomato sauce, it also works well as a side to grilled sausages or fish. Red cabbage can be blended with green cabbage for slaw, or even used entirely on its own. Braised red cabbage (with red wine, vinegar, and a little sugar) makes a wonderful accompaniment to hearty winter meat dishes.

Chinese

These varieties (such as Napa, Maruba Santoh, and Tokyo Bekana) require less cooking time by far than Western-style cabbages. They also may be cut up raw in salads. Whole heads can be halved (washed again), briefly marinated and grilled.

Savoy

Large and round like a green cabbage, savoy cabbage leaves have a crinkly texture. The leaves are tender enough to eat raw, but have enough body to use for cooking or as a wrap for stuffed cabbage.

Carrots

With really fine carrots, peeling is not necessary, though some people find the outer layer slightly bitter. Be sure to wash them once more. The large ones are often more tender (best for raw); the smaller perhaps best for gentle simmering or glazing in honey and butter.

Cauliflower

Though the leaves are edible, most people eat just the white florets. The florets tightly grip a tough core in the center. Cut the cauliflower in half to expose and cut out the core. Cooked cauliflower does not last long in the refrigerator but can be easily frozen for longer storage.

Celeriac

Celeriac is a variety of celery with small stalks and is grown for its root. The celery root has a fuzzy skin that needs to be peeled before cooking or eating. It has a mild celery flavor with a hint of turnip, and can be used in place of (or mixed with) potatoes for mashed or gratins. Thinly sliced, it can be served raw, and tossed with mayonnaise for the traditional French rémoulade, a variant on coleslaw. See illustration on page 119.

Celery

Though rarely cooked on its own, celery's distinctive flavor enhances French, Chinese, and Southern cooking. Its crunchy texture makes it a staple in egg, chicken, or tuna salads.

Chervil

A classic French herb with a delicate flavor akin to a blend of nice parsley with sweet fennel. Outstanding in salads, or added late to sautéing chicken breast or white-fleshed fish. Makes a superb Dijon-based salad dressing. Heating past 210°F destroys most of the flavor.

Cilantro

An herb many people adore and a similar number cannot abide. We use it in salads, salsas, marinades for grilled shrimp and rockfish, and, of course, in many Thai dishes, Chinese soups, and vegetarian bean-and-rice burritos. Heating past 190°F kills most of the flavor. See illustration on page 102.

Corn

Popping

Popping corn comes from a starchier variety than the sweet corn. Its tough outer skin traps just enough moisture to pop the corn into a low-fat, highly satisfying snack.

Sweet

Corn is one of the most cherished summertime crops for its sweet and crunchy flavor. Corn's sugar converts quickly to starch, so

cutting corn off the cob

it's best to eat the corn as soon as you can. Boiling whole ears is perhaps the easiest way to prepare it: Put corn in a pot of boiling salted water—after the water returns to a boil, cook just for 2–5 minutes. It can also be grilled in or out of the husks, or cut off the cob and sautéed in butter.

To wipe silk off an ear of corn, rub with a wet paper towel. To cut kernels off the cob, lay the ear on its side and run a sharp paring knife straight down the sides. Then scrape with the back of the knife to extract the very sweet "milk."

Cucumbers

Small cucumbers are more crisp, rarely peeled, and are most convenient for snacking. Cut lengthwise and dipped in soy sauce, they can tempt even the most stubborn child. Small cukes are traditionally sliced and marinated with onions, sugar, dill, and cider or white wine vinegar. Medium cucumbers are the most versatile but can become bitter in the scorching days of August. Peeling and then soaking in water for about 5 minutes before slicing can obviate bitterness in any size.

We prefer mediums to the other sizes because they need no deseeding and you can do practically anything with them. They are fine for snacks, salads, cold soups, nori-roll sushi, etc., and are the best size for slicing and immersing in yogurt mixed with herbs. Larger cucumbers are usually the sweetest but often need peeling. Their large and juicy seed cavity is often discarded, especially if making gazpacho or other soups. Just peel, cut in half lengthwise, and scoop out the seeds and pulp with a teaspoon or melon-baller.

Dill

Home-grown dill has superior and balanced flavors relative to commercial herbs. Excellent in cold bean salads; in salads of greens, potato, cucumbers, or egg; mixed with sour cream for baked potatoes; in omelets; with dips for vegetables or in lemon-juice salad dressings; or with cooked fish or chicken dishes, added late. Heating past 210°F destroys most of the flavor, except when baked into breads. See illustration on page 99.

Edamame (soy beans)

Traditionally, the whole pod is simmered with salt, beer, and ginger for 10 minutes, or until the pods are bright green. Once chilled, the beans pop out and make a great snack. Once shelled, they can be added to a succotash or other summer salads.

Eggplant

Eggplant is a superbly malleable vegetable. It takes on the flavors of any meat or broth or seasoning you add while cooking, and offers an almost meaty feel to the palate. Different eggplant varieties present an amazing spectrum of firmness, bitterness, and mild flavors versus strong, seediness, and propensity to melt (in contrast with staying firm) upon lengthy cooking. Japanese, Chinese, and Italian varieties are favored for their mildness and tender skins; Thai and Indian varieties have firmer textures and more pronounced flavors. Eggplant should be stored on the counter until ripe, then refrigerated (refrigerating too soon can lead to small brown streaks in the flesh). The sweetest and most mild eggplants are permitted to ripen at room temp until they soften and slightly wrinkle. Like a peach, this softening and wrinkling means you've handled the eggplant perfectly, and you now need to use within a day or refrigerate.

The jury is still out as to whether salting eggplant before cooking reduces any bitterness. Without doubt, however, salting it for 15 minutes before cooking prevents the eggplant from absorbing oil when sautéing or frying.

Fennel Bulbs

Fennel is another lover of cool and relatively moist conditions. In truth, it really wants to grow in the mild springs of Italy and California. The bulbs ought to be separated into individual petioles (the pale green-white fleshy things that subtend the leafy parts, similar to celery). The petioles and tops should then be washed. Both are very usable, but with slightly different applications. The leaves are outstanding minced and added to bread or pizza dough before cooking, or minced and added to salads or salad dressings. The stems can be cut into ¾-inch pieces and barely simmered, with garlic and butter added late. And the tenderest petioles are really fine served separated and raw but whole, smeared with nice soft cheese or butter. Alternately, use any recipe for the classic Italian dish of braised fennel, which uses the entire thing, cut up. Fennel also pairs beautifully with tomatoes and seafood dishes like paella or bouillabaisse. See illustration on page 163.

Garlic

Garlic can have a strong bite when raw, but mellows with cooking. To roast garlic: toss peeled cloves with 1–2 Tbs olive oil. Wrap in an aluminum foil pouch. Bake at 350°F

to best release all the dirt. Soak them in cold water, the dirt will settle to the bottom, and the leeks should be lifted out before draining. Properly washed, they are also wonderful sliced in half lengthwise, simmered until soft, (chilled, if desired) and then tossed with vinaigrette. See illustration for washing greens on page 41.

Lima Beans

Lima beans (also referred to as butter beans) have a starchy, creamy texture. They are a wonderful textural complement to many dishes including succotash or rice. The pod of the lima bean is flat, oblong, and slightly curved, averaging about 3 inches long. Within the pod are the two to four flat kidney-shaped seeds, which are the lima beans.

Melon

Cantaloupe

Sometimes not as sweet as other melons, cantaloupes pair well with blueberries, mint, and ginger. A fully ripe cantaloupe is soft, very sweet, and musky (remember its other name, muskmelon). Serve plain for breakfast, or as an appetizer with prosciutto. Cantaloupe puréed into a soup is a refreshing first course to a summer meal.

Watermelon

In the best of summers—hot and tending toward drought—watermelons are at their finest. In cool, wet summers they are not as sweet or perfect, but they are still better than store-bought. Good watermelons are not just for eating as cut fruit. They are also excellent (after deseeding) in daiquiris or as the base for a sorbet. For the latter, blend watermelon meat to make 3 cups. Add 3 Tbs corn syrup or no sugar at all, the juice of 1 lime, and (optional) 1 Tbs vodka. Put through an ice cream machine; refreeze if necessary. Superb, healthy, and refreshing!

Watermelons will ripen a little more on the counter if they are harvested under-ripe. To tell if one is ripe, tap on the shell: it should sound like a taut drum. If you

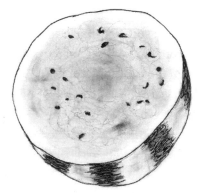

Cutting watermelon rind to expose the internal cylinder of seeds

end up with a slightly underripe melon, sprinkle a little sugar and lemon juice on the flesh to sweeten and brighten the flavor. While smaller watermelons are undoubtedly more convenient, the larger ones will generally be better flavored.

The seeds are in a cylinder that runs lengthwise. Inside the cylinder is seed-free flesh; between the rind and the seed cylinder is another zone, about three-quarters of an inch thick, of seed-free flesh. To efficiently deseed a watermelon, use a stainless steel knife. Place the melon on a rimmed cookie sheet to catch the juice and cut off the two caps (either end of the melon). Stand it on one of its cut ends. Skin by arcing your knife, following the curve of the melon, from top to bottom. A typical 10-pound melon needs 8–12 such skinning slices. Trim off any white rind that remains and throw away the rinds. Now cut about ¾-inch thick slices from each face of the melon; these will be pretty free of seeds. The seed cylinder is right under those slices. Cut that seedier flesh away in slices about 1½ thick for tedious hand deseeding. Underneath the seedy slices is the seed-free core, often the best in flavor.

Yellow Moon and Stars
Firm, sweet, crispy, yellow flesh. Nice flavor balance, not as sweet as other varieties. Shelf life is shorter than Crimson Sweet: about 3 weeks, or 10 days on the counter.

Crimson Sweet
Melting, slightly crisp flesh. Superior flavor balance; sweet, but not cloyingly sweet.

Seedless
Undoubtedly most convenient, but consistently less flavorful than the seeded varieties. The demand for seedless has forced farmers into the arms of multi-national seed monopolies.

Yellow Doll
Very old Japanese variety developed in the 1930s. Crisp, sweet flesh when at its best; requires perfect growing conditions.

Orangeglo
Like Yellow Doll, requires perfect growing conditions (slightly cool) for best flavor. The pale orange flesh is semi-crisp and fairly sweet.

Sugar Baby
Super sweet, more sugar than any other flavor. Crisp. Bright yellow spot on the belly of the melon is the best ripeness indicator. Caution: these have very think skins; handle gingerly.

Mint
Given its prolific growth, it's a good thing mint is so versatile—from desserts to grilled meats to drinks. Toss a few leaves with berries, steep leaves in hot water for

tea, puréed for a sauce for lamb or salmon, or mixed with cucumbers or peas for a refreshing salad. It even brightens up a gin and tonic on a hot summer afternoon.

Mushrooms (wild and cultivated)

Lucky indeed is the farmers market customer who can buy fresh mushrooms. We strongly advocate washing mushrooms, despite conventional wisdom against it. Growing on the forest floor means lots of grit and pine needles, and these can ruin the most delectable meal. Wash mushrooms as we advise for leafy greens. Drain well.

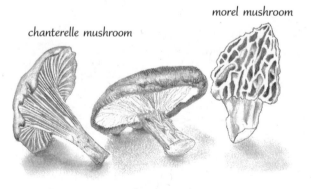

chanterelle mushroom

morel mushroom

shiitake mushroom

Chanterelles

Deeply floral aromas make this second only to the truffle in our passion. More gritty than other varieties; washing is critical. Superb with cream. Use low to medium heat when cooking.

Honeys

They are close kin to the shiitake. With a clean, woodsy flavor, they are less thick and rubbery. They are best sautéed quickly over high heat. They don't store well; use quickly.

Morels

The most woodsy of all wild mushrooms. Its bizarre conical shape easily distinguishes it from other mushrooms. Without doubt, best sautéed slowly with cream.

Oysters

Mild, meaty, and versatile. These have superior shelf life compared to most wild mushrooms. Use in place of button mushrooms for outstanding flavor. Great in omelets and pizzas.

Porcini

Porcinis (Cèpes) are unique and very expensive mushrooms. Chefs and consumers forgive its most poor shelf life because of its perfectly nuanced flavors. Outstanding grilled, but adds an oyster-like texture to sauces when sautéed. Amazing (though pricey) in mac-n-cheese.

Puffballs

They are the most mild of the wild mushrooms, like tofu. Best peeled and marinated before cooking to absorb more flavors. The bigger ones can be sliced and grilled, the smaller are nice mixed with other mushrooms.

Nasturtiums

These edible flowers make a lovely garnish for any dish, or mix them with lettuce leaves for a bright salad. The leaves are soft and velvety with a peppery taste. They are quite delicate so they shouldn't be cooked, and if using in a salad, just minimally dress them.

Nectarines

Nectarines are, in fact, a variety of peach, and differ only in the fuzz-less skin. The fruit should smell sweet and "peachy" when ripe. While peaches and nectarines have a slight give when ripe, you don't want to test too often this way as they will end up bruised.

Okra

Okra is a much-maligned vegetable that we treasure sliced raw in salads, stewed, or deep-fried. Really fresh and tender okra is as delicate in flavor as baby green beans. The uses are many, from barely steamed, then shocked and chilled and finally dressed with vinaigrette, to deep-fried, to stewed. Raw and sliced thinly into summer tomato salads, okra adds great sweet crunchy contrast as well as pleasant thickening to any vinaigrette. See illustration on page 62.

Onions

Cipollini

Small, sweet, squat onions are typically served as a vegetable rather than chopped and cooked as an aromatic like larger storage onions. Once peeled, they can be roasted or cooked with cream, or added to braised meats.

Dry Skin

Also referred to as "storage onions," they need not be refrigerated. They are a staple of all types of cooking. There are many tips to avoid tearing up when cutting, though none is foolproof. The best solution is to use a sharp knife and cut quickly to minimize the exposure time. Better yet, have someone else cut the onions for you.

Candy

These are regular storage onions that are a sweeter and milder variety than what you'd find in the supermarket, and like storage onions need not be refrigerated.

Green and Spring

Tend to be sweeter than storage onions, but should definitely be stored in the refrigerator to maximize shelf life. Excellent raw in salads or peeled and simmered whole. The big bulb onions can be cut in half or grilled whole, depending on their size.

Oregano

A common seasoning in both Mexican and Mediterranean cuisines, its flavor is a blend of mint, thyme, and camphor. Some varieties have a slightly peppery/spicy taste. It is similar to marjoram, but less sweet and more pungent. It pairs well with other strong herbs and flavors: rosemary, thyme, and sage; with potatoes, and meats.

Parsley

Mild, with a slight carrot flavor, parsley brightens most dishes with a sprinkle at the end. It's an essential ingredient when making soups and stews and adds a subtle backdrop of flavor. See illustration on page 129.

Parsnips

They resemble carrots in their shape, and they grow in the ground. But these sweet root vegetables have a flavor all their own. They must be peeled before cooking. Roasting brings out their sweetness, but they are also good boiled or mashed. You can use them in any recipe that calls for potatoes. The really large ones (about 2 inches in diameter at the widest point) will be tougher.

Peaches

Most of peaches' nutrients are in the skin. Washing them in cold water rids them of the fuzz. Nonetheless, many dessert recipes suggest peeling as the skin will fall off during the cooking and is considered unappealing. To peel a peach, score the bottom of the peach with a sharp paring knife. Put them in a pot of boiling water for 30 seconds. Scoop them out and plunge them into an ice bath to stop the cooking. The skin will now easily peel off.

Peas

English

Anyone who does not like peas surely never had a sweet English pea fresh in the springtime. Sautéed in butter or tossed with mint, they are a refreshing side dish to lamb or salmon. They also work well in pasta dishes tossed with Parmesan and a little bacon.

Snow, Sugar Snap

Oh, what joy a sugar snap pea is! Best destringed by snapping and pulling on the stem end gently. Excellent raw or very briefly cooked (no more than 30 seconds).

Pea Shoots

The tender leaves of the pea vine are snipped before the plant starts to flower and produce pods. With their soft leaves and pea-like flavor, they can be added raw to salad mixes, quickly sautéed with garlic and ginger, or mixed in with pasta. See illustration on page 206.

Peppers

Sweet Green

Green peppers are excellent counterpoints when used raw in salads or crudités. Cooked, they add character to stir-fries, pastas dishes, but shine most brightly when braised, Italian style, with pork sausage or other meats.

Hot

Either you love them or you hate them. To most safely handle hot peppers, wear protective gloves. Chop raw peppers and store in a glass container, covered with vinegar. They will keep indefinitely if refrigerated. When you want to add some heat to a dish, use a spoon and spare your fingers.

The hottest part of the pepper tends to be the white membranes, and the seeds are second (though this can vary by variety). Remove these parts to create a milder heat in your recipes. Be careful not to touch your eyes or any other sensitive area after handling. Washing your hands with baking soda and cold water also helps to neutralize the burn.

Sweet Red

Best all-around pepper for raw, dicing in salads, or stuffing and baking. To roast and peel red peppers, carefully blacken skin under an oven broiler or over an open flame. Remove from heat, and place in a bowl. Cover with plastic wrap or damp cloth. Let cool and then the skin will easily peel off. These can be stored packed in olive oil in the freezer indefinitely, or in the refrigerator for 10 days or more. See illustration on page 58.

Elongated (many types)

The US is going through a pepper revolution, with countless heirloom and new varieties now available. Most of the long types have richer pepper flavors than the classic bell. Some have no heat (like *Jimmy Nardello*), others have a touch or more (like *anchos* and *poblanos*). These long peppers are often best cut up and add superb flavors to other dishes, or as focal points for sauces and relishes (e.g., Romesco, see recipe on page 270).

Plums

The flesh of the plum is quite sweet while the skin is tart, giving this stone fruit a wonderfully balanced flavor. It's a versatile fruit that can be dried for prunes, fermented for wine, or baked into tarts and pies. Plums can be substituted for any recipe that calls for peaches.

Potatoes ("Irish")

Regular, non-sweet potatoes are often called Irish, but in fact, potatoes originated from the Andes. When locally grown the skins are safe to eat, unlike commercial, conventional potatoes, which have some of the highest tested levels of added chemicals for "storage reasons." So don't eat skins from lesser grade spuds.

When the potatoes are freshly harvested (new), they are best gently simmered at low temperatures (skins left on) until barely soft, with a small amount of butter added late. Or gently simmer in lightly salted water, drain when just soft, and then chill to dress very minimally as a salad. Their flavors are so clean that heavy seasoning wastes them.

If using promptly, do not refrigerate, as cold temperatures lead to increased (and unwelcome) sugars. When boiling always start with cold salted water.

Blue

With deep blue skin and flesh that almost appears purple, here is another potato to brighten your table and your favorite potato salad. A favorite for making French fries or oven fries.

Green Mountain

This white potato is more oblong than round shaped. Like other high-starch potatoes, it's excellent for boiling and baking—great flavor! Deep eyes make this not so pretty—but the flavor makes up for it.

Katahdin

A low-starch potato, traditional to Maine. Waxy white flesh and thin buff skin.

Kennebec

Kennebecs are superb boiled, mashed, fried, hashed, or baked. Good jacket potato—smother it in sour cream, cheese, chives, and bacon.

Red Norland

Smooth skin, white flesh, medium to large tubers. Excellent boiled and in salads. This potato has just enough starch that makes it good for frying as well as boiling for potato salad.

Red Pontiac

Round tubers with red skin, medium-deep eyes, and moist, crisp, white flesh. They are good for baking, salads, and roasting.

Yukon Gold

With attractive, smooth, thin yellow skin, and yellow flesh, it's versatile for most potato preparations—roasted or mashed. Their sweet flavor yields a rich mashed potato even without butter.

Pumpkins

To create your own "pumpkin pack" like those purchased in cans at the supermarket: cut the pumpkin in half, and bake in a shallow dish with water, cut side down for an hour until soft. Scoop out seeds and set aside for another use. Purée the pulp in a food processor and freeze in portion controlled containers. For a moister pie, simmer peeled chunks until soft. The seeds can be depulped, rinsed and roasted with soy sauce, or olive oil and salt.

The seeds used for pepitas are from a different variety of pumpkin than what you find at the farmers market, and these should not be used as a substitute.

Jack-O-Lantern

Lovely to look at, lovely to carve, but have been bred more for Halloween than for cooking; often flavor-deficient.

Neck Pumpkin

Also called the Pennsylvania Dutch Crookneck, these pumpkins look more like a butternut squash on steroids, often weighing as much as 15 pounds each. You can get enough "pumpkin pack" from each one to bake 6–8 pies, which is the best use for these. Rated by many as the best for pure pumpkin flavor and ease of use.

Pie Pumpkin

Often ovoid in shape, typically more moist than neck or jack-o-lantern pumpkins. Excellent for cooking.

Spookies

These flavorful pumpkins are a bit moister than the crooknecks, making them perfect for pie filling. Their medium size is great for carving, too.

Purslane

Some people consider it a weed, but it has a tangy flavor that can provide a nice contrast to an otherwise rich meal. Both the leaves and stems are edible and are high in omega-3s. They can be sautéed with olive oil, garlic, and tomatoes or mixed with other cooking or salad greens.

Radishes

Really nice sliced thinly in sandwiches of crusty bread, good cheese, and/or roast beef, turkey, or ham. If they are too peppery for your taste, they can be roasted with butter and soy sauce for a refreshing spring or autumn side dish.

Cherry Belle

Small red radish that's crisp and juicy.

China Rose radish

French breakfast radish

watermelon radish

daikon radish

China Rose

Classic pungent winter radish, best sliced but not peeled; not at all mild. Very nice sliced thinly and smeared with Brie, chèvre, or butter. Can also be chopped and added to cold salads of cucumbers, greens, tuna, beans, or egg. The tops can be cooked like turnip greens.

Daikon

Daikon is an Asian variety: crisp, white, mild sweet radish. They're about 2–3 inches in diameter and 6–12 inches long. Unlike other radishes, this variety can be peeled. Daikon and carrots can be mixed together for an easy, quick pickle: Season matchstick-cut veggies with equal parts sugar and vinegar. Add salt to taste.

French Breakfast and Pink Beauty

The mildest of radishes, fine any way you use the traditional red radish.

Misato Rose

Larger radishes, with a greenish/white skin and red or pink flesh. Sweet and spicy, they are larger than the typical red radish. Sliced thin, they make a terrifically colorful alternative to crackers for dips and cheese platter.

Watermelon

An heirloom variety of the Asian winter radish, they are larger than a French Breakfast and rounder than a daikon. They can be peeled, exposing the bright fuchsia center. Sliced raw, they add brilliant color to salads or crudités platters. They can also be cooked, but best with honey added to the simmering liquid.

White Icicle

Midway in pungency between China Rose and French Breakfast, with similar uses. Probably related to the daikons.

Raspberries

With just a touch of acidity, raspberries have a perfectly balanced sweetness that makes them ideal for desserts, savory dishes, or just snacking. If puréing to make a dessert sauce, be sure to strain out the seeds.

Rhubarb

An early spring crop (April–June): get it while you can! It freezes superbly; for when the season is over, it's over. Its tart flavor and thickening qualities are unique and much appreciated in many cultures. Very nice in many desserts as well as savory Middle Eastern dishes. Be sure to remove the inedible leaves before preparation.

Rosemary

The pine-like scent of rosemary comes alive when grilled. The woody stems can act as kebab skewers for grilled vegetables. A few sprigs enhance roasted potatoes, chicken, steak, or lamb. Sprinkled on fresh baked breads or infused in olive oil, rosemary is quite versatile. Like sage, a little rosemary can go a long way, so it is best to be judicious.

Rutabaga

Two possible varieties: one more elongate and more intense than turnips, the other round like a turnip and milder in flavor. Excellent raw or in soups, stews, purées, risotto, or roasted. Balance and complexity superior to that of turnips. We don't peel them. Rutabaga can be used for recipes that call for turnips, but is more of a performer when slow-cooked.

Sage

Sage is a tricky herb—added fresh to a dish, a little, no more than a tablespoon chopped, goes a long way. But if you fry the leaves and sprinkle with a little salt, they entice like potato chips. Deep-fry (see page 42) the leaves in plain oil until just translucent. Strain with a slotted spoon and drain on a paper towel, and season them with salt. The leaves seem thinner and melt in your mouth.

Sage has many medicinal qualities, including: reduces bad breath, reduces perspiration, reduces the symptoms of menopause and premenstrual cramps, increases brain concentration, and reduces blood sugar in people with diabetes. Be cautioned, if you are pregnant, you should not consume sage in great quantity.

Squash Blossoms

Squash flowers are a favorite in France and Italy, but are rarely served in the US. They can be scrambled with eggs, mixed into light risotto or pasta dishes, broiled at the last minute on top of mostly cooked focaccia or white pizza, or stuffed and then deep-fried. Squash flowers are extraordinarily perishable, must be kept chilled at all times after harvest and must be used within 3 days. See illustration on page 65.

Squash, Summer

Yellow squash tends to be sweeter and crunchier than the green zucchini. Yellow squash pairs well with traditional American summer flavors like corn and tomatoes. Zucchini blends well with Mediterranean flavors like tomatoes, olives, and eggplants. Both varieties can be grilled or sautéed. Smaller squash are more tender and can also be cut into sticks as a great addition to traditional crudité platters. Larger squash have a tough texture and are ideal for zucchini breads, puréed soups, ratatouille, or caponata.

Some of the more traditional yellow summer squashes, especially from the South, can have tough skins even when picked young. Despite the tough skin, the flesh is sweeter and soft. Simply peel the squash as you would a carrot or cucumber.

Squash, Winter

Winter squash are not squash grown during the winter. They are squash grown in the warm months and harvested in August or later; their thick skins let us store them for later use. Some can even keep until winter. Because of their shape, winter squash can be difficult to peel and handle raw. We recommend cooking them first and then scooping out the flesh. If you decide to cut them before cooking, it's easiest when they are at room temperature. These varieties of winter squash are particularly well-suited for puréed preparations—served as a "mash," or as a base for creamy soups.

Acorn

Classic New England winter squash for roasting or baking with maple syrup and butter. Its shape makes it ideal for stuffing.

Butternut

One of the longest-storing of all winter squash. Much appreciated in creamy autumn soups. It can be cubed and baked, or boiled and puréed.

Spaghetti

This is one of the few winter squash that merits special non-baked handling. Can be briefly microwaved or steamed and the strands "forked" out. Very versatile in salads, mixed in sautés, etc.

Forking spaghetti squash

Buttercup

A superb winter squash, with some of the finest flavor of all varieties. Slow, gentle cooking yields a sublime, custard-like texture and flavor.

Blue Hubbard

These tough-skinned winter squash with a golden yellow flesh can weigh as much as 15 pounds. Texturally, they tend to be dry and sometimes mealy, but the flavor is nutty and sweet, and extremely popular in New England. They are best roasted and puréed, in either a soup or pie.

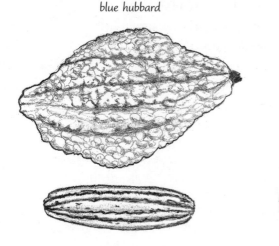

blue hubbard

delicata

acorn

kabocha

Safely break open a Hubbard by placing it in a large plastic or paper bag and then dropping it on the ground.

Delicata

An elongated winter squash that's yellow with green streaks. Unlike most winter squash, it has a thin skin so it doesn't need to be peeled (though you still need to scoop out the seed cavity). Once it's deseeded, it can be stuffed and roasted, or sliced and sautéed as you would summer squash.

Strawberries

Strawberries are the delicate jewels of spring. They are best eaten straight from the container to savor their sweet, juicy flavor. They are also a lovely addition to a spring salad, dressed simply with red wine vinegar, olive oil, and fresh thyme.

Best washed by immersion: fill a large bowl or sink with cold water. Add the strawberries and swish them around a little. Let the dirt settle to the bottom, no more than 30 seconds, and then lift the strawberries out to drain in a colander. You will see the grit that simple rinsing under the faucet does not get rid of.

Sweet Potatoes

Fingerling sweets potatoes are starchier than big ones and are outstanding left skin-on, chunked, and then roasted with garlic. The really big sweet potatoes are the most easily peeled for subsequent steaming, grating, or pie-making, but are also the fastest to chunk for a quick roast. Novices unjustly scorn very large sweet potatoes, but old-time Southern cooks treasure the mammoths for ease of use. They also know that a slowly grown but big sweet potato is more flavorful than a typical conventionally grown, smaller sweet potato whose growth was rushed and babied with agricultural chemicals. Finally, the classic middle sizes are good for baking whole and for individual servings. Sweet potatoes should be washed once more and then stored in the pantry.

Recent studies have confirmed that lowering the baking temperatures to 325°F or 340°F maximizes sweetness. If you want your sweet potatoes consistently sweet, keep the baking temperatures low.

Beauregard

Orange, creamy, not too sweet, and with very full and nuanced flavors. Our absolute favorite orange type.

Covington

Orange as well but so sweet that it oozes sugary syrup while cooking!

White Hamon

Beige to milk-white and with a nutty, nuanced suite of flavors. Absolute best for frying but fine baked as well. Never boil, as this can turn the flesh grey-green.

Japanese, Purple Skin

A great white sweet potato. Has typical nuttiness and subtlety, but has unique chestnut-like flavor if slowly baked past the softened stage.

O'Henry

Smooth-skinned and mild; is most like Irish potatoes in texture and flavor. Can be creamy and very sweet under ideal growing conditions.

Tarragon

The soft leaves have a flavor reminiscent of licorice and basil. They enhance many dishes—tomatoes, asparagus, beef, and salmon.

Thyme

A great all-purpose herb. A few sprigs add zest to sautéed mushrooms, stewed meats, chicken soup, or roasted potatoes.

Tomatillos

These are the husk tomatoes that so confuse many non-Mexican cooks. The sticky papery husk obscures a potential gem and must be removed. Store-bought tomatillos are nearly always picked very underripe and are usually dark green and bitter. In contrast, local farmers can let them fully ripen on the vine, where they sweeten wonderfully, develop nearly apple- or melon-like flavors, and turn a very pale green-yellow or even purple. Tomatillos can be grilled or roasted or turned into a green chile salsa, but properly ripened ones are so good that we prefer them raw.

After husking, slice raw into salads, use for dipping, or top slices with a nice cheddar, Gouda, chèvre, or fresh mozzarella. Less ripe ones can be baked with olive oil and salt to become the vital base for salsa verde. See illustration on page 249.

Tomatoes

All tomatoes should be taken out of their packaging once you get them home. Larger tomatoes are best stored on their shoulders (where the stem was attached), separated from each other on a counter until fully ripe. Set on a windowsill if you want to speed ripening. Once ripe, tomatoes that cannot be eaten within 12–24 hours should be refrigerated before they rot. The transition from gloriously ripe to beginning to turn (the wrong way) is fastest in August, September, or whenever the tomatoes have been harvested right after intense summer heat or violent rains.

We use two iron-clad rules for tomatoes: 1) the ripening enzymes inside each tomato are killed at 53° F by refrigeration, so chilling an underripe tomato dooms you to poor flavors; and 2) a ripe but refrigerated tomato is much better than a tomato that slowly rots at room temp because you didn't get around to eating it fast enough.

Cherry tomatoes are superbly convenient fast snacks for kids and adults, make lovely salsas and salads, and are usually more intensely flavorful than bigger tomatoes. Store cherries the same as regular tomatoes, though they cannot easily be stored on their shoulders.

Tomatoes fall into four basic categories: plums, cherries, currants, and larger slicers (the beefsteak types, weighing between 3 ounces and 2 pounds). The plums are generally the least flavorful, least juicy and best for cooking: they won't water down your sauces. Cherries and currants are best for snacking, but together with the beefsteak types, can be used for cooking. Simply drain and reserve the extra juice (see stewed tomato recipe on page 237).

Heirlooms vary widely in color and ugly form, but have incredible flavor. Some are sweeter, others more acidic. Typically they are juicier. As such, when cooked, they require long simmer times to reduce the liquid, and also to concentrate the flavors. There are thousands of varieties. Here are some of the more popular ones we've seen available.

Aunt Ruby's German Green
These have a strong tomato flavor, and are green when ripe, with light pink strips and slightly translucent skin.

Big Rainbow
Similar to pineapple tomatoes but slightly smaller, these tomatoes are uniformly medium-sized beefsteaks whose multi-colored stripes go from yellow to candy red. Juicy and super sweet.

Black Prince
One of the saladette tomatoes, Black Princes are smaller, with dark brownish-purplish flesh. Their higher acid content makes them great for a mozzarella salad and pairing with olive oil.

Bolseno
They have green shoulders even when ripe. This Italian variety is slightly acidic, so vinegar is not necessary when making a salad.

Brandywine
Most suitable for regions with cool summer nights, Brandywine is difficult to grow, but produces an amazing tomato. Only moderately acidic with superb depth of flavors and an almost buttery texture.

Celebrity
A hybrid tomato that produces deep red, medium to large fruit. Full flavored with a nice balance of sweetness and acidity. It's a great slicing tomato for sandwiches.

Cherokee Purple
A really ugly tomato, with green shoulders even when ripe, frequent cracking and purple-red-auburn mottled skin and flesh. But what flavor! Full, deep taste, with enough acidity to make you take notice. Very juicy as well. A really fine, bold heirloom; grown under the right conditions, among the most intense.

Cherry and Grape Tomatoes

Superbly convenient fast snacks for kids and adults! For salads and salsas, they are halved with a serrated knife.

Chocolate Pear

Yellowish-red cherry tomatoes that have a balanced flavor of sweet and tangy.

Eva Purple Ball

A flatter version of Cherokee Purples, with the same green shoulders and full flavor.

Goldie

This is a beautiful golden-colored beefsteak with a really nice texture. They're also more drought tolerant than your average tomato.

Homestead and Rutgers

These large red beefsteak types are classic American tomatoes, with lots of juice, moderate acidity, and good sweetness. Very good, though juicy, for sandwiches.

Not as fully flavored or aggressive as many others, but very popular.

Indigo Apple

A cherry tomato that is deep red, with purplish black shoulders. Very sweet.

Moreton

The classic "Jersey" tomato: outstanding flavor, large and meaty.

Mortgage Lifter

Mortgage Lifters are legendary for their size (as much as 3 pounds for one tomato) and flavor. As the story goes: They were developed in the 1930s by a gardener who crossbred 4 of the largest plants he had. People drove as far as 200 miles to buy his plants, which sold for $1 each (in the 1940s!). He was able to pay off his $6,000 mortgage in 6 years; hence the name.

Mountain Jubilee

A gold beefsteak heirloom with superb balance of flavors, low to moderate acidity, low juice, and buttery texture.

Orange Blossom

A yellow-orange tomato with a mild flavor and low acidity.

Pink Girl

A hybrid tomato, large and juicy. These tomatoes are slightly sweet with a smooth skin.

roma tomato

pineapple tomato

cherry tomato

Plum Tomatoes

Lower water content (i.e., less juicy), makes them ideal for sauces and grilling. They typically have less flavor than cherries or heirlooms. The intensely flavored and juicy heirlooms can easily make too soupy a sauce, hence the plums. Frequently grown plum varieties are Roma, Amish Paste, San Marzano, and Speckled Roman.

Pruden's Purple

Really complex flavors, excellent texture, and only moderate acidity make this a worthy competitor to the venerable heirloom Brandywine. Pruden's is a bright pink to mottled purple, often large, and nearly as funny looking as the Cherokee Purple.

Red Zebra

A small red tomato with orange stripes. They have excellent flavor, but are rather acidic, making them a great complement to grilled cheese sandwiches or caprese salads.

Rose

A large pink beefsteak, tasting similar to Beefsteak. Its versatility and its refreshing texture adapt equally well to cooking or salads.

Striped German

A beautiful juicy tomato with red and yellow stripes. It has sweet, complex flavors with a smooth texture.

Stupice

These super small tomatoes are bigger than cherries, but still good for popping in your mouth for a snack!

Sunbrite

Firm, meaty tomato, less sweet than other varieties. When dressing these tomatoes, use less vinegar than the typical ratio of 3:1, oil:vinegar.

Sungold

A hybrid cherry tomato that revitalized the commercial cherry tomato world with its superb intense flavor.

Sun Sugar

Yellow cherry tomato.

Sunstart

Large firm fruit produce early in the season.

Sweet One Hundred

A red cherry tomato with flavors often as intense as Sungold.

Sweet Tangerine

Medium-sized fruit with a tangerine color, they ripen earlier than other varieties. They are very sweet and flavorful—perfect for salads.

Sweethearts

A very sweet cherry tomato.

Yellow and Red Brandymaster

Firm and juicy tomatoes, with rich tomato flavor.

White Wonder

With its off-white color comes a milder flavor, not as puckering as the more acidic tomatoes.

Turnips

Tender and outstanding roasted, braised, or simmered. Very nice raw, sliced 1/16"–1/8" thin, then dipped into soy sauce or a vegetable dip. Peeling optional. Tops (greens) may be washed once more and sautéed or braised as per any of the chard recipes. Both roots and tops are very high in calcium and potassium.

Coletto Viola

An absolutely perfect heirloom turnip for simmering and then finishing with butter. Long and slender, violet and white.

Gilfeather

An egg-shaped turnip that has a mild flavor, which becomes sweeter after the first frost.

Hakurei

Snow white and perfectly round, they are sweet and slightly earthy, crisp, and juicy. They are wonderful raw or lightly cooked.

Purple Top

The traditional turnip in much of the US; it can be boring when grown for supermarkets, but its crisp texture and gentle flavors really shine when cold grown.

Scarlet Queen

They look like a radish, but have a stem similar to a beet. They have more kick than the other varieties. They can be eaten raw or cooked.

Scarlet Ohno

Smaller than the classic purple-top turnip, these roots have a scarlet skin that resembles a radish, with magenta streaks when you cut it open. It can be eaten raw, braised, or pickled. The leafy tops are delicious and nutritious. Most esteemed of the Asian turnips. Nice flavor, good in salads or cooked.

Tokyo

Slightly spicy when raw, they are buttery sweet when cooked.

Storing Your Produce for Optimal Freshness 3

Most fruits and vegetables can be grouped into simplifying categories that really help busy home cooks and chefs:

Produce that wants to be kept as cold as possible without freezing and preferably in a lidded container like a large Tupperware. Examples are most leafy greens, ripe berries, wild mushrooms, cucumbers, and radishes.

Produce that hates any refrigeration and wants a cool (or room temperature) pantry, basement, or kitchen. Examples are sweet potatoes and winter squash.

Produce that wants the warmer part of the refrigerator but suffers if too cold. Includes basil, sorrel, and a few others.

Produce that likes refrigeration but can briefly be kept on the counter. Examples are watermelon and carrots.

Fruits that need ripening, but once ripe must be eaten soon or refrigerated. This group is the most complex and takes the most care. Refrigeration of these fruits will irreparably destroy the ripening enzymes within the fruits, thus dooming the foods to be underripe, boring shadows of what they could have become. Examples include peaches and nectarines, but premature cooling of commercial tomatoes has made more Americans dissatisfied with mass-marketed tomatoes than with any other crop. Whenever possible, fruits in this category should be placed on a counter, slightly separated from each other, and not on their bellies but rather on their shoulders. The shoulders, most obvious with big tomatoes, are the part that surrounds where the stem was (or is). Once ripened at room temperature, fruits in this group are at the peak of flavor. At this point they must be eaten very soon or refrigerated, as rotting will begin within 12 to 24 hours. A refrigerated ripe tomato, nectarine, or avocado will keep for a few days and is much better than one that festers on the counter until thrown out. To maximize flavors, bring refrigerated ripe fruits back to room temperature before eating.

Storage areas also have subtle temperature differences that can also help you keep foods best:

The coldest areas of the refrigerator are usually the bottom, back, and crisper drawers; the door shelves are generally the warmest (e.g., better for basil).

Basements are usually cooler than pantries or closets. If dry, they are excellent for winter squashes and sweet potatoes.

Windowsills ripen tomatoes much faster than countertops.

Canning Tomatoes

Canning foods safely protects them from rot or off-flavors for 1 to 3 years. Canning used to be how many American families survived through winter before the advent of freezers and cheap (and more boringly flavored) commercial foods. It is still a superb technique to learn and use as part of the repertoire of accomplished cooks. The approach below uses tomatoes as an example, but also works well with jellies, jams, and other vegetables packed in an acidic liquid.

The one thing to remember when canning tomatoes (or any other acidic foods) is that you need to boil everything. Boil the jars, boil the tomatoes, and boil the tomatoes in the jar. The first two boils are necessary to sterilize the jars and the tomatoes; the third boil is to create a vacuum seal in the jar. This technique also works well for sauces and jams. For more tips on canning, refer to *The Joy of Cooking* by Rombauer and Becker.

The process goes like this:

1. Purchase canning jars. We prefer the wide mouth because they are easier to fill. Consider buying a variety of sizes. Even if you are only canning one kind of sauce, the variety will enable you to maximize your tomatoes—if a recipe calls for a small amount of tomato, you open a small jar, instead of opening a large jar that may not be completely used. Also, buy a pair of canning tongs. These tongs are specially designed to lift the jars out of the water.

2. Wash the jars. Put the lids and bands in one pot and the jars in another pot. The pot for the jars should be deep enough that the top of the jars can be covered by at least 1 inch of water.

3. Cover the jars completely with water and bring them to a boil. Continue boiling them for 10 minutes.

4. Cover the lids and bands completely with water and put them on the stove. Bring to a boil, and turn off the heat. Let them sit in the water until you're ready to use them.

5. Meanwhile, wash and coarsely chop tomatoes. Put them in a stainless steel (non-aluminum) pot. Bring the tomatoes to a boil, and continue cooking them for at least 10 minutes. Even if you smoked the tomatoes, you still need to boil them.

6. Remove the jars from the water, draining the water out. Fill each jar with tomatoes; be sure to leave at least a ½-inch gap at the top. With a clean towel, wipe the lip of each jar clean.

7. Drain the water from the lids and cover each jar. Screw on the metal band, but not too tightly.

8. Return the jars to the boiling water and let boil for 10 minutes. Remove from the water and let stand for 20 minutes. Remove the band and test the seal of the lids—if it comes off easily, then the seal did not work and you must repeat the process. If the lid is tight, then you are all set! Otherwise, remove lid and wipe rim of jar clean with a sterilized towel. Reseal jar with lid and band, and return to pot of boiling water for 5 minutes more.

More Detailed Storage Guide

We have prepared this list to help you best enjoy your seasonal produce, and how to time which foods to eat first when you pick up your CSA subscription or arrive home from the farmers market.

We have used our decades of experience as restaurant chefs to advise you on how to best store your foods. While there are numerous beliefs on correct storage, the approaches that follow have been tested on many thousands of cases of wholesale produce.

Enjoy your great local fruits and vegetables, and store them well!

Asparagus
Shelf Life: Up to 10 days
Cold part of the refrigerator, with the cut end in an inch or 2 of water. Upright, in a plastic container.

Apples
Shelf Life: 5–26 weeks
Coldest part of the refrigerator. Soften after some months, but fine for cooking after that.

Basil (*all types*)
Shelf Life: 2–5 days
Cut stems in vase with water on countertop is best, or in the warmest part of the refrigerator. Excessive cold blackens the leaves.
Long-term Storage: Wash and dry leaves. Purée in a food processor with about 1 Tbs olive oil for every 1 cup of leaves. Spoon into ice cube trays and freeze. When frozen solid, cubes can be transferred to a Ziploc bag.

Beans (*fava*)
Shelf Life: 7–10 days in the refrigerator
Refrigerator—loose and dry.

Beans (*yard-long*)
Shelf Life: 5–7 days in the refrigerator
Refrigerator—loose and dry.

Beets
Shelf Life: roots: 5 weeks; greens: 5 days
Best in refrigerator, but OK in basement. Separate greens—must be refrigerated. Wash greens just before cooking.

Blackberries
Shelf Life: 3–5 days
Must be refrigerated: coldest part of refrigerator. If storing in a plastic container, pack loosely. It's also okay to store in an open container. Wash right before eating/using. Excess undrained water leads to fungal growth.

Blueberries
Shelf Life: 1–2 weeks
Must be refrigerated: coldest part of refrigerator. Wash only before eating/using. Excess water leads to fungal growth.
Long-term Storage: Line a cookie sheet with parchment or wax paper. Lay blueberries in a single layer and freeze overnight. Once frozen, they can be transferred to a Ziploc bag.

Broccoli
Shelf Life: 1–2 weeks
Refrigerate in coldest part of refrigerator. Best with a moist towel on top to keep crisp.

Brussels Sprouts
Shelf Life: Keeps 3–4 weeks
Coldest part of the refrigerator.

Cabbage (green)
Shelf Life: Refrigerate up to 4 months
Best anywhere in the refrigerator. Can be stored in a very cold basement if needed, but not ideal.

Cabbage (Chinese)
Shelf Life: 5–21 days
Any part of refrigerator.

Carrots
Shelf Life: 3 months, properly stored
Coldest part of the refrigerator. Best to store dry (in a bag). If they are too wet, they will start to sprout or rot. Out of the bag, they begin to go flaccid. Cellar only with great care.

Cauliflower
Shelf Life: 1–2 weeks
Refrigerate in coldest part of refrigerator.

Celeriac
Shelf Life: Up to 3 months
Refrigerator is best, but pantry or cellar works okay too.

Celery
Shelf Life: 1–3 weeks
Coldest part of refrigerator. Leaves like to be dry in a bag. Stems like to be loose in a bag.

Cilantro
Shelf Life: 3–14 days
Washed, drained, and then refrigerated. In a sealed Tupperware, with a paper towel or cloth underneath to help regulate the moisture.

Corn (popping)
Shelf Life: 9 months

Sealed jar in pantry is best. Pops best if used within 9 months of harvest.

Corn (sweet)
Shelf Life: Best to eat immediately, but will retain sweetness up to 4 days
Coldest part of the refrigerator. Typically loses sweetness during storage.
Long-term Storage: Cut kernels off the cob. Store in a Ziploc bag in the freezer for up to 6 months.

Cucumbers
Shelf Life: 3–10 days
Refrigerate.
Long-term Storage: See Pickles for pickling suggestions.

Dill
Shelf Life: 3–14 days
Washed, drained, and then refrigerated. In a sealed Tupperware, with a paper towel or cloth underneath to help regulate the moisture.
Long-term Storage: Wash and thoroughly dry. Put in a Ziploc bag and freeze. No need to defrost before using.

Edamame (soy beans)
Shelf Life: 7 days
Store refrigerated, unwashed.

Eggplant
Shelf Life: 7–10 days upon refrigeration
On counter until ripe and soft (and a little wrinkly)—this is mildest and most tender. When ripe put in refrigerator.

Fennel Bulbs
Shelf Life: 1–3 weeks
Coldest part of refrigerator. Leaves like to be dry in a bag. Stems like to be loose in a bag.

Figs
Shelf Life: Best eaten immediately
Even in the refrigerator, they will only keep for 2 days before starting to mold.

Garlic
Shelf Life: Best flavor when eaten within 6 weeks, but can keep up to 4 months
Pantry.

Ginger
Shelf Life: 1 month
In the refrigerator, in a brown paper bag, for up to 1 month in the warmer part such as the crisper drawer.
Long-term Storage: Peel and freeze up to 6 months.

Green Beans/String Beans
Shelf Life: 3–10 days
Refrigerator—loose and dry.

Greens
All greens should be washed and drained before storing in the refrigerator. Longest shelf life is had by placing greens on top

of a paper towel or clean cloth inside a lidded Tupperware container. Whole heads store longer and better than cut leaves.

Shelf Life:

Arugula: 3–14 days

Bok Choy: 1–3 weeks

Collards: 3–14 days

Cress: 3–7 days

Endive (Belgian): 1–8 weeks

Frisée: 5–14 days

Hon Tsai Tai: 3–5 days

Kale: 3–14 days

Lettuce: 3–7 days

Mesclun: 2–5 days

Mizuna: 7–10 days

Mustard Greens: 3–10 days

Pak Choi: 3–21 days

Pea Tendrils: 3–5 days

Radicchio: 1–3 weeks

Sorrel: 1–7 days

Spinach: 2–5 days

Swiss Chard: 3–14 days

Tat Soi: 1–3 weeks

Yukina Savoy: 3–5 days

Horseradish

Shelf Life: Many months
Coldest part of refrigerator.

Jerusalem Artichokes

Shelf Life: Many months
Coldest part of refrigerator, loose and dry in paper or plastic bag.

Kohlrabi

Shelf Life: 1–6 weeks
Coldest part of refrigerator, loose and dry in plastic bag.

Lima Beans

Shelf Life: Up to 10 days
Refrigerator. Shell as soon as pods slightly soften.

Long-term Storage: Freeze shelled beans for up to 6 months.

Leeks

Shelf Life: 5–30 days
Coldest part of refrigerator, loose and dry in plastic bag.

Melons (cantaloupe)

Shelf Life: Up to 2 weeks (after ripe) in refrigerator
On counter until ripe. Refrigerating will slow or stop the ripening if necessary. Cantaloupe smells perfumed and ripe from the stem end when perfect; the flesh will be meltingly soft when fully ripe. At this point, eat within 24 hours or refrigerate.

Melons (honeydew)

Shelf Life: Up to 5 weeks in the refrigerator
Treat as per cantaloupe; however, honeydews have little, if any, scent. Store on the counter until ripe, when it will be more white than green on the outside with a little yellow blush over parts of

the skin (5–30%); store in the refrigerator when ripe.

Melons (watermelon)
Shelf Life: 3–5 weeks
Counter storage will not help ripening. Watermelons have much more tolerance for pantry, refrigerator, or basement storage than other melons.

Mint
Shelf Life: 2–5 days
Cut stems in vase with water on countertop is best, or in the warmest part of the refrigerator. Excessive cold blackens the leaves.
Long-term Storage: Wash and thoroughly dry. Put in a Ziploc bag and freeze. No need to defrost before using.

Mushrooms (wild)
Shelf Life: 1–5 days
Immediately refrigerate when you return home from the market. Best stored in a paper bag or in Tupperware with a paper towel. Do not store in a plastic bag. Wash immediately before using. Porcinis and honeys are ideally used within 12 hours. Morels, oysters, maitake, and shiitake can last up to 2–4 weeks in the refrigerator. Once cooked, they freeze superbly.

Nectarines
Shelf Life: Once ripened and refrigerated, 3–5 days

On countertop, loose and separated on platter, until just soft. Fruit should sit on its shoulders. Once ripe, eat within 12 hours or refrigerate.

Okra
Shelf Life: 3–7 days
Refrigerated, dry and loose in bag. Wash only immediately before using.

Onions (dry skin)
Shelf Life: 2–20 weeks
Pantry or basement.

Onions (green and spring)
Shelf Life: 3–14 days
Must be refrigerated.

Oregano
Shelf Life: 2–5 days
Do not wash! Store loose in a bag in the warmest part of refrigerator. Best if used quickly.

Parsley
Shelf Life: 4–21 days
Washed, drained, and then refrigerated. In a sealed Tupperware, with a paper towel or cloth underneath to help regulate the moisture.
Long-term Storage: Wash and thoroughly dry. Put in a Ziploc bag and freeze. No need to defrost before using.

Parsnips
Shelf Life: 3 months
Coldest part of the refrigerator. Best to store dry (in a bag). If they are too wet, they will start to sprout or rot. Out of the bag, they begin to go flaccid. Cellar only with great care.

Peaches
Shelf Life: Once ripened and refrigerated, 3–5 days
On countertop, loose and separated on platter, until just soft. Fruit should sit on its shoulders. Once ripe, eat within 12 hours or refrigerate.

Peas (English)
Shelf Life: 1–3 weeks, but sweetest eaten within 1–4 days after harvest
Refrigerator, keep in the bag. Shell as soon as pods soften.

Peas (snow, sugar snap)
Shelf Life: 3–14 days
Coldest part of refrigerator.

Peppers (green, sweet)
Shelf Life: 1–5 weeks
Refrigerate, loose and dry.

Peppers (Hot)
Shelf Life: 1–5 weeks
Refrigerate, loose and dry.
Long-term Storage: Cut into rings, then pack in vinegar or freeze.

Peppers (red, sweet)
Shelf Life: 3–21 days
Refrigerate, loose and dry.
Long-term Storage: Place peppers over a gas burner (or under a broiler) until the skin is blackened on all sides. Put peppers in a bowl, cover with plastic wrap and let steam for 10 minutes. When peppers are cool, peel or rub away blackened skin. Cut in half; remove and discard the stem and seeds. Toss with olive oil. Freeze in 1-cup containers.

Plums
Shelf Life: Once ripened and refrigerated: 3–5 days
On countertop, loose and separated on platter, until just soft. Once ripe, eat within 12 hours or refrigerate.

Potatoes ("Irish", but actually from the Andes)
Shelf Life: Up to 4 months in refrigerator, 6 months maximum in cool cellar or pantry
Pantry, cellar, or warmest part of the refrigerator. Very cold temperatures lead to increased sugar/sweetness; nice for some people, unexpected for others. New potatoes, on the other hand, must be refrigerated.

Pumpkins
Shelf Life: 3–8 weeks
In a cool basement (55–65°F) or pantry. Hate refrigeration.

Purslane
Shelf Life: 2 days
Wrap in a damp paper towel, store up to 2 days in the refrigerator.

Radishes
Shelf Life: 1–5 weeks
Washed, drained, and then refrigerated in a Tupperware with a paper towel or cloth underneath to help regulate the moisture.

Raspberries
Shelf Life: 1–3 days
Must be refrigerated in coldest part of refrigerator. If storing in a plastic container, pack loosely. Okay to store in an open container. Wash only before eating/using: excessive or premature washing leads to fungal growth.

Rhubarb
Shelf Life: Maximum 3 weeks, coldest part of the refrigerator in a plastic bag
Long-term Storage: Wash stems, cut into ½-inch chunks, slowly simmer until soft (see Stewed Rhubarb recipe on page 252). Freeze. Great for pies and other fillings.

Rosemary
Shelf Life: 1–2 weeks
Do not wash! Store dried, loose in a bag in any part of refrigerator.

Rutabaga
Shelf Life: 2–7 weeks
Loose and dry in any part of the refrigerator.

Sage
Shelf Life: 2–5 days
Do not wash! Store loose in a bag in the warmest part of refrigerator. Best if used immediately.

Squash Blossoms
Shelf Life: 1–3 days
Refrigerate ASAP! Store in a lidded Tupperware with a moist paper towel in the bottom.
Long-term Storage: May be stuffed, dredged, and then frozen (see Stuffed Squash Blossoms recipe on page 65).

Squash (summer, all)
Shelf Life: 3–10 days
Refrigerate.

Squash (winter: acorn, buttercup, delicata, hubbard, kabocha)
Shelf Life: 1–5 months, depending on variety and growing conditions
In a cool basement, pantry, or countertop (55–65°F). Hates refrigeration.

Squash (winter: butternut, spaghetti)
Shelf Life: 3 weeks–6 months, depending on variety and growing conditions
In a cool basement, pantry, or countertop (55–65°F). Hates refrigeration.

Strawberries
Shelf Life: 1–3 days
Must be refrigerated in coldest part of refrigerator. If storing in a plastic

container, pack loosely. Best to store in an open container. Wash only before eating/using: excessive or premature washing leads to fungal growth.
Long-term Storage: Wash and stem berries. Put in a pot with ¼ cup of water and 1–2 Tbs of sugar for every cup of berries. Simmer over medium heat until soft. Purée and freeze.

Sweet Potatoes
Shelf Life: 5 weeks–8 months, depending on variety and previous handling
Hate refrigeration: NEVER in refrigerator. Basement or pantry. Ideally at 55–65°F, but tolerates up to 80°F or higher.

Tarragon
Shelf Life: 4–7 days
Dry, loose in a plastic bag in the coldest part of the refrigerator. Wash just before using. If you pack it in vinegar or white wine, it will keep indefinitely.

Thyme
Shelf Life: 1–2 weeks
Do not wash! Store loose in a bag in any part of refrigerator.

Tomatillos
Shelf Life: 10–14 days in refrigerator
Keep on countertop until ripe (pale yellow/green inner skin and softening of fruit).

Tomatoes (big slicing)
Shelf Life: Once ripened and refrigerated: 3–5 days
Countertop, loose and separated on platter, until just soft. On shoulders as per peaches and nectarines.
Long-term Storage: See canning directions (see page 32). Alternatively, make sauce (see page 271) or stewed tomatoes (see page 237) and freeze.

Tomatoes (cherry)
Shelf Life: in refrigerator: 7–10 days
Assuming they arrive ripe, eat within 12 hours or refrigerate. If underripe, store in open container on counter until fully ripe.

Tomatoes (plum)
Shelf Life: in refrigerator: up to 10 days
Store loose on counter, separated from each other, until ripe. Use or refrigerate within 24 hours.
Long-term Storage: See canning directions (see page 32) . Alternatively, make sauce (see page 271) or stewed tomatoes (see page 237) and freeze.

Turnips
Shelf Life: 2–7 weeks
Loose and dry in any part of the refrigerator.

Key Techniques and Definitions of Terms 4

Washing Leafy Greens: Most vegetables can be washed under cool (not cold) running water. The exception to this is the leafy greens which need a soaking to remove all the dirt. Nothing ruins a meal more than biting into a mouthful of sandy, gritty greens.

To properly wash greens and rid them of dirt: fill a large bowl or sink with cool water. Put the greens in the water and gently swish them around. Let them sit for a minute to let the dirt settle to the bottom. Lift the greens out of the water and place them in a colander to let the water drain. Do not pour the greens with the water into the colander as the grit that has settled to the bottom will reintroduce itself into the leaves. For really **gritty greens**, repeat this process with clean water. This technique is also recommended for leeks, parsley, cilantro, wild mushrooms, and berries.

Baking and Roasting are often used for the vegetables of late summer, especially the winter squash (grown during the summer, but suitable for storage and use during the colder months) and sweet potatoes. Farm-fresh eggs also perform superbly in baking. They are so fresh relative to store-bought that cakes and soufflés made with them are much more airy, as is the fried-then-baked Italian omelet, the frittata.

Roasting is a subset of baking. In this simplest of cookbooks, roasting usually means adding seasoning and olive oil, baking between 340°F and 425°F until nearly soft, then adding (if desired) chopped onion, garlic, and herbs.

Blanching is to steam or boil briefly (10–90 seconds), usually followed by

washing greens

shocking in an ice bath. Used more with winter cooking greens.

Boiling is unjustifiably looked down upon as a "common" cooking technique, but it can make tough greens or old stewing chickens more tender than can anything except a pressure cooker. Boiling can also dispel or dilute the occasionally bitter flavors of some vegetables. We always add about 1 tsp salt per quart of water to preserve the color and some of the nutrients that can be lost by non-careful boiling. Be sure, too, that the water is fully boiling (medium and small bubbles coming up from the pot's bottom) or rolling more vigorously. Simmering, a gentler boil with only small bubbles coming up, is the key technique for a great tomato sauce.

Braising is to cook under low to moderate heat, with plenty of water, broth, beer, or wine, until soft. Excellent for bigger summer squash, for the winter squash, for non-bitter, cold-season greens, for some meats, and for comfort food approaches. Cooking times vary from only 20 or 30 seconds (the most tender greens) to as long as 2 hours (some meats).

Grilling means cooking over an open flame and usually on top of a grate. We grill many summer vegetables: summer squash, plum tomatoes, skewered cherry tomatoes, tomatillos, sweet peppers, sweet potato slices, and even parboiled potatoes. Even at its simplest, good grilling should involve

brushing vegetables sparingly with oil and seasoning with salt and pepper. More complex marinades can include soy sauce, wine, minced onion and garlic, herbs, ginger, etc.

Deep frying adds textural contrast and interest to many vegetables, but given that it adds many calories to a recipe, we recommend saving this technique for special occasions. To deep-fry properly, you will need a heavy-bottomed 3-quart pot and plenty of plain oil. If you have a "fry daddy," even better. A slotted spoon or Chinese wire-mesh spoon is the best tool for fetching food out of the oil. Always drain on a paper towel or newspaper to absorb excess grease.

The secret to non-greasy deep-fried foods is making sure the oil is properly heated and the pot is not overcrowded. A candy thermometer is the best tool to ensure the oil is properly heated. In a pinch, a wooden spoon acts as a good gauge. Put the spoon in the oil; when vigorous bubbles form around the spoon, the oil is hot. By not adding too much food at a time, the oil maintains its temperature. Heat the oil over a medium-high heat. When the oil reaches the proper temperature, 350°F to 375°F, turn the heat down to medium and monitor to make sure the temperature stays within that range.

Nearly all fried foods signal they are done not by color, but by sound. Food that has just been put in the oil crackles very loudly from all the moisture. Once the food floats, it will turn down the volume somewhat, but there's an abrupt shift to pretty quiet just when it hits the perfect point.

Oil here means oil from vegetables, seeds, or nuts. We advocate using oils to protect broiling, grilling, or roasting foods from drying out; to conduct heat while grilling; and in the more traditional sense, to prevent foods in a skillet from sticking. In the Italianate approach we prefer, we rarely fry or sauté in pure butter (which is a fat, not an oil), but rather add butter late and sparingly to a sauté or even as a final seasoning.

We recommend stocking three oils: extra-virgin olive oil; any relatively neutral or plain oil like peanut, corn, or canola; and dark sesame oil. Extra-virgin olive oil is strongly perfumed, outstanding in salads or roasted vegetables, but easily burned and costly for sauté. Sesame oil acts in much the same way but is of Asian origin. We therefore often blend either of the two strongly flavored oils above with the intentionally neutral corn, peanut, or canola oil. The neutral oils elevate the temperatures at which the olive or sesame oils alone would burn, as well as decreasing cost and toning down the overwhelming flavors of the premium oils. A neutral oil such as canola or peanut is ideal for deep-frying.

Poaching is a temperature-sensitive, gentle technique. It means barely cooking greens, eggs, or most famously fish in water or broth that is just below 212°F and that is rigorously guarded against that boiling point. Poaching respects tender foods better than any other cooking approach, though with chewier or tougher foods, boiling remains a better choice. Poaching or blanching large whole tomatoes let us then shock them with ice water, peel the skins, and have skin-free tomato meats.

Shocking is an essential step that follows boiling or steaming of many foods, from tomatoes, greens, and other vegetables to eggs and even shrimp. Shocking stops the cooking process precisely when you want by immediately plunging the really hot food into an ice water bath (recall that foods continue to cook from the time they are taken from the stove until the time they cool to room temperature). They are then drained promptly. This keeps the lovely bright green of asparagus, beans, and leafy vegetables, as well as keeping textures crisp rather than becoming mushy. Nearly all vegetables and plain shrimp served in many restaurants are blanched and shocked, later seasoned, and possibly reheated. Shocking gives busy cooks insurance against overcooking. Ice water is our friend.

Steaming is one of the hottest and fastest ways to cook, but adds little flavor (in contrast with sautéing or grilling). Western steamers are good, but a wok and stackable bamboo steamers, available in good Asian markets, remain our favorite. Be sure to start with at least ¾-inch of water for fast steaming and at least 3 cups of water for long steaming. Put your food in the steamer after it has fully heated up and is vigorously steaming.

On Pots and Pans: We urge you to consider pruning your kitchens of potentially hazardous cookware. Cookware coated with Teflon or other synthetics always slowly and imperceptibly lose their finish, and molecules of Teflon are now being routinely discovered in alarming amounts in human tissues and in the environment. Enameled pots (e.g., Le Creuset) are outstanding, but only if the enamel finish is entirely intact. Solid aluminum pots require fewer cautions: aluminum appears to be OK except for acidic cooking (like tomato sauces), but conclusive data on the health effects of aluminum aren't yet present.

So what pans to use? Cast iron makes the absolute best for skillets and woks, and cultures that still favor cast iron have lower incidences of anemia (any iron that leaches out into your food acts as a vital nutrient; not so with aluminum or Teflon). The only drawbacks are that iron pans weigh more and react with acidic foods. For deep frying and large volumes of stew, we use cast iron Dutch ovens, though the weight necessitates lifting these with two hands when full.

And for boiling water, as well as all sizes of saucepans, high-quality, thick-bottomed stainless steel is super.

Finally, having both a blender and a food processor will make cooking much easier. We loathe any surplus of kitchen gadgets but find these indispensable. It should also be noted that a blender makes a poor substitute for a food processor, and a food processor rarely purées as smoothly as a blender—hence the need for both.

The Recipes 5

The recipes in this book range from super-simple with just a few ingredients to more complex, multi-component dishes. There are soups, salads, side dishes, entrees, and desserts. All give you new and interesting ways to enjoy your fresh produce.

We've each cooked professionally for over 15 years. Like many chefs, we've tired of our own cooking, so when we get together we love eating each other's creations. But we have distinct personalities, which perhaps you will pick up on.

Most notably, Julia seasons all her recipes with salt, pepper, and lemon juice, whereas Brett is more likely to use beer or wine for a final flourish.

The other big distinction, perhaps less obvious, is Brett's substantially larger appetite than Julia's—no doubt from hours working in the fields planting, harvesting, and working the land. By Julia's standards, Brett's recipes could feed a family of four for a week. And Brett could easily make a single meal out of a recipe Julia thinks would feed 6.

Unless otherwise noted, the recipes generally yield four to six servings. The number of servings you get will depend on whom you're serving and what you're serving with the dish.

Cooking for Dietary Restrictions

We don't profess to be vegetarian or gluten-free. But certainly, if you prefer to eat that way, many of the recipes can accommodate dietary restrictions and preferences.

We've noted recipes that accommodate vegetarian, vegan, and gluten-free diets. Some recipes are inherently friendly—that is, they don't have gluten and/or animal products. And some recipes are easily adapted: as an example, olive oil often makes a fine substitute for butter. Those recipes are also noted accordingly. But in some cases, we feel the notation would be disingenuous—like suggesting a pasta dish is gluten-free because there is gluten-free pasta available on the market. That shouldn't stop you from trying any dish!

Vegan recipes do not have any animal products or by-products (like dairy or eggs), or those ingredients can easily be omitted.

 Gluten-free recipes do not have any gluten, or those ingredients can easily be omitted.

 Vegetarian recipes do not have any animal flesh, or those ingredients can easily be omitted.

Breakfast

Pumpkin Bread

◆ ◆ ◆ ◆ ◆

1¾ c	all-purpose flour
1 tsp	baking powder
1 tsp	baking soda
¾ tsp	salt
¾ tsp	cinnamon
¼ tsp	nutmeg
1½ c	pumpkin purée (see page 20)
½ c	sugar
½ c	brown sugar
½ c	vegetable oil, plus extra for brushing pans
2	large eggs
½ tsp	minced fresh ginger
¾ c	buttermilk or ¾ cup milk mixed with 1 tsp lemon juice

—————— Optional ——————

1 c	raisins, walnuts, and/or pepitas (pumpkin seeds)

*Nice as a breakfast food with fresh fruit,
or as a less caloric dessert for dinner or lunch.
Keeps very well tightly wrapped and refrigerated.*

1. Preheat the oven to 350°F. Brush two 9-inch loaf pans with oil.

2. Combine flour, baking powder, baking soda, salt, cinnamon, and nutmeg in medium bowl; whisk to blend. Mix in any of the optional additions. Mix pumpkin and both sugars in a large bowl until blended. Gradually whisk in oil, then eggs 1 at a time, then minced ginger. Stir in dry ingredients in 4 additions alternately with buttermilk. Divide batter among prepared pans.

3. Bake breads until tester inserted into center comes out clean, about 1 hour. Cool in pans.

Raspberry Pancakes

*We like to add the raspberries at the end
so they hold their shape and texture.*

1. Sift flour, salt, sugar, and baking powder together into a bowl and make a well in the center.

2. Mix together milk, eggs, and butter. Pour into the well of dry ingredients. Mix until just incorporated.

3. Heat a frying pan over medium heat. Add butter. Ladle in about 2 ounces of batter per pancake. Dot each pancake with a few berries. Cook for about 3 minutes. Flip, continue cooking. Serve immediately, or keep warm in a 200°F oven until ready to serve.

4. When finished making all the pancakes, add the remaining berries to the pan along with some maple syrup. Pour the berry syrup over the pancakes just before serving.

1½ c	all-purpose flour
1 tsp	salt
3 Tbs	sugar
1 Tbs	baking powder
1½ c	milk
2	eggs, lightly beaten
3 Tbs	melted butter
1 c	raspberries
½–1 c	maple syrup
	butter for cooking

3 Tbs	butter
4 slices	bread
3	eggs
1 c	milk
½ tsp	salt
3 Tbs	fresh herbs: basil, scallions, tarragon, and/or parsley
1 Tbs	finely diced celery
2	large tomatoes, sliced
8 oz ball	fresh mozzarella, sliced

Tomato Mozzarella Strata

Strata is a breakfast dish, similar to a quiche or frittata.

1. Preheat the oven to 350°F. While the oven is heating, melt butter in a 9-inch square Pyrex dish.

2. Lay bread slices on top of melted butter.

3. In a mixing bowl, combine eggs, milk, herbs, and celery. Season with salt.

4. Pour egg mix over the bread.

5. Layer tomatoes, mozzarella, and basil on top. Sprinkle with a little extra salt and pepper for seasoning.

6. Bake at 350°F for 45 minutes or until eggs are set. Serve immediately.

Zucchini Bread

Less dense than pumpkin or carrot breads, and generally less sweet. A fine breakfast food or light dessert, and an excellent way to use zucchini when you have too much.

1. Preheat the oven to 325°F.

2. Grease the insides of two 9-inch × 5-inch bread pans.

3. In a large mixing bowl, combine zucchini, oil, eggs, and vanilla. Mix thoroughly.

4. Add sugars to the above and mix until it is thoroughly blended.

5. In a separate bowl, combine the flours, baking soda, baking powder, salt and cinnamon. Whisk together to break up any clumps. Add the flour mix to the above. Mix until batter is well blended and even in texture. The batter should be smooth, except for the zucchini shreds. If it's not, add a few tablespoons of milk. Stir in the walnuts or raisins.

6. Divide the batter evenly between the two pans.

7. Bake for approximately 1 hour, or until bread is brown and springs back when gently pressed in the middle. Let cool for 10 minutes before serving.

2–2½ c	zucchini, shredded
1 c	vegetable oil
3	eggs
1 tsp	vanilla
¾ c	white sugar
¾ c	brown sugar
2 c	all-purpose flour
1 c	whole wheat flour
1 tsp	baking soda
¼ tsp	baking powder
1 tsp	salt
1 tsp	cinnamon
1 c	walnuts, chopped, or raisins, or a combination of the two

VEGETARIAN

◆ ◆ ◆ ◆ ◆

Appetizers,
Hors d'Oeuvres,
and Snacks

Arugula Soufflé

3 Tbs	butter, plus extra for buttering the soufflé dish
4 Tbs	flour
1½ c	half–n–half
6	eggs separated + 2 egg whites (for a total of 6 yolks and 8 whites)
4	bunches arugula (about 3–4 cups), washed, with tougher stems removed
4 oz	soft goat cheese
	pinch cayenne pepper
	pinch nutmeg
⅛ tsp	cream of tartar
	salt and pepper to taste

This recipe is adapted from the Silver Palate Cookbook. *It makes an elegant start to an early spring dinner.*

1. Preheat the oven to 375°F. Butter a 2-quart soufflé dish.

2. Make the soufflé base: Melt the butter in a medium sauce pan over medium heat. Add the flour and cook, stirring constantly until the butter starts to foam. While still on the heat, slowly whisk in the half and half. Remove from heat, and whisk in the egg yolks.

3. Finely chop the arugula in a food processor or by hand. Mix into the soufflé base, along with the goat cheese. Season with cayenne, nutmeg, salt, and pepper.

4. Combine the egg whites, a pinch of salt, and the cream of tartar in a bowl. Whisk at a high speed (with an electric mixer) until the whites are stiff.

5. Gently fold egg whites into soufflé base. Pour into soufflé dish and bake for 35–45 minutes, or until well puffed and golden. The center should be just firm or have the slightest bit of wiggle.

Serve immediately.

arugula

Braised Endive with Watercress and Apple Salad

*This salad is fully flavored and balanced with bitter endive,
spicy watercress, earthy cheese, and sweet apples.
Served with crusty bread, you could make a meal of it.*

1. Put endive in a pot with sugar and lemon juice. Cover with water. Season water to taste with salt and pepper, and additional lemon juice or sugar as necessary. Bring water to a boil, reduce heat to simmer. Let endive simmer for 30 minutes, or until tender.

2. When the endive are tender, remove from liquid. Put endive in an ovenproof dish. Cover with cheese. Melt cheese in the oven (350°F) for 5 minutes.

3. Meanwhile, core and slice apple thinly (do not peel). Toss apples and watercress with vinegar, olive oil, and shallots. Season to taste with salt and pepper (and fresh thyme if you'd like).

4. Serve half a large endive or 1 whole small endive per person with a small watercress and apple salad.

2	endive, large, cut in half lengthwise, or 4 small endive
2 Tbs	sugar
2	lemons, juiced
¾ c	grated Gruyère or Swiss cheese
1	red apple
1 bunch	watercress
1 Tbs	cider vinegar
3 Tbs	extra virgin olive oil, salt and pepper to taste
1	shallot, diced

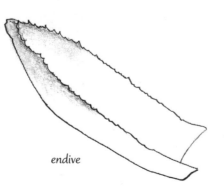

endive

◆ ◆ ◆ ◆ ◆

2 Tbs	butter
4	leeks, dark green tops removed, cut in half lengthwise and washed
1 sprig	thyme
¼ c	white wine
1 c	chicken or vegetable broth
2 slices	bacon, diced (or ¼ cup toasted walnuts)
1 c	arugula
	mustard vinaigrette
	salt and black pepper

—— **Mustard Vinaigrette** ——

1 tsp	whole grain mustard
2 tsp	red wine vinegar
¼ c	extra virgin olive oil
	salt and pepper to taste

Braised Leeks with Mustard Vinaigrette

This is a classic French appetizer.

1. Melt butter in a skillet and add the leeks in a single layer, cut side down. Brown a little before adding a sprig of thyme and the wine. Let the wine reduce and then add the stock, salt and pepper to taste.

2. Put leeks in a 350°F oven for 20 minute to braise, or until softened. Set aside.

3. Put the diced bacon in a pan in the oven to render the fat and get crispy. Drain the bacon on a paper towel. If using walnuts, toast in the oven for 10 minutes or until they become fragrant.

4. To serve, dress the arugula in mustard vinaigrette and put on a plate. Lay the leeks on the plate and sprinkle bacon bits or walnuts on top.

Mustard Vinaigrette
Whisk everything together.

Chinese Turnip Cakes

This traditional recipe is often seen in Dim Sum houses, and is adapted from Florence Lin's Complete Book of Chinese Noodles, Dumplings and Breads. *This recipe easily halves or doubles. The recipe, as we give it below, makes two loaf pans (9" × 4" × 3"). It is really easy to make, doesn't necessarily taste "radishy," and is absolutely delicious!*

1. Wash roots well. Grate by hand or with a food processor.

2. Heat oil in wok or heavy-bottomed skillet; stir-fry the grated roots with oil for 1 minute on medium heat. Add the salt and pepper, cover and simmer over medium heat for 10 minutes, stirring often.

3. Meanwhile, line two loaf pans with plastic wrap.

4. Mix rice flour with 3½ cups water, then pour mixture into roots, stirring constantly. Cook an additional 3–4 minutes. Remove from heat. Stir in scallions and optional (but highly encouraged) meat.

5. Spoon mixture into loaf pans. When full, push down to remove air bubbles.

6. Steam these loaf pans in a wok or large pot with a steamer basket for 45 minutes. Check the water level regularly to make sure you don't burn the bottom of the pan.

7. Let cool in loaf pans and then refrigerate.

8. When cold, remove turnip cakes from pan and slice ½-inch thick.

9. Heat a skillet over high heat. Add second set of oil. Pan-fry until crispy on both sides.

10. Serve with garnishes.

3 lbs	turnips or radishes
4 Tbs	neutral oil
2 tsp	kosher salt
½ tsp	white pepper or ¾ tsp black pepper
4 c	rice flour
1 bunch	scallions, chopped
2 Tbs	neutral oil + 1 tsp dark sesame oil
½ lb	bacon or ground pork, precooked until edges are browned, then crumbled (optional)

——— **Garnishes** ———

soy sauce, tamari, chili paste, minced scallions, hoisin, and/or cilantro.

◆ ◆ ◆ ◆

2 slices	diced bacon
¼ c	diced red onion
3 ears	corn, kernels cut off cob
½ c	diced red pepper
¼ c	diced scallions or chives
½ c	cornmeal
1½ c	flour
1 Tbs	baking powder
¼ tsp	cayenne pepper (optional)
1 c	milk
2	eggs
	salt and pepper to taste
	canola oil for frying

——— **Red Pepper Salsa** ———

1	large tomato
½	red onion
2 cloves	garlic (optional)
4	scallions, cut into rounds
2	red chili peppers, or 1 canned chipotle pepper
2	sweet red peppers
4 Tbs	chopped cilantro or to taste
2 Tbs	extra virgin olive oil
2	limes juiced, or to taste salt to taste

Corn Fritters with Red Pepper Salsa

While not as healthy, these fritters are also terrific with chipotle aioli (see Cuban Sandwiches recipe, page 213).

1. In a large skillet, cook bacon until half crisp. Add onions and corn, and cook until onions are soft. Cool mixture. Add red peppers and scallions. Season with salt and pepper to taste.

2. In a bowl, mix dry ingredients together (cornmeal, flour, baking powder, cayenne pepper, and salt). Make a well in the center and add the milk and eggs. Stir just to incorporate all ingredients.

3. Combine corn mixture with batter, and stir to mix everything together.

4. Fry 2 Tbs of batter per fritter in oil on medium-high until golden brown on all sides. Drain on paper towel. Serve with salsa.

Red Pepper Salsa
Chop vegetables. Mix together with everything else. Adjust seasoning to taste.

pepper

Eggplant with Fresh Tomato Sauce

A simple but very satisfying vegetarian dish of high summer, when tomatoes and eggplants abound. Good on its own, with crusty bread, alongside pasta, or to accompany grilled meats, poultry, or peppers and zucchini. Fresh basil or herbs of Provençal can substitute for the tarragon.

1. Heat 3 Tbs olive oil in a sauce pan. Add garlic and onions and cook until they are soft. Add tomatoes and continue cooking until most of the liquid is reduced and the sauce is thick. Stir in tarragon. Remove from heat and set aside.

2. Cut eggplant into slices. Season with salt and pepper, toss with olive oil. Broil (or grill) for 5 minutes (turning once), or until they are half soft.

3. Top eggplant with mozzarella, and some tomato sauce. Bake at 400°F for 5 minutes more, until eggplant is soft and cheese is melted.

4. Garnish with fresh basil.

6 Tbs	olive oil
2 cloves	garlic, chopped
1	onion, chopped
2 lb	plum tomatoes, diced
2 Tbs	fresh tarragon
3	Italian eggplants, about 2 pounds
1 Tbs	olive oil
1 lb	fresh mozzarella cheese
	salt and pepper to taste
	basil to garnish

Fried Green Tomatoes

♦ ♦ ♦ ♦ ♦

3   green tomatoes

1 c   buttermilk, or 1 cup regular milk mixed with 1 Tbs sour cream or yogurt

½ c   flour

¼ c   cornmeal

1 tsp salt

½ tsp black pepper

       pinch (or more) cayenne

½ tsp garlic powder

¼ tsp cumin

¼ c   plain oil or bacon grease

A classic Southern dish that deserves to be enjoyed each and every autumn; a traditional way to prepare tomatoes when frost threatens to kill the vines before the tomatoes have a chance to ripen. Superb alongside barbeque, baked chicken, or fish. Using shiny bright green tomatoes with no blush whatsoever ensures best texture.

1. Slice tomatoes ½-inch thick and soak in buttermilk.

2. Mix together flour, cornmeal, salt, and other spices.

3. Heat a large skillet on high. Add oil and/or bacon grease. When oil is hot, dredge tomato slices in flour mix and gently place in pan. Cook on both sides until brown and crispy.

4. Serve with rémoulade (see page 119) or red pepper salsa (see page 58).

Fried Zucchini with Mint

You can fry the zucchini slices in advance and reheat them in the oven. Toss with vinegar and mint just before serving.

1. Wash and dry zucchini. Cut into quarters. Season with salt to taste.

2. Dust zucchini with flour. Toss in egg wash, and coat in bread crumbs.

3. Heat pan on medium. Add oil and butter. Fry zucchini on all sides until bread crumbs are browned and crispy. Drain on a paper towel.

4. In a separate pan, heat sugar and vinegar, and cook until sugar dissolves. Stir in mint. Pour over zucchini.

♦ ♦ ♦ ♦ ♦

6	small zucchini
2 Tbs	all-purpose flour
1	egg, lightly beaten and mixed with 1 Tbs water
1 c	bread crumbs
4 Tbs	olive oil
4 Tbs	butter
3 Tbs	white wine vinegar
1 Tbs	sugar
1 Tbs	mint
	salt to taste

Okra Fritters

◆ ◆ ◆ ◆ ◆

1 c	flour
½ c	cornmeal
¼ c	grated Parmesan
1	medium onion, peeled and diced
3	eggs, lightly beaten
1¼ c	buttermilk
1 tsp	baking soda
2 tsp	salt
½ tsp	cayenne
1 lb	okra, trimmed and sliced thin, about ¼ inch
1 c	canola oil

*Excellent served with a dipping sauce.
Some of our favorites are Romesco (page 270),
Ketchup (page 265), Dreamy Green Goddess (page 260),
and Agrodolce (page 250).*

1. Make a batter by mixing together flour, cornmeal, Parmesan, onions, eggs, buttermilk, baking soda, salt and cayenne. Mix in okra.

2. Heat a large skillet over medium-high heat. Spoon in 4–5 fritters (2–3 Tbs) at a time. Fry until golden brown on each side, about 3 minutes. Drain on paper towels. Keep in a warm place while cooking remaining fritters.

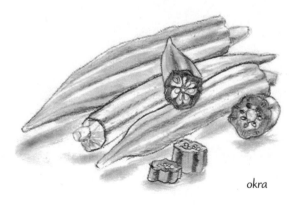

okra

Potstickers

*Even' Star Farm CSA subscriber Ange Funya makes
these Chinese-inspired dumplings with whatever
cooking greens show up in her weekly share.
Makes 20–36 depending on wonton wrapper size.*

1. Place chopped greens in large bowl and toss with salt.
   Let greens wilt for about 30 minutes.

2. Squeeze liquid out of greens.

3. Combine pork, garlic, green onion, ginger, sesame oil, soy
   sauce, and pepper with the wilted greens. Mix well.

4. Place approximately 1 tablespoon filling mixture into a
   wonton skin. Fold in half to form a triangle, corner to corner.
   Seal the dumpling with water. Place dumplings onto an oiled
   plate or cookie sheet and cover with a damp cloth until ready
   to cook.

5. To cook dumplings: heat a heavy skillet over medium-high
   heat. Add oil. Place dumplings into skillet and brown on one
   side (or both) and then add ½ cup water to steam. Cover and
   steam for 3–5 minutes.

◆ ◆ ◆ ◆ ◆

1 lb	greens (loosely packed), coarsely chopped
2 Tbs	kosher salt
1 lb	ground pork
2–3	cloves garlic, minced
4	green onions, chopped fine
2 tsp	minced fresh ginger
2 tsp	toasted sesame oil
1 Tbs	soy sauce
¼ tsp	ground pepper
	wonton skins
2 Tbs	canola or peanut oil

8	figs
1 tsp	fresh thyme
8 slices	prosciutto
2 c	balsamic vinegar
¼ c	white wine
1	shallot, diced
3 oz	Roquefort or other blue cheese
2 Tbs	butter

——————— Optional ———————

arugula salad

Prosciutto-Wrapped Grilled Figs with Blue Cheese and Balsamic

*If you can manage to save the figs for cooking
(we could easily eat every single one raw), they are delicious
grilled or roasted with a little balsamic.*

1. Slice figs in half. Sprinkle with thyme. Wrap in prosciutto and secure with a toothpick.

2. Put 2 cups of balsamic vinegar in a pot, reduce over high heat until about ½ cup remains and the balsamic is syrupy. Remove from heat.

3. In medium sauce pan, add white wine and shallots. Reduce over high heat until only 2 Tbs of liquid remain. Reduce heat to low (or turn heat off completely), and vigorously whisk in blue cheese and 2 Tbs of butter. Set aside in warm place (does not reheat well).

4. Grill figs until prosciutto is slightly charred and figs are heated through. (Alternatively, set under the broiler for a few minutes.) Serve with blue cheese sauce and the balsamic glaze.

5. Garnish with an arugula salad, if you'd like.

Stuffed and Deep-Fried Squash Blossoms

This makes a great hors d'oeuvre, served with a tart dipping sauce such as Agrodolce (page 250).

1. Sauté the garlic, onion, and optional ingredients in the olive oil until the garlic has barely browned. Let cool.

2. In a large bowl, combine the three cheeses, onion-garlic mix, salt, pepper, basil, 1 bowl of egg (i.e., ½ beaten egg), and the bread crumbs, cornmeal, or semolina and gently mix. Fill each blossom only ⅔ full with this mix (a tsp works best) and gently twist the petal tips to close; lay on a cookie sheet after stuffing.

3. Start heating the oil for deep frying. Meanwhile prepare an egg wash by beating the reserved ½ egg with the milk in a medium-sized bowl. Dredge the stuffed blossoms in the commercial coating or into seasoned flour or cornmeal. Then carefully roll these in the egg wash and redredge in the dry flour mix.

4. When oil is hot (use a thermometer to read 350°F, or test by putting a wooden spoon in the oil—when bubbles vigorously form around the spoon, it is properly heated), deep-fry about 5 at a time, until they float; drain on paper towels.

5. Serve immediate*

squash blossom

1 Tbs	olive oil
2 cloves	garlic, chopped
¼ c	minced onion
1 c	ricotta cheese
⅓ c	grated mozzarella
2 Tbs	grated Romano cheese
1	large egg, beaten and divided into 2 bowls
½ tsp	each salt and pepper
⅓ c	coarsely chopped fresh basil
3 Tbs	bread crumbs, semolina flour or coarse cornmeal
20	squash blossoms, picked over to remove any stray insects
¼ c	milk
2 qt	peanut or corn oil (possibly more)
	commercial chicken coating or seasoned flour*

——— Optional ———

½ c	minced ham, baby shrimp, or sweet corn kernels

VEGETARIAN

* To make your own seasoned flour: Mix 1 cup flour, cornmeal, or semolina, plus ¾ tsp salt, and ½ tsp each pepper and dried thyme.

Sweet Potato Latkes

◆ ◆ ◆ ◆ ◆

1   small sweet potato
1   medium russet potato
1   onion
2 Tbs   flour
1   egg
1 tsp   baking powder
¼ c   plain oil
     salt and pepper to taste

The trick to crispy latkes is to squeeze as much liquid out of the potatoes as you possibly can.
Serve with apple sauce (page 236), sour cream, or both.

1. Peel potatoes and onion. Grate using the largest hole of a cheese grater or food processor. Pour into a colander and squeeze out any liquid.

2. Mix potatoes and onion with flour, egg, salt, pepper, and baking powder.

3. Heat a large skillet over medium-high heat and add about 2 Tbs oil. Spoon about 2 Tbs of batter per latke—about 4 latkes per batch. Cook for about 5 minutes or until brown, flip and cook on other side. Drain on a paper towel. Repeat until all the batter is used.

Tomato Bruschetta

When summer evenings grow so hot that dinner cooking is wearisome, tomato bruschetta can be a most welcome main course or big appetizer. Easy, delicious, light, satisfying but low calorie, the only negative is that preparing bruschetta with out-of-season tomatoes will disappoint. Think SUMMER!!

1. Mix the tomatoes and salt in a china, glass, or steel bowl. Let sit 30–45 minutes while you prepare the rest of your meal.

2. Put all into a colander to drain the juice. Mix in the other ingredients, add more vinegar, salt, or pepper to taste, and serve alongside the warm toasted bread slices.

1 lb	Roma or other plum tomatoes, chopped into ⅓-inch pieces
1 lb	ripe cherry tomatoes, quartered, or heirloom tomatoes, cut into ⅓-inch pieces
¾ tsp	kosher or sea salt
2 cloves	garlic, chopped (or more)
¼ tsp	freshly ground black pepper
½ tsp	balsamic or red wine vinegar
2 Tbs	coarsely chopped basil
10 slices	toasted bread, preferably from a baguette-type loaf

Turnip Bruschetta

◆ ◆ ◆ ◆ ◆

2	medium turnips
1	medium red onion
¼ c	(or less) olive oil
4 oz	prosciutto (optional)
1–2 Tbs	balsamic vinegar (more or less depending on how much olive oil used)
1 Tbs	fresh rosemary (or 1 tsp dried)
8 slices	baguette

This recipe comes courtesy of Even' Star CSA member Jennifer LaRoche. She suggests serving it as an appetizer/hors d'oeuvre for a winter cocktail party or open house.

1. Dice the turnips and red onion.

2. In a medium skillet, heat olive oil over medium-high heat. Add the turnips and onions and sauté for 10 minutes, or until onions are soft and turnips are tender.

3. Add the prosciutto (or ¼ tsp of salt) to the turnips, season with the balsamic vinegar and rosemary.

4. Toast the baguette slices.

5. Just before serving top each slice of baguette with turnip/prosciutto mix.

Baba Ganoush I

*Traditionally, raw garlic is added to the dip,
but Julia prefers the flavor of roasted. If you like raw garlic,
reduce the quantity to one or two cloves.*

1. Prick whole eggplant with a fork. Place directly over a fire (a gas burner or grill) and cook until they are blackened on all sides and the flesh is tender. Let cool.

2. In a piece of aluminum foil, wrap up the garlic and olive oil. Roast in a 350°F oven for 30 minutes, or until the garlic is soft and golden brown.

3. Peel the charred, black skin away from the eggplant and discard.

4. Put the eggplant pulp, tahini, cumin, garlic, and lemon juice in a food processor. Blend until smooth. Season to taste with salt and pepper.

5. Garnish with scallions or parsley.

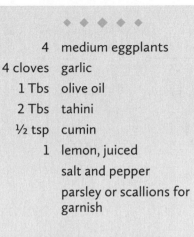

4	medium eggplants
4 cloves	garlic
1 Tbs	olive oil
2 Tbs	tahini
½ tsp	cumin
1	lemon, juiced
	salt and pepper
	parsley or scallions for garnish

Baba Ganoush II

Adapted from Tess Mallos,
The Complete Middle East Cookbook.

◆ ◆ ◆ ◆ ◆

3	large eggplants
3 cloves	garlic
⅓ c	tahini
1–2 Tbs	olive oil
¼–⅓ c	fresh lemon juice
2–3 tsp	salt, or to taste
	black pepper or Tabasco to taste
¼ c	basil, Provençal herb mix, or parsley

———— Optional ————

2 Tbs	freshly toasted sesame seeds

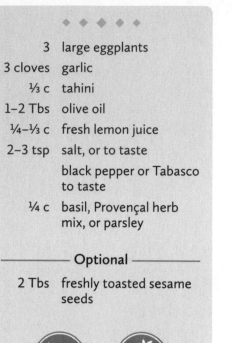

1. Bake the whole eggplant in a lightly oiled, heavy roasting pan or iron skillet at 375°F until soft. Remove from the oven and peel and destem while still warm.

2. Purée eggplant, garlic, and tahini in a Cuisinart until smooth, then drizzle in first the olive oil and then the lemon juice, with the motor running all the while.

3. Add herb(s), salt, and pepper. Adjust seasoning. Sprinkle with the freshly toasted sesame seeds.

4. Serve with crusty bread, crackers, or as a dip for raw vegetables. Keeps very well frozen if well-covered. When thawed, it may be best to add some bread crumbs to absorb the fluid that results from the freezing. Excellent to have stored in the freezer for quick entertaining or snacking.

Edamame Hummus

This recipe can be simplified by skipping the second step and leaving the garlic raw and the cumin untoasted. If you opt to skip this step, you may also want to reduce the amount of garlic to 1 clove. The spinach adds a bright green hue to the dip.

1. Bring a large pot of salted water to a boil. Add edamame and cook for 2–3 minutes or until bright green. Drain and run under cold water to preserve the color.

2. In a small skillet, simmer the garlic with 2 Tbs olive oil over medium heat. After 3 minutes, when the garlic is slightly golden, stir in the cumin. Turn off heat and set aside.

3. In a food processor, combine everything. Purée until smooth, scraping down the sides as necessary.

4. Adjust seasoning to taste with more lemon or salt. Serve with pita chips, crackers, or crudité.

1 c	shelled edamame
2 cloves	garlic, coarsely chopped
4 Tbs	olive oil
¼ tsp	cumin
2 Tbs	tahini
3+ Tbs	lemon juice
¼ tsp	(or more to taste) salt
1 c	loosely packed spinach, arugula or kale, washed

edamame

Basic Popcorn

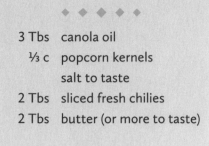

3 Tbs   canola oil
⅓ c   popcorn kernels
        salt to taste
2 Tbs   sliced fresh chilies
2 Tbs   butter (or more to taste)

———— Optional ————

2 strips bacon, diced

*Popcorn is a great afternoon snack.
Our favorite is popcorn with bacon.*

1. Heat the oil in a 3-quart saucepan on medium-high heat.

2. Put 3 or 4 popcorn kernels into the oil and cover the pan.

3. When the kernels pop, remove pan from heat. Add the rest of the kernels in an even layer with a generous pinch of salt. If using chilies and/or bacon, add to pot with kernels. Cover.

4. Return the pan to the heat. The popcorn should begin popping soon, and all at once. Once the popping starts in earnest, gently shake the pan by moving it back and forth over the burner. Try to keep the lid slightly ajar to let the steam from the popcorn release (the popcorn will be drier and crisper). Once the popping slows to several seconds between pops, remove the pan from the heat, remove the lid, and dump the popcorn immediately into a wide bowl.

5. If you are using butter, place it in the now empty but hot pan to melt. When melted, pour over popcorn.

Kettle Popcorn

Add peanuts at the end for a homemade Cracker-Jack.

1. Heat the oil in a 3-quart saucepan on medium-high heat.

2. Put 3 or 4 popcorn kernels into the oil and cover the pan.

3. When the kernels pop, remove pan from heat. Add the rest of the kernels in an even layer, plus a generous pinch of salt and the sugar. Cover.

4. Return the pan to the heat, and give it a good shake. The popcorn should begin popping soon, and all at once. Once the popping starts in earnest, gently shake the pan by moving it back and forth over the burner. Once the popping slows to several seconds between pops, remove the pan from the heat, remove the lid, and dump the popcorn immediately into a wide bowl.

5. If you are using butter, place it in the now empty but hot pan to melt. When melted, pour over popcorn.

3 Tbs	canola oil
⅔ c	popcorn kernels
⅔ c	white sugar
	salt to taste
2 Tbs	butter (or more to taste)

• • • • •

Soups
and
Salads

Butternut Squash and Ginger Soup

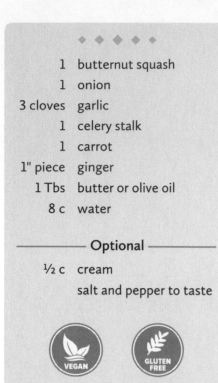

1	butternut squash
1	onion
3 cloves	garlic
1	celery stalk
1	carrot
1" piece	ginger
1 Tbs	butter or olive oil
8 c	water

—————— Optional ——————

½ c	cream
	salt and pepper to taste

If doubling this recipe, consider using two different winter squash varieties, such as acorn or kabocha.

1. Cut butternut squash in a half. Roast in a 350°F oven with a little water for 1 hour, or until tender (a butter knife will pierce the flesh easily).

2. Meanwhile, cut onion, garlic, celery, carrot, and ginger into small pieces.

3. Heat soup pot over medium heat and add butter or oil. Add onions, let sit until they begin to turn golden, add garlic, ginger, carrots, and celery. Stir for 2 minutes.

4. Add water and salt.

5. When the squash is tender, scoop out the seeds and discard. Scoop out pulp and add to soup. Purée.

6. Return soup to pot and simmer for 10 more minutes to let flavors blend.

7. Add cream if desired. Salt and pepper to taste.

Alternative Flavorings

This same method for squash can be used with different seasonings. Omit the carrot, celery, and ginger and replace with: a) 1½ tsp curry powder and 1 apple cored and chopped; or b) ¼ tsp each: cardamom, cinnamon, and nutmeg.

ginger

Celery Soup

A great way to tenderize tougher late-summer celery.

1. Trim leaves off celery. Cut into 1-inch pieces.

2. Heat a skillet over medium heat. Add olive oil. Then add carrots, garlic, and onions. Cook for 3 minutes, or until soft.

3. Add celery to the skillet and toss to coat in oil and veggies. Add chicken broth.

4. Bring to a boil, and reduce heat to simmer. Cover and cook for 15 minutes, or until celery is tender.

5. Purée soup in a blender (be sure to crack the lid a little to let the steam escape). Add cream or yogurt. Purée again.

6. Return soup to pot and season to taste with salt, pepper, and lemon juice.

7. Garnish with herbs or peppers before serving.

♦ ♦ ♦ ♦ ♦

1 head	celery, washed well
2 Tbs	olive oil
1	carrot, peeled and diced
2 cloves	garlic
1	onion, peeled and diced
3 c	chicken broth
½–1 c	cream or plain yogurt salt, pepper and lemon juice to taste

—————— Garnish ——————

chopped dill, parsley, or sweet red pepper

GLUTEN FREE

Classic Italian Greens and Garlic Soup

◆ ◆ ◆ ◆ ◆

3 cloves	garlic, chopped
1 tsp	olive oil
¼ c	white wine
1 qt	good poultry or vegetarian broth
¼ lb	tortellini, ravioli, capellini, egg noodles, etc.
½ tsp	black pepper
½–1 tsp	salt
1 bunch	prewashed cooking greens (such as kale, collards, arugula, Swiss chard, or bok choy), coarsely chopped
1	baguette or similar crusty bread
1 bottle	good to very good wine, red or white

—————— Optional ——————

1 tsp	(per diner) pesto or chopped fresh basil

Working outside in the winter for his living has taught Brett the value of great simple soups on frigid days. This one works best with homemade chicken or turkey broth, but vegetarian or purchased stocks can also do nicely.

1. In a large pot, sauté garlic in olive oil until soft; immediately add ¼ cup white wine. Add broth and bring to boil. Add pasta of your choosing, continue boiling until pasta is just cooked, remove pot from heat, taste and adjust seasoning. (If meal will be delayed, remove pasta immediately with a slotted spoon. It overcooks easily.) Stir in greens and immediately serve.

2. The good bread really complements the dish, as does the basil, stirred in by each diner. Commercial pesto is easier to get in the depths of winter than is fresh or frozen basil. This recipe on its own justifies having a stock of basil in oil in your freezer, prepped during the glory days of summer.

3. The wine is for you to drink, especially if you needn't return to work.

Coconut-Sorrel Soup with Shrimp or Chicken

Fresh tomatoes would be a nice addition to this soup.

1. Bring the water to a boil. Add the lemongrass, shallots, ginger and chilies. Reduce heat to low and simmer for 10 minutes and strain. Season to taste with fish sauce and lime juice.

2. Return the broth to a pot. Add the coconut milk, chicken or shrimp, and mushrooms. Simmer over medium heat for 5 minutes, or just until chicken is cooked. Stir in sorrel and cook for 1 minute more or until wilted.

3. Garnish with cilantro. Adjust seasoning with salt and pepper.

◆ ◆ ◆ ◆ ◆

3 c	water
2	lemongrass stems, chopped
3	shallots or 1 large onion, peeled and coarsely chopped
5 slices	ginger or galangal
3–4	hot chili peppers, chopped
2–4 Tbs	fish sauce
4 Tbs	lime juice
2 c	coconut milk
1	chicken breast (boneless, skinless), sliced thin, or ½ pound shrimp
½ c	sliced button mushrooms
1 bunch	sorrel, coarsely chopped
2 sprigs	cilantro, chopped
	salt and pepper to taste

GLUTEN FREE

Cold Cucumber Soup

♦ ♦ ♦ ♦ ♦

6	large cucumbers, peeled, seeded, and very coarsely chopped
1 qt	plain yogurt, non-fat or full fat
½	lemon, juiced
1 Tbs	olive oil
½	yellow onion, coarsely chopped
½ tsp	salt
½ tsp	black pepper
¼ c	basil leaves

—————— Garnish ——————

chopped parsley, scallion, basil, or dill

This soup keeps very well, so you can make a big batch to serve for several meals. Perfect for extended heat waves. Very good served with thincrisp crackers.

1. In a blender, combine cucumber, yogurt, lemon juice, and olive oil. Purée until just a little texture remains. It may be necessary to blend in several batches.

2. Leave 1 cup of cucumber purée in blender, and add onion. Purée until smooth. Then add salt, pepper, and basil and pulse until the basil is just chopped.

3. Refrigerate for 1 hour and then taste for seasoning—you may want to add more salt, lemon juice, herbs, a dash of white wine or beer.

4. Garnish with additional herbs.

Creamy Corn Chowder

Serving the soup in roasted onion cups makes for an impressive presentation. If you prefer to more simply serve the soup in bowls, then just use 1 onion.

1. Remove corn kernels from cob. Place cobs in a large pot with cream and chicken stock. Simmer over medium heat for 20 minutes. Remove cobs, scraping out the juices with a butter knife. Discard the cobs.

2. Cut onions in halves along the poles. Place them on a greased cookie sheet (or Pyrex dish), cut side down. Roast in a 400°F oven for 40 minutes, or until tender. Scoop out inner part of the onion (leaving the 3 outer rings that create a cup) and add to corn stock. Reserve outer part of the onion for serving.

3. In a large pan, over medium heat, cook the salt pork or bacon until about 1 Tbs of fat releases. Alternatively, melt the butter. Add garlic and half the corn. Cook until garlic is lightly browned. Add to above corn stock.

4. Purée soup in a blender or with an immersion blender. Season to taste with salt and pepper.

5. Prepare garnish for soup: Heat a large sauté pan on medium heat. Add butter and let melt. Add potatoes and remaining corn. Sauté until potatoes begin to crisp. Turn off heat and stir in scallions rounds.

6. To serve: place an onion cup in each soup bowl, and ladle soup inside onion cup; it's okay if the soup spills out of the onion into the bowl. Top with garnish.

loading corn chowder into an onion cup

5 ears	corn
1 pt	light cream
1 pt	chicken or corn stock*
3	large onions
¼ c	diced salt pork or bacon (vegetarian option: 2 Tbs butter)
2 cloves	garlic
1 Tbs	butter
2	small new potatoes, cut into small dice, and parboiled (about ½ cup)
4	scallions, cut into rings

* **To make corn stock:** put corn cobs (with kernals cut off) in a pot and cover with cold water. Bring to a boil and let simmer for one hour. Strain the broth and scrape any excess juice out of the cobs.

French Onion Soup

◆ ◆ ◆ ◆ ◆

4 Tbs	butter
6 c	sliced onions
2 tsp	sugar
1 Tbs	flour
3½ c	beef stock, boiling
2 c	water
¼ c	Cognac or brandy
1½ tsp	salt
½ tsp	black pepper
12	stale French bread slices
1½ lb	Gruyère or Swiss cheese, grated

You can prepare this soup with standard storage onions. If you're at the farmers market and have the option, a medley would be great too.

1. Melt butter over medium heat in a large sauce pan. Add onions and sugar, stir well, and cover. Cook, stirring occasionally, for about 20 minutes or until onions are wilted and golden. Cook onions for another 20 minutes, uncovered, until they are a deep golden brown.

2. Add flour to the pan and stir well to fully incorporate flour into onions. Slowly stir in stock, water, Cognac, salt, and pepper. Bring to a boil, reduce heat to a simmer and cook for 30 minutes.

3. Toast bread slices. Ladle soup into ovenproof bowls. Arrange 2 pieces of toast on top of each bowl, sprinkle cheese on top. Put in the oven, until cheese is melted and bubbly. Alternatively, melt cheese on top of toasts in the oven and then put them on top of the soup when serving.

Garlic Scape Vichyssoise

*This vichyssoise has more than normal zing.
Scapes have intense garlic flavors coupled with hints of greenery.
The season for garlic scapes is brief, so exploring creative
scape approaches in that short month is wise.*

1. Heat pot over medium heat. Add butter. Add scapes and leeks. Cook for about 5 minutes, or until soft. Deglaze with white wine. Cook for 5 minutes more, or until the pan is mostly dry again (about 1 Tbs of liquid remains).

2. Add potatoes and water. Season with salt and pepper. Simmer for about 30 minutes, or until potatoes are tender.

3. Purée soup in a food processor. Add cream. Adjust seasoning with salt and (white) pepper.

4. Chill soup before serving. Garnish with scapes.

3 Tbs	butter
12	garlic scapes, coarsely chopped
1	leek, white and light green, chopped and then washed
½ c	white wine
1 lb	potatoes, peeled and diced
6 c	water
¼ c	cream
	salt and pepper to taste
	more scapes, scallions, or chives, chopped, for garnish

Gazpacho

♦ ♦ ♦ ♦ ♦

3	Roma or other plum tomatoes, coarsely chopped (optional: 1 smoked tomato, page 248)
1	heirloom beefsteak tomato, coarsely chopped
1	red onion, peeled and coarsely chopped
1	bell pepper, seeded and coarsely chopped
1	spicy chili pepper, coarsely chopped (remove seeds for a milder soup)
1	large cucumber, peeled and coarsely chopped
1 Tbs	lime juice
1 Tbs	lemon juice
1 Tbs	red wine or balsamic vinegar
3 Tbs	extra virgin olive oil
⅔ bunch	scallion, diced
	salt and pepper to taste

On its own, this soup is a great way to start off a summer meal. You can give it an extra loving touch with grilled bread or shrimp.

1. Purée first 6 ingredients in a blender.

2. Adjust seasoning with lime juice, lemon juice, vinegar, olive oil, salt, and pepper.

3. Chill soup for at least one hour in the refrigerator. Taste for salt, pepper, and acidity once more.

4. Garnish with scallions just before serving.

Macomber Turnip Soup

*Great on its own or garnished with scallions,
tarragon, and/or lobster meat.*

1. In a large soup pot, combine turnip base, chicken stock, and leeks. Simmer for 20 minutes.

2. Purée in a blender (in two batches if necessary) until smooth. Add cream.

3. Return to pot to keep warm until ready to serve.

◆ ◆ ◆ ◆ ◆

1	recipe Roasted Turnips II (see page 132)
1 qt	chicken stock or broth
1	small leek, white and light green parts, cut and washed
¼ c	heavy cream
	salt and pepper to taste

Potato Leek Soup

◆ ◆ ◆ ◆ ◆

4	leeks, whites and light green parts only
3 Tbs	butter
¼ c	white wine
3	medium-sized potatoes (about 1 pound), peeled and cut into large pieces
1 qt	chicken or vegetable broth
3 Tbs	butter
1 c	heavy cream
1½ tsp	fresh thyme leaves, finely chopped
	salt and pepper
	chopped scallions, for garnish (optional)

A classic soup, more subtle and earthy than the garlic scape vichyssoise. Sublime if you are using new potatoes (in which case peeling is not necessary). Fresh parsley or chervil may substitute for the thyme.

1. Cut leeks in half and wash in a bowl of cool water (see directions for washing leafy greens page 53). Let the dirt settle to the bottom and lift out the leeks.

2. In a soup pot over medium heat, melt the butter. Add the leeks and a heavy pinch of salt and sweat for 5 minutes. Decrease the heat to medium-low and cook until the leeks are tender, approximately 15 minutes, stirring occasionally. Add the wine.

3. Add the potatoes and the broth, increase the heat to medium-high, and bring to a boil. Reduce the heat to low, cover, and gently simmer until the potatoes are soft, approximately 25 minutes (this will depend on how large the potato chunks are).

4. Remove the pot from the heat. Purée the mixture with an immersion blender until smooth. Alternatively, purée in batches in a blender. Be sure to crack the lid to let the steam escape! Stir in the heavy cream and pepper. Taste and adjust seasoning if desired. Sprinkle with scallions and serve immediately, or chill and serve cold.

Sweet Potato Vichyssoise

This soup freezes superbly. Just omit the cream.

1. Heat pot over medium heat. Add 2 Tbs butter. Add half the shallots and garlic, all of the leeks and celery. Sweat for about 5 minutes. Deglaze with white wine.

2. Add potatoes, carrots, and water. Simmer for about 30 minutes, or until potatoes are tender.

3. Purée soup. Add cream. Season to taste with salt and pepper. Chill soup.

4. While soup is chilling, heat a large sauté pan over high heat. Add remaining butter, corn, shallots, and garlic. Sauté, without shaking the pan, for 3 minutes, or until the corn becomes sweetly aromatic. Season to taste with salt and pepper.

5. Purée chipotle peppers with ¼ cup water and 1 Tbs red wine vinegar.

6. When soup is chilled, garnish with corn and a drizzle of the chipotle purée. Sprinkle with chives, if you like.

◆ ◆ ◆ ◆ ◆	
3 Tbs	butter
2	shallots, peeled and chopped
4 cloves	garlic, chopped
2	leeks, white and light green parts, washed and chopped
1	celery stalk, chopped
¼ c	white wine
1	sweet potato, peeled and diced
1	potato, peeled and chopped
1	carrot, peeled and diced
6 c	water
¼ c	cream
2 ears	corn, kernels cut off cob
	salt and pepper to taste
2	chipotle peppers
1 Tbs	red wine vinegar
	chives or scallions, minced, for garnish (optional)

♦ ♦ ♦ ♦ ♦

— The Leek and Stock Base —

3 Tbs	unsalted butter
1 lb	leeks, white and tender green portions, rinsed, halved, and thinly sliced
1	onion, peeled and finely chopped
	sea salt
1 qt	homemade chicken stock
2 c	heavy cream (or whole milk)

— The Cress —

3 Tbs	sea salt
1 lb	English cress or curly American mustard, or 4 bunches watercress, roots and stems removed; washed

— The Cream —

1 c	heavy cream
	juice of 1 lemon
	sea salt
	freshly ground white pepper (or black pepper, but this will leave flecks in an otherwise pure white cream)
2 Tbs	caviar; lumpfish works and is more ecologically defensible than sturgeon

Taillevent's Cream of Cress Soup with Caviar

Patricia Wells describes Taillevent Restaurant in Paris as "a place that my husband, Walter, and I reserve for special occasions." She describes its watercress soup as "the perfect choice for a celebratory New Year's Eve dinner. Like so much of the fare at this august restaurant, this soup shines with simple elegance."

The recipe is a lot of work and is absolutely worth it. This is one of the finest soups we've ever eaten, and 90% of non-caviar lovers have added caviar to their second serving. It is adapted from National Public Radio.

1. In a 6-quart stockpot, combine the butter, leeks, onions, and a pinch of sea salt. Cook, covered and over low heat, until soft but not browned, about 3 minutes. Add the chicken stock and cream. Simmer gently, uncovered, for 30 minutes.

2. Purée the soup in a blender, food processor, or with a handheld immersion blender until emulsified into a smooth-textured mixture.

3. Return the mixture to the saucepan, increase the heat to high, and bring to a gentle boil. Using a slotted spoon, skim off any impurities that may rise to the surface. Set this base aside. (This mixture can be prepared up to 1 day in advance. To store, cover and refrigerate.)

4. Prepare a large bowl full of ice water.

5. In a 6-quart pasta pot fitted with a colander, bring 4 quarts water to a boil over high heat. Add the sea salt and the greens. Blanch, uncovered, until soft and wilted, 2 to 3 minutes. Immediately remove the colander from the water, drain the

cress, and plunge the colander into the ice water to stop the cooking. Drain again, and purée the cress in a food processor. Place the purée in a fine-mesh sieve, and carefully press out (and discard) any remaining liquid. Set the purée aside.

6. In the bowl of a heavy-duty mixer fitted with a whisk (or with a handheld mixer), whip the cream at high speed until stiff. Add the lemon juice, and season to taste with sea salt and white pepper. Set aside.

7. At serving time, reheat the soup base until simmering. Remove it from the heat and add the cress purée, stirring until thoroughly blended. Serve the soup in warm shallow soup bowls, placing a scoop of the whipped cream in the center of each bowl. Top with a small spoonful of caviar, and serve.

Makes 6 servings.

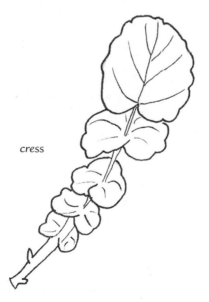

cress

Tomato Soup

◆ ◆ ◆ ◆ ◆

1 Tbs	butter or olive oil
2 cloves	garlic, chopped
1	shallot or small onion, chopped
¼ c	white wine
4 c	diced tomatoes, a variety is good
	salt and pepper to taste

——————— Optional ———————

¼ c	cream

VEGAN   GLUTEN FREE

In the height of summer tomato season, little embellishment is needed for tomato soup. If you'd like, serve with a dollop of pesto (see page 253) and a grilled cheese sandwich.

1. In a soup pot, melt butter over medium-high heat. Add garlic and shallots and cook for 5 minutes, or until soft. Add wine. Then add tomatoes and stock.

2. Simmer tomatoes for 20 minutes. Transfer to a blender and purée until smooth. If you want, you can then strain the soup through a mesh strainer to get rid of the seeds. Brett doesn't like to do this because you also get rid of a lot of nutrients, but Julia prefers the smoother texture.

3. Season to taste with salt and pepper. Stir in cream, if using.

White Bean and Greens Soup with Chicken Sausage

A great hearty autumn or winter soup that can serve as a complete meal with a baguette and a glass of red wine. If smoked chicken sausage is hard to source, andouille or even kielbasa can substitute.

1. Heat oil in a large pot over medium heat. Add onions, garlic, celery, and carrots, and cook until soft, about 4 or 5 minutes. Add beans, liquid, cheese rind, and thyme. Season to taste with salt and pepper. Bring to a boil and reduce to a simmer. Cook uncovered for about 20 minutes.

2. Meanwhile, brown sausage in batches over medium heat. Cut into chunks.

3. Stir greens and sausage into soup. Cook for 2–5 minutes or until greens are wilted and tender.

4. Add water, if necessary to thin soup. Adjust seasoning with salt and pepper to taste.

2 Tbs	olive oil
1	onion, coarsely chopped
4 cloves	garlic, coarsely chopped
½ stalk	celery, coarsely chopped
1	large carrot, peeled and coarsely chopped
2 c	cooked white beans
5 c	chicken broth, water, or combination of the two
1 piece	Parmesan rind
1 sprig	fresh thyme, chopped
½ lb	smoked chicken sausage, sliced
1 lb	turnip greens, kale, Swiss chard, or collards, coarsely chopped
2 tsp	salt
½ tsp	black pepper

½	red cabbage
6	scallions
2 Tbs	canola oil
1 Tbs	sesame oil
¼ c	sliced almonds
¼ c	raw sesame seeds
1 Tbs	sugar
1 tsp	salt
2–3 Tbs	rice vinegar

Asian Red Cabbage Slaw

*Half a cabbage makes plenty of slaw.
If you don't want to double the recipe, consider making
braised red cabbage (page 148) with the other half.*

1. Cut the core out of the cabbage and slice as thinly as possible.

2. Julienne the scallions. Put in a mixing bowl with the cabbage.

3. Heat the oils in a skillet over medium heat. Add the almonds and sesame seeds. Cook, stirring frequently until the nuts begin to brown. Immediately pour over the cabbage.

4. Add the sugar, salt, and vinegar to the cabbage. Mix well. Let sit for 10 minutes so the flavors can meld.

1 lb	asparagus
¼ c	olive oil
½	lemon, juiced, about 2 Tbs
2 Tbs	mixed fresh herbs: any combination of tarragon, chives, parsley, chervil, and thyme (no more than ½ tsp of thyme)
1	small shallot diced
	croutons to garnish
	salt and pepper to taste

———— Optional ————

2 Tbs	freshly grated Parmesan

Asparagus Salad
with Soft Herb Dressing

The soft herbs such as tarragon, parsley, chives, and chervil have delicate textures and alluring scents. They pair beautifully with the earthy sweetness of the asparagus and cheese. A little bit of thyme adds roundness to the flavor, but can easily overpower the dish, so use judiciously. Parmesan cheese tuilles would be an excellent garnish in addition to (or in place of) the croutons.

1. Trim asparagus. Toss with 2 Tbs olive oil, and place in a single layer on a sheet pan. Season with salt and pepper. Roast in a 425°F oven for 10 minutes, or until water has evaporated and asparagus begins to brown on the bottom.

2. To make the vinaigrette: Mix lemon juice, herbs, and shallots in a bowl. Whisk in remaining oil. Season to taste with salt and pepper.

3. When asparagus is cooked, place on a serving platter. Drizzle lemon vinaigrette on top. Garnish with croutons (and Parmesan).

Baby Spinach Salad with Warm Sherry Vinaigrette and Dried Cherries

Serve this as an elegant salad course or as a side to roasted duck or venison.

1. Make the vinaigrette: heat olive oil in a pan over low heat. Add shallots, and cook until they begin to wilt, about 3 minutes. Add garlic, thyme, and dried cherries. Cook for 1 minute more. Add lemon juice and vinegar.

2. Put spinach in a bowl. Toss with warm dressing. Garnish salad with croutons. Serve immediately.

½ c	extra virgin olive oil
1	shallot or small onion, sliced
1 Tbs	chopped thyme
2 cloves	garlic, chopped
¼ c	dried cherries or cranberries
1 Tbs	fresh lemon juice
2 Tbs	sherry or malt vinegar
1 lb	baby spinach, washed
	croutons
	salt and pepper to taste

Beet Horseradish Salad

A passionate courtship of sweet and pungent, deep and spicy. A perfect dinner side dish or main vegetable course for lunch.

1. Put beets in a pot and cover with cold water by 1 inch. Bring to a boil, and reduce heat to simmer. Cook beets for 20 minutes, or until tender: a paring knife can be easily inserted.

2. Drain beets and let cool.

3. When beets are cool enough to handle, peel and slice them.

4. Toss beets with remaining ingredients. Season to taste with salt and pepper. Let stand for at least 20 minutes to let the flavors marry, though overnight would be ideal.

6	medium beets (any variety, color)
¼ c	red wine vinegar
½ c	olive oil
2 tsp	sugar
2 tsp	prepared horseradish
3	scallions, chopped
	salt and pepper to taste

Beets and Goat Cheese Napoleon with Buttered Walnuts

• • • • •

1 lb	red beets
2 Tbs	olive oil
1	red onion, finely diced
1 Tbs	red wine vinegar
1–2 Tbs	fresh thyme, chopped
4 oz	creamy goat cheese
	salt and pepper to taste

Balsamic Vinaigrette and Mesclun

3 Tbs	balsamic vinegar
2 tsp	chopped shallots
1 tsp	thyme
1 tsp	mustard
½ c +	extra virgin olive oil
	pinch sugar
½ lb	mesclun or lettuces
	salt and pepper to taste

———— **Buttered Walnuts** ————

1 c	walnuts
2 Tbs	(or more) butter
	salt and pepper

*Beets and goat cheese are a classic combination.
This recipe combines the two into an impressive salad with
an added depth of toasted walnuts.*

1. Put beets in a pot and cover in cold water. Season water with salt. Bring to a boil over high heat. Reduce heat to a simmer. Continue cooking for 30 minutes, or until skins easily peel off.

2. When beets are cooked, let cool. Peel beets. Slice ¼-inch thick. Toss beets with red onions, vinegar, olive oil, and thyme.

3. Put beets on a plate and dollop goat cheese on top. Garnish with mesclun and buttered walnuts.

Balsamic Vinaigrette and Mesclun

1. Put balsamic, shallots, thyme, and mustard in a blender. Purée. With the motor running, slowly drizzle in the oil. Season to taste with salt, pepper, and sugar.

2. Use this to dress the mesclun or lettuce. Leftover dressing will keep for several weeks in the refrigerator.

Buttered Walnuts

1. Melt butter in skillet. Toss in walnuts and toast until lightly browned and fragrant.

2. Season with salt and pepper.

beet and goat cheese Napoleon

Bell Pepper, Okra, and Tomatillo Salad

This wonderful dish is essentially a "high summer" chilled succotash. Excellent on its own or to accompany grilled chicken or fish.

1. Sauté the bell peppers in oil until soft. Remove these from the frying pan, but leave oil in pan.

2. Add chopped garlic and the okra. Sauté at high heat until the garlic barely browns, then remove from heat and let cool.

3. Meanwhile, peel and coarsely slice the tomatillos. Thinly slice the slender Italian peppers. Mix this together in a bowl along with the cherry tomatoes, the fresh herb and beans. Toss all together, then let sit 5 or 10 minutes. Mix in the bell peppers and okra.

4. Add salt, pepper, and more vinegar or lemon juice to taste.

1	large red or green bell pepper, cut into chunks
1 Tbs	olive oil
1–2	garlic cloves, chopped
1½ c	okra, cut into 1½-inch pieces
1–2 c	ripe tomatillos
2	red peppers, sweet slender Italian slicing or bell
1 c	red cherry tomatoes, halved
2 Tbs	fresh basil, lemon basil, or cilantro, chopped
1 c	black beans or navy beans, cooked and drained
2 Tbs	fresh lemon juice or any vinegar
	salt and pepper to taste

Celery Salad

◆ ◆ ◆ ◆ ◆

Celery is used in the dressing as well as in the salad mix. Save the tender inner stalks for the salad, and use the tough outer stalks for the dressing.

―――――――― Dressing ――――――――

1 tsp	salt
½ bunch	celery, with leaves
1	onion, coarsely chopped
1	egg, at room temperature or slightly warmer (free-range if possible)
1 Tbs	Dijon mustard
3 Tbs	extra virgin olive oil
¼ can	anchovy fillets (optional)
½ bunch	parsley
½ bunch	basil
1 Tbs	fresh chopped garlic
½ tsp	black pepper
½	lemon, juiced (or to taste)

―――――――――― Salad ――――――――――

4	large stalks of celery, sliced thin
2 c	mixed greens, including romaine, arugula, and/or mesclun
¼ c	grated Romano
	salt and pepper to taste
	croutons

1. Bring a medium pot to a boil with 2 cups of water. Season with salt. Add the celery and onion (from the dressing list). Cook covered until the celery is almost fully soft, about 20 minutes; remove lid and continue cooking until fully soft. Drain well and reserve liquid.

2. To make the dressing: crack the egg into a food processor bowl. Run the machine until the egg is pale yellow, add the mustard and then slowly drizzle in the olive oil running the machine all the while. The mix should thicken substantially and whiten. Add the anchovies, celery, parsley, basil, garlic, black pepper, and lemon juice. Continue running the machine until the dressing is smooth and creamy. Let sit for 15 minutes, pulse again, and then taste for seasoning. Excellent optional additions are white wine, cayenne, or Worcestershire sauce.

3. In a large salad bowl, combine the thin slices of celery and lettuces. Add the grated Romano and toss with ¼ cup of the dressing. Remaining dressing will keep for 6 weeks.

4. Adjust seasoning. Garnish with croutons.

Cherry Tomato Salad

Superb served alongside grilled meat, sausage, or poultry.
A serrated knife is the best tool for slicing the tomatoes.
Four cups serve six as salad, and can easily be halved.

Mix everything together. Adjust seasoning to taste with lemon or lime juice.

4 c	(heaping) cherry tomatoes, halved
½	onion, very thinly sliced
1 clove	garlic, finely chopped
½ bunch	cilantro or basil, washed and chopped
½ tsp	salt
½ tsp	freshly ground black pepper
1 Tbs	olive oil
	lemon or lime juice to taste

———— Optional ————

½	green or red bell pepper, thinly sliced in 1-inch strips
½ c	pitted manzanilla olives, sliced

Chilled Spinach Salad with Sesame Dressing

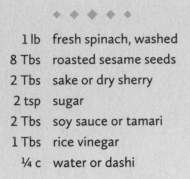

1 lb	fresh spinach, washed
8 Tbs	roasted sesame seeds
2 Tbs	sake or dry sherry
2 tsp	sugar
2 Tbs	soy sauce or tamari
1 Tbs	rice vinegar
¼ c	water or dashi

This recipe is inspired by the traditional Japanese dish, Gomae Spinach.

1. Heat a large skillet on high. Add spinach (no oil, just the residual water from washing). Cook the spinach just until it wilts, turning occasionally.

2. Chill spinach in refrigerator.

3. Meanwhile, in a food processor, combine the remaining ingredients. Blend until smooth, approximately 3 minutes.

4. Squeeze out excess water from spinach. Drizzle dressing on top just before serving.

Cool Crunchy Cucumber Salad

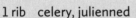

1 rib	celery, julienned
1	pear, julienned
2	small carrots, peeled and julienned
1	cucumber, peeled and julienned
6	scallions, julienned
1½ tsp	vinegar
1½ tsp	lemon juice
2 tsp	sugar
1 Tbs	sesame oil
½ tsp	salt

The vegetables in this salad are cut into long strips. This allows the dressing to season them in short order. If you choose to cut the vegetables larger, let sit for at least one hour before serving.

Mix everything together.

Israeli Salad
with Cucumbers and Dill

*In Israel, this salad of chopped tomatoes and cucumbers
is usually served at breakfast with smoked, cured, or pickled fish.
It's also a great condiment for falafel, or tossed with Israeli
cous cous for a refreshing side salad.*

1. Coarsely chop tomatoes. Toss with salt and pepper. Let sit for 10 minutes.

2. Meanwhile, coarsely chop cucumbers (unpeeled) and red peppers.

3. Drain excess liquid from tomatoes. Toss with remaining ingredients. Adjust seasoning to taste with salt, pepper, lemon juice, and/or olive oil.

2	heirloom tomatoes
3	small cucumbers
1	red bell pepper or mildly hot red pepper
3	scallions
3 Tbs	extra virgin olive oil
1 Tbs	lemon juice
1½ Tbs	fresh dill
½ tsp	salt
¼ tsp	freshly ground black pepper

Kohlrabi Salad

*When visiting Vietnam a few years ago, Julia noticed
many chefs using kohlrabi in place of green papaya for their
crispy salads. This recipe follows that example.*

1. Peel kohlrabi. Slice very thin, or shred with a mandolin.

2. With a mortar and pestle (or in a food processor), grind the shallots, salt, half the chilies and garlic.

3. Toss kohlrabi with garlic paste. Season with sugar, lime juice, and fish sauce.

4. Toss with beans and tomatoes.

5. Garnish with peanuts.

2	kohlrabi
2	shallots or 1 red onion, chopped
3–4	chilies
4	garlic cloves
½ tsp	salt
1 Tbs	sugar
1	lime, juiced
3 Tbs	fish sauce
2	tomatoes, diced
6	green beans, cut into thin strips
2 Tbs	unsalted, roasted peanuts

Kohlrabi and Apple Slaw

♦ ♦ ♦ ♦ ♦

1–2   kohlrabi

1–2   red crisp or snacking apples, such as Gala or Honeycrisp

fresh herbs, such as basil, tarragon, mint, and/or parsley, chopped

This recipe scales up or down very easily. The important factor is to have equal parts of kohlrabi and apple.

1. Combine ingredients for the dressing.

2. Peel kohlrabi and cut into small matchsticks.

3. Core apple (but do not peel: the skin adds a nice texture, color, and flavor). Cut into matchsticks.

4. Toss kohlrabi with apples, dressing, and fresh herbs.

Dressing

¼ c   mayonnaise

1 Tbs   sour cream or plain yogurt

1 Tbs   lemon juice

½ Tbs   Dijon mustard

½ tsp   sugar

salt and pepper to taste

(VEGETARIAN) (GLUTEN FREE)

Korean-Style Spinach Salad

1 lb   spinach, washed

2 Tbs   soy sauce or tamari

½ Tbs   sugar

1 Tbs   rice vinegar

1 Tbs   chopped scallion

½ Tbs   ground sesame seeds

A typical Korean meal will have many small dishes of pickles and vegetables, called banchan. This along with kim chi and pickled carrots and daikon (recipes pages 240 and 228) would be wonderful additions to a larger feast.

1. Heat a large skillet on high. Add spinach (no oil, just the residual water from washing). Cook the spinach just until it wilts, turning occasionally. Remove from pan and let cool.

2. Mix remaining ingredients together and toss with spinach.

Optional

½ tsp   chopped garlic

(VEGAN) (GLUTEN FREE)

Mexican Cucumber and Jicama Salad

Excellent in the heat of summer.
Great with vegetarian burritos or grilled fish.

1. Mix everything together. Refrigerate at least 10 minutes before serving.

◆ ◆ ◆ ◆ ◆

1	jicama (slightly bigger than a baseball), peeled and cut into 2-inch x ¼-inch strips
3	large or 4 medium cucumbers, cut in half, seeded if desired and then cut into 2-inch strips
½	yellow or red onion, sliced thinly
1 clove	garlic, chopped fine
1	lime, juiced
1–2 Tbs	olive oil
½ tsp	salt
4 Tbs	cilantro leaves torn, or 1 Tbs basil, either lime or lemon
½ tsp	dried red chili flakes or ½ jalapeño pepper, minced

Mexican Red Cabbage Slaw

Serve this with fish tacos.

♦ ♦ ♦ ♦ ♦

¼ c   mayonnaise

⅓ c   sour cream

½ tsp cumin

1   chipotle pepper (canned and packed in adobo juice) or ¼ tsp chipotle powder

2 c   shredded red cabbage or lettuce

2   ripe tomatoes, coarsely chopped

¼ c   finely sliced red onion

1   jalapeño, seeded and minced (omit if you prefer mild)

¼ c   chopped cilantro

salt and lime juice to taste

1. In a large bowl, mix together the mayonnaise, sour cream, cumin, and chipotle.

2. Toss in cabbage, tomatoes, red onion, jalapeño, garlic, and cilantro. Season to taste with salt and lime juice.

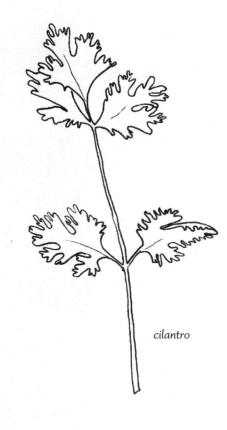

cilantro

Panzanella

Recipes abound for panzanella. Most suggest that stale bread needs to be soaked in water and then squeezed out. We don't fully understand the purpose of this step—obviously, the bread needs to soften up. But why not soften it in tomato juice?

1. Slice cucumbers. Toss with salt and let sit for 30 minutes.

2. Meanwhile, cube tomatoes and set aside in a small bowl. Cube mozzarella.

3. Drain excess water off the cucumbers.

4. The tomatoes should start to give off water after 15 minutes of sitting. Strain this liquid and toss it with bread cubes.

5. Mix the remaining ingredients just before serving. Adjust seasoning with salt, pepper, and lemon juice to taste.

♦ ♦ ♦ ♦ ♦

1	large cucumber
1 tsp	salt
2	large heirloom tomatoes
8 oz	fresh mozzarella
2 c	cubed bread, stale or toasted
3–4	sprigs (or to taste) fresh basil, chopped
2 Tbs	extra virgin olive oil
	salt, pepper, and lemon juice to taste

Moroccan-Style Beet Salad with Mint

* * * * *

6	baby beets or 3 medium beets
3 Tbs	extra virgin olive oil
½ tsp	cumin
¼ tsp	coriander
	salt, pepper, and lemon juice to taste
8	large mint leaves, cut into thin strips

Julia discovered this flavor combination when traveling in Morocco, where they serve this salad with boiled potatoes and carrots.

1. Put beets in a pot of cold water. Bring to a boil over high flame. Cover pot and let simmer for 20 minutes, or until beets are tender and you can insert a paring knife easily.

2. Remove beets from heat and let cool. The skins should peel off easily.

3. Cut beets into eighths.

4. Heat olive oil in a skillet over medium flame. Add cumin, coriander, salt and pepper. Cook until spices become aromatic, about 2 minutes. Add the beets, and warm through, tossing to coat in scented oil.

5. Remove from heat and serve. Sprinkle mint on top, and a squeeze of lemon.

Variation: add cooked potatoes and/or carrots to this salad.

Rainbow Tomato Salad

This is a celebration of ripe, diverse summer tomatoes; store-boughts or out-of-season tomatoes will not work. A summertime must-have in fine restaurants that seek out local farmers.

1. Pick a large wooden or china platter, chosen to maximize color contrasts between the tomatoes and the platter.

2. Cut each large tomato in half, then each half into ⅓-inch slices. Fan these slices in a thin layer on the platter. If you have red and other colored tomatoes, put the red ones down first to maximize color contrasts (gold or purple is lovely in the upper layers). Cut the cherry tomatoes in half, and place these in discrete groups, sorted by color, on top of or alongside the slices of bigger tomatoes. We try to have the most contrast and most height in the center of the platter.

3. Sprinkle salt and pepper over the tomatoes, then drizzle on the olive oil.

4. Right before serving, drizzle on the vinegar and sprinkle on the basil or arugula.

5. Excellent with a layer of freshly made mozzarella below the first slices of tomatoes. Appropriate wines to accompany this include a red Sancerre or Pinot Noir at slightly below room temperature, or a sangria, or a Portuguese vinho verde. Serve with crusty bread.

◆ ◆ ◆ ◆ ◆

2–4 c	(heaping) cherry tomatoes, preferably of different colors
1–1½ lb	heirloom or very farm-fresh bigger tomatoes, preferably of different colors
2 tsp	olive oil
2 tsp	your favorite vinegar
¼–½ tsp	sea or kosher salt
¼ tsp	fresh ground black pepper
	fresh basil or arugula if available

♦ ♦ ♦ ♦ ♦

1 lb	kale, washed
¼ c	sesame seeds
½ c	pepitas or hulled sunflower seeds
1	small red onion
¼ c	lemon juice
¼ c	soy sauce or tamari
¼ c	olive oil
	black pepper

Refreshing Raw Kale Salad with Sesame Seeds

Julia is addicted to this salad, to the point where she has a jar of toasted seeds and dressing in the fridge at all times. You can easily double (or quadruple) the recipe; just dress the greens as you need it.

1. Remove stems/ribs from kale. Cut into thin strips. Put into a large salad bowl.

2. In a small skillet, attentively toast the sesame and pepitas over medium heat, stirring frequently. When the sesame seeds begin to turn golden, remove from heat and set aside.

3. Peel the onion and slice as thin as possible.

4. Mix the dressing: combine the soy sauce, lemon juice, and olive oil.

5. Toss the kale with the seeds, dressing and onions. Let sit for at least one hour, mixing occasionally.

6. Season with black pepper to taste.

Roasted Pears with Arugula and Prosciutto

It's best to use firm pears such as Bosc.

1. Peel pears. Slice in half, and scoop out core. Season with balsamic, thyme, salt and pepper. Put in a roasting pan, add butter and bake at 425°F for 15 minutes, or until soft.

2. Toss arugula with olive oil, then with lemon juice. Season to taste with salt and pepper. Divide arugula into 6 bundles and wrap each bundle with a prosciutto slice.

3. When pears are cooked, slice thinly. Drape over arugula bundles. Sprinkle Parmesan on top.

2	Bosc pears
2 Tbs	balsamic vinegar
1 Tbs	fresh thyme, chopped
2 Tbs	butter
2	bunches arugula
2 Tbs	extra virgin olive oil
1	lemon, juiced
6 slices	prosciutto
¼ c	fresh shaved Parmesan salt and pepper to taste

Roasted Red Peppers with Arugula and Cheese

This sensuous salad is meant to be eaten with a fork and sharp knife.

1. Blacken the skin of the peppers over a gas burner (or under a broiler) until blackened on all sides. Put in a bowl, cover with plastic wrap, and let steam for 10 minutes. When peppers are cool, peel away blackened skin. Cut in half; remove and discard the stems, interior white membrane and seeds.

2. Put arugula on a large serving platter. Drape peppers on top.

3. Sprinkle with salt and pepper. Drizzle vinegar and oil on top. Sprinkle on cheese and basil.

3	red bell peppers
2 c	arugula or mesclun, washed and drained
1 tsp	red wine or sherry vinegar
1 Tbs	olive oil
¼ c	freshly grated Romano, Asiago, or Parmesan cheese
	fresh basil, shredded
	salt and freshly ground black pepper

Roasted Pepper and Tomato Salad

♦ ♦ ♦ ♦ ♦

2   bell peppers, red or yellow

2   ripe tomatoes

2 Tbs   fresh basil

2 tsp   balsamic vinegar

2 tsp   extra virgin olive oil

salt and pepper to taste

Refreshing and clean with deep summer flavors, this salad may best be paired with a milder main course like chicken or fish. The peppers can be charred and peeled; they'll last 5–7 days in the fridge thereafter.

1. Blacken the skin of the peppers over a gas burner (or under a broiler) until blackened on all sides. Put in a bowl, cover with plastic wrap and let steam for 10 minutes.

2. Meanwhile, dice the tomatoes.

3. When peppers are cool, peel away blackened skin. Cut in half; remove and discard the stems, interior white membrane and seeds.

4. Cut the peppers into ½-inch wide strips. Mix with the tomatoes. Coarsely chop the basil and add to the peppers. Add the balsamic and olive oil. Season to taste with salt and pepper.

5. Let stand for 10 minutes before serving.

Smoky Coleslaw

Most slaw recipes start with a base of cabbage, but consider it just a canvas to express your creativity. This is a basic recipe but feel free to make it your own by adding more variety of vegetables (green beans, bell peppers or tomatoes) and other seasonings, such as blue cheese or caraway seeds.

1. Using a food processor with the shredder attachment, thinly slice the cabbage, carrots, and onion. Alternatively, finely chop vegetables with a sharp knife.

2. In a large bowl, combine the remaining ingredients to create the dressing. Adjust seasoning with salt and pepper.

3. Add the shredded vegetables to the dressing. Mix well to evenly coat and distribute the dressing. Let sit for 1 hour before serving.

1	small head of cabbage
2	carrots
1	red onion
½ c	mayonnaise
3 Tbs	cider vinegar
1 tsp	sugar
½ tsp	celery seed or one celery stalk, finely chopped
1	chipotle pepper
	salt and pepper to taste

Strawberry Salad

A simple salad that lets the flavors of the strawberry sparkle.

1. Wash strawberries, cut out stems and quarter.

2. Put strawberries and greens in a serving bowl. Toss with olive oil to well coat the leaves. Sprinkle with salt and pepper. Finally, drizzle vinegar on top.

3. Serve immediately.

1 pt	(¾ lb) strawberries
1 bunch	arugula, 2 cups mesclun, or 1 small bunch watercress
2 Tbs	olive oil
	salt and pepper to taste
1 Tbs	red wine vinegar

◆ ◆ ◆ ◆ ◆

2–3 c	baby turnips or cubed rutabagas, washed, trimmed, but unpeeled
	water to cover, in a lidded pot
1 tsp	salt
	any good salad dressing or vinegar and oil
	salt and pepper

Tender Turnip Vinaigrette

Excellent as an alternative to green salads, or as a small appetizer preceding a heavy meal.

1. Simmer the roots until just tender in the salted water (about 15–25 minutes). Drain. Let cool.

2. Add generous amounts of the salad dressing or drizzle with vinegar and olive oil. Season to taste with salt and pepper.

――――― Vinaigrette ―――――

2 tsp	Dijon mustard
2 tsp	red wine vinegar
2½ Tbs	extra virgin olive oil
½ tsp	fresh thyme
	salt and pepper to taste

――――― Salad ―――――

2 slices	bacon or 2 Tbs olive oil
1	small red onion, peeled and thinly sliced
1 bunch	frisée
¼ lb	baby spinach

Warm Frisée and Spinach Salad with Mustard Vinaigrette

With a poached egg on top, this is a wonderful lunch salad.

1. Combine mustard and vinegar in a bowl. Whisk in olive oil. Season with thyme, salt and pepper.

2. Cut bacon into cubes. Cook in skillet over medium heat until it is just starting to brown (but not fully crispy). If using olive oil, heat over medium heat.

3. Add onions, turn heat to high and continue cooking for 3 minutes or until bacon and onions are crisp.

4. Drain excess fat from bacon, and toss warm bacon over greens.

5. Dress salad with the vinaigrette. Season to taste with salt and pepper.

frisée

Watermelon and Goat Cheese Salad with Minty-Citrus Vinaigrette

Extremely popular summer salad.

1. Peel watermelon and cut into 1-inch cubes. Scrape out seeds.

2. To make the vinaigrette, combine salt, pepper, lemon juice, and olive oil.

3. Chop mint and basil. Combine mint, basil and mesclun in a salad bowl. Add watermelon, red onion, and crumble goat cheese on top.

4. Toss with the vinaigrette.

2 lb	watermelon (1 small, or portion of a large one)
2 Tbs	fresh lemon juice
¼ c	extra virgin olive oil
2 Tbs	fresh mint leaves
2 Tbs	fresh basil leaves
½ lb	mizuna or lettuce greens
½	red onion, sliced thin
4 oz	plain goat cheese or feta
	salt and pepper to taste

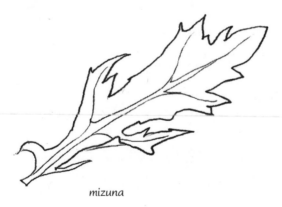

mizuna

Side Dishes

Acorn Squash with Sunflower Seeds and Dried Cranberries

◆ ◆ ◆ ◆ ◆

1	acorn squash, sliced in half lengthwise, seeded, and then cut into 4 wedges per half
3 Tbs	olive oil
1	lime, juiced
2 Tbs	honey
3 Tbs	dried cranberries
3 Tbs	pepitas or hulled sunflower seeds
	salt and pepper to taste

An atypical approach to winter squash. Conceived as an homage to the Native Americans (the three main ingredients were all grown and harvested here before the Europeans invaded) and as a way to do something special and delicious with an autumn/winter staple.

1. Preheat the oven to 400°F.

2. Spread the squash slices on a cookie sheet. Toss with 1 Tbs olive oil. Season with salt and pepper. Roast for 20 minutes; then turn the slices over and roast for an additional 10 minutes.

3. While the squash are baking, combine lime juice, honey, remaining olive oil, salt, and pepper. Mix well.

4. When the squash are cooked, arrange them on a serving platter. Sprinkle the dried cranberries and sunflower seeds all around. Spoon the dressing on top.

Apple and Hazelnut Hash

*This is a perfect autumnal accompaniment
to roast chicken or pork.*

1. In a large sauté pan, heat oil over a high heat. Add the sage leaves (whole) and the hazelnuts. When the hazelnuts begin to brown, add the garlic slices. When the garlic slices begin to brown, remove from heat. Scoop out "crispies" with a slotted spoon and drain on a paper towel. Leave remaining oil in the pan. Season "crispies" with salt and pepper.

2. Return pan to heat, add onions. When the onions begin to turn translucent, add apples. Let apples sit for a few minutes, without stirring, so that they brown. Season with salt, pepper, and thyme.

3. Right before serving, mix apples with "crispies."

2 Tbs	canola oil
½ bunch	sage, stems removed
¼ c	hazelnuts, coarsely chopped
2 cloves	garlic, sliced
1	red onion, thinly sliced
3	apples (3 different kinds is ideal), cored and sliced, skin left on
1 tsp	fresh thyme
	salt and pepper to taste

Basic Sautéed Shiitakes or Wild Mushrooms

♦ ♦ ♦ ♦ ♦

½ lb	wild or shiitake mushrooms
1 Tbs	olive oil, butter or a combination of the two
½	small onion, minced
1 clove	garlic, minced
2 Tbs	white wine, brandy, bourbon, sherry, or beer
	salt and pepper to taste

Nearly all mushroom cooking starts with this sauté or with grilling. The sauté precedes subsequent cream reductions for luscious mushrooms sauces, mixing into quiche batters or adding to already-cooked dishes, such as burgers or pastas. The onions and garlic are added after the mushrooms if the latter take longer to cook, e.g., maitake, shiitake, or chicken of the woods. The onions and garlic are added first to the skillet if you have fast-cooking species like honey mushrooms or chanterelles.

1. Wash the mushrooms by immersing the caps in water (see greens technique page 41). Drain well. Cut into chunks.

2. Heat olive oil and/or butter in a large skillet over high heat. Add mushrooms first, then onions and garlic. Season with salt and pepper. Cook for 3–5 minutes without stirring until mushrooms begin to brown at the edges and then add the booze. Cook until mushrooms are just soft.

3. Excellent with poultry, fish, omelets, and especially red meat.

Basic Whole Baked Sweet Potatoes

Especially for freshly dug sweet potatoes, baking at low temperature (e.g., 340°) maximizes conversion of the starches into sugars. Higher-temperature baking is fine for sweet potatoes that you've stored at room temperature for a long time.

Bake one 5-inch-long sweet potato, or a similar chunk cut from bigger sizes, per person in a 340°F oven about 40 to 55 minutes, until a squeezed one is fully soft.

Note: Baking sweet potatoes in a pan will prevent the natural sugars from dripping onto the bottom of the oven and burning.

Beet Risotto

Adding beets to the classic risotto
gives it a brilliant pink hue.
For a total shock of color, serve it as a side dish
with salmon and broccoli.

1. Bring chicken stock to a boil. Keep hot while making the risotto.

2. Heat large sauté pan over medium-high heat. Add half of the butter. When it is melted, add shallots, and sweat for 2 minutes. Add rice, stirring to ensure each grain is coated in butter.

3. Add the wine to the pan. When the rice has absorbed the wine, add ½ cup of the stock and beets. Gently stir, to ensure that nothing is sticking to the bottom of the pan. Add ½ cup of remaining liquid. Cook rice, uncovered and without stirring, until most of the liquid is absorbed. Add remaining liquid, ½ cup at a time, and continue cooking in the same method.

4. Test risotto to ensure that it is cooked almost completely. If not, add more hot water, and continue cooking. Otherwise, season with salt and pepper. Stir in Parmesan and butter. Adjust seasoning with fresh lemon juice, if desired.

3 c	chicken or vegetable stock
4 Tbs	butter
1	large shallot, diced
¾ c	Arborio rice
¼ c	white wine
1½ c	raw diced beets (approximately 2 beets, peeled first)
⅓ c	Parmesan
	lemon juice
	salt and pepper to taste

Butternut Squash with Vanilla and Curry

♦ ♦ ♦ ♦ ♦

1   butternut squash, peeled, seeded, and cut into ¼-inch slices

1 Tbs   butter

2 Tbs   olive oil

½   vanilla bean or 1 tsp vanilla extract

1 tsp   Madras curry powder

salt and pepper to taste

Curry is a wonderful, all-purpose spice; along with the vanilla, it gives the squash an alluring scent and flavor.

1. Preheat the oven to 375°F.

2. Melt the butter with olive oil in a small skillet over medium-low heat. Add the curry powder and vanilla bean (if using). Let simmer for 5 minutes.

3. In a baking dish, combine the butter/curry mix with the squash (and vanilla extract, if using). Season to taste with salt and pepper.

4. Bake squash for 20 minutes or until tender.

Celeriac Purée

2 knobs   celery root (celeriac)

½ c   cream

salt, pepper, and lemon juice to taste

This makes a great side dish for roasted meats or fish.

1. Peel celery root and cut into chunks.

2. Put celeriac in a pot and cover with cold water. Add a generous amount of salt, about 1 tablespoon per quart of water. Bring to a boil, reduce heat to simmer. Cook for about 20 minutes, or until celeriac is tender.

3. Drain the celery root and reserve 1 cup of water. Put root in a food processor and purée with cream. If it seems too thick, add some of the reserved cooking liquid. Add lemon juice, 1 squeeze at a time, until it is seasoned to your taste. Adjust seasoning with salt and pepper.

Celeriac Rémoulade

A variant on coleslaw, rémoulade makes a great side dish for crab cakes or grilled fish.

1. In a small bowl combine ingredients for dressing: mayonnaise, parsley, lemon juice, capers, mustard, tarragon, and salt and pepper to taste. Mix until combined well. Toss with celery root.

   Chill until ready to serve.

¼ c	mayonnaise
1 Tbs	minced fresh parsley leaves
2 tsp	fresh lemon juice
½ tsp	minced bottled capers
1 tsp	Dijon mustard
1 tsp	fresh tarragon, minced, or ¼ tsp dried
2	small celeriac, peeled and cut into matchstick pieces or shredded coarse
	salt and pepper to taste

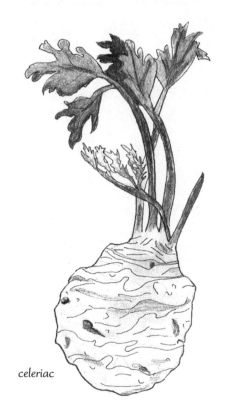

celeriac

Chunked Roasted Sweet Potato with Garlic

♦ ♦ ♦ ♦ ♦

3	sweet potatoes (to yield 3 cups of chunks) or 1½ lb of fingerling sweet potatoes, washed but not peeled
2 tsp	olive or vegetable oil
½ tsp	salt
¼ tsp	black pepper
1–2 tsp	chopped garlic
½ c	chopped onion
½ tsp	fresh rosemary, sage, or oregano

In a sweet potato rut? Tired of simple baking or of the "add sugar or marshmallows" less healthy approach? Try this fast savory recipe! Excellent with chicken or grilled sausage or steak.

1. Cut potatoes into 1-inch chunks, skin on (3 cups of potato serves 3 or 4). Drizzle oil on top, and then stir in salt and pepper.

2. Microwave for 4 minutes, or skip this step and just roast in a heavy pan at 400°F until the edges start to soften. Add garlic, onions, and herbs.

3. Lower heat to 350° F and continue roasting until garlic has slightly browned and sweet potato has softened, about 8–10 minutes.

Classic Southern–Style Lima Beans

Lima beans and butter beans are interchangeable, though butter beans are considered superior. This is the way to cook lima beans in the South where they are most esteemed. This recipe works well with black-eyed peas and crowder peas. Best served alongside roasted chicken, white fish, or pork roast.

1. Melt butter or fat in a saucepan over medium heat. Add onions and stir frequently until translucent or slightly caramelized.

2. Add stock/broth and beans. Season with salt (approximately ½ tsp). Cover and simmer until just tender; the skins will start to peel away. The beans will take 30 minutes or so, but start checking after 20 minutes to test for doneness.

3. Mix in optional ingredients and thyme. Adjust seasoning with salt, pepper, and more butter if you'd like.

2 tsp	lard, chicken fat, olive oil, or butter
½ c	diced onion
3 c	(or more) chicken stock, vegetable broth, or pork stock
2 c	fresh shelled lima beans (do not use dried beans)
	precooked bacon bits, ham hock, precooked (leftover chicken chunks) (optional)
2 tsp	chopped fresh thyme
	salt and pepper to taste

Honey-Roasted Acorn Squash

◆ ◆ ◆ ◆ ◆

2	whole acorn squash
1–2 Tbs	olive oil
	salt to taste
1 stick	(4 ounces) butter, room temperature
½ c	honey
1 Tbs	minced fresh thyme
½ tsp	minced fresh rosemary or sage

Sweet, savory, and simple. A good approach for little kids or adults who may dislike the slightly astringent flavor of some acorn squash.

1. Preheat the oven to 350°F.

2. Cut squash in half. With a large metal spoon, scoop out the seeds and discard. Cut each half into 4 wedges.

3. Place wedges in a baking dish and drizzle with olive oil. Sprinkle lightly with salt. Roast in the oven for 20 minutes.

4. Combine butter, honey, salt, and herbs in a bowl and mix into a paste.

5. Remove squash from the oven and spoon butter/honey mix all over squash. Return to the oven for 15 minutes, and bake until brown and caramelized.

Oregano Potato Salad

Serve either warm, just after you've finished preparing, or cold. New potatoes are smaller spuds dug while the potato plant is still alive, and this makes new potatoes sweeter, nuttier, more tender-skinned, and with superior texture compared to older spuds.

1. In a small bowl, combine the onion, pepper, garlic, vinegar, and pinch of salt.

2. Wash and cut potatoes into about ½-inch chunks. Put in a large pot and cover with cold water. Add a generous amount of salt (approximately 2 tsp per quart). Bring to a boil over high heat and reduce the heat to simmer. Continue cooking until the potatoes are tender, approximately 10 minutes. Test for doneness; you should be able to insert a paring knife easily into the potatoes.

3. Drain potatoes. Let cool slightly, and toss potatoes with onion mix, olive oil, olives, and fresh herbs. Season to taste with salt and pepper.

♦ ♦ ♦ ♦ ♦

½	onion, peeled and diced
1	red bell pepper, seeded and diced
1 clove	garlic, minced
¼ c	balsamic vinegar
2 lb	new potatoes
¼ c	olive oil
¼ c	chopped fresh mint
¼ c	chopped fresh parsley
2 Tbs	fresh oregano
	salt and pepper to taste

—— Optional ——

black olives, pitted and coarsely chopped

◆ ◆ ◆ ◆ ◆

2 lb	parsnips
½ c	cream or chicken stock (or combination)
	Salt, pepper, and lemon juice to taste

Parsnip Purée

This is a great alternative to mashed potatoes.

1. Peel parsnips and cut into 2-inch cubes. Put in a large pot, and cover with cold water. Season generously with salt. Bring to a boil over high heat, and then reduce the heat to a simmer. Cook until parsnips are tender, about 20 minutes. Drain.

2. Purée parsnips with cream, and season to taste with salt, pepper, and lemon juice.

2 Tbs	butter
1 Tbs	olive oil
½ c	diced fennel
½ c	diced onion
2 c	peeled (optional) and diced potatoes
¼ c	white wine
1 qt	chicken stock
2 Tbs	grated Parmesan cheese
	salt, pepper, and lemon juice to taste

Potato Fennel "Risotto"

Risotto is usually prepared with rice, but this variation uses potatoes instead.

1. Melt 1 Tbs butter and olive oil in a large sauce pan. Add fennel, onion and potato. Season with salt and pepper. Cook for 2 minutes, stirring every so often.

2. Add white wine and stir.

3. Add chicken stock, ½ cup at a time, stirring regularly.

4. Cook for 10 minutes, or until potatoes are tender.

5. Stir in remaining butter and Parmesan. Adjust seasoning with salt, pepper, and lemon juice.

Quinoa with Roasted Brussels Sprouts

It's very important to rinse quinoa before cooking as the grains often have a bitter residue on them that comes from processing.

1. Put quinoa in a fine mesh strainer and rinse under cold water. Put in a small saucepan and cover with water by 1 inch. Add 1 tsp salt. Cover the pot and cook over medium heat for 10 minutes, or until quinoa has popped and is cooked through.

2. Meanwhile, cut Brussels sprouts in half and then slice thin.

3. Heat a large skillet over high heat. Add the olive oil, and let heat for 1 minute. Add the garlic and cook for 3 minutes or until aromatic. Add the Brussels sprouts and cook, stirring regularly, until they are bright green and soft. Remove from heat.

4. When quinoa is cooked, drain excess water. Toss with Brussels. Add juice from ½ lemon and season to taste with salt and pepper. Stir in almonds, if using.

◆ ◆ ◆ ◆ ◆

½ c	quinoa
½ lb	Brussels sprouts
2 Tbs	olive oil
3 cloves	garlic, sliced thin or chopped
½	lemon
	salt and pepper to taste

—————— Optional ——————

¼ c	toasted, slivered almonds

Roasted Beets with Onions and Bacon

◆ ◆ ◆ ◆ ◆

4	medium-sized beets
2 Tbs	olive oil
1 slice	bacon, diced
1	small onion, peeled and finely diced
	salt and pepper to taste

Roasting beets intensifies the flavors and sweetness. It also makes peeling easier.

1. Scrub the beets well to remove all the dirt. Toss them, unpeeled, in olive oil, wrap in foil, and bake in a 425°F oven for 30 minutes. To test for doneness, a paring knife should insert easily.

2. Let beets cool slightly. Peel with a paring knife or butter knife. Cut into quarters and set aside.

3. In a small skillet, cook bacon over medium heat, stirring occasionally until it starts to release its fat. Drain all but 1 Tbs. Add onions and cook until soft.

4. Toss beets with bacon and onions. Season to taste with salt and pepper.

Roasted Jerusalem Artichokes with Sage

A nice autumn dish to serve as the main starch.
An old toothbrush and running water is perhaps the best way
to scrub soil from the nooks and crannies of most sunchokes.

1. Scrub and wash well Jerusalem artichokes (but do not peel) and cut into ¼-inch chunks. Toss with olive oil and season with salt and pepper.

2. Put Jerusalem artichokes on a baking sheet or Pyrex dish. Roast at 375°F for 10 minutes.

3. Remove pan from the oven and stir in garlic, sage, and butter. Continue baking for an additional 10 minutes or until artichokes are tender and garlic is lightly golden.

4. Squeeze lemon juice on top just before serving.

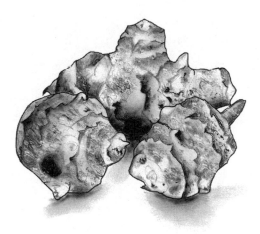

Jerusalem artichokes

◆ ◆ ◆ ◆ ◆

1 lb	Jerusalem artichokes
2 Tbs	olive oil
3 cloves	garlic, chopped
2–3 Tbs	thinly sliced fresh sage
2	Tbs butter
	salt, pepper, and lemon juice to taste

Roasted Kohlrabi

◆ ◆ ◆ ◆ ◆

1½ lb	kohlrabi, ends trimmed, thick green skin sliced off with a knife, and diced
1 Tbs	olive oil
1 Tbs	garlic
2 slices	bacon, chopped (optional)
1–2 Tbs	red wine vinegar
	salt

A return to the concept of members of the brassica family (e.g., cabbage, kale, collards, Brussels) being so easily wed to bacon and maybe a hint of vinegar.

1. Preheat the oven to 425°F.

2. Toss the diced kohlrabi with olive oil, garlic, bacon (if using) and salt in a bowl. Spread in a single layer on a rimmed baking sheet and put into the oven (it needn't be fully preheated) and roast for 30–35 minutes; after 20 minutes, stir every five minutes.

3. Sprinkle with vinegar just before serving.

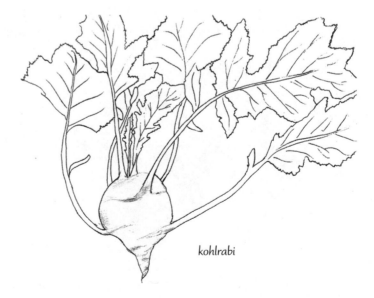

kohlrabi

Roasted Potatoes with Lemon Zest and Parsley

Tossing the potatoes in cornstarch before roasting
gives them a lovely crust.

1. Preheat the oven to 400°F.

2. Wash and dry potatoes. Cut into sixths, to yield about 3 cups.

3. Toss potatoes with oil, cornstarch, salt, and pepper. Make sure potatoes are evenly coated.

4. Place potatoes on a cookie sheet in a single layer. Roast in the oven for 20 minutes, or until crispy on the outside and tender on the inside.

5. Toss potatoes with lemon zest and parsley.

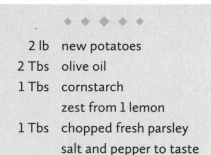

2 lb	new potatoes
2 Tbs	olive oil
1 Tbs	cornstarch
	zest from 1 lemon
1 Tbs	chopped fresh parsley
	salt and pepper to taste

 VEGAN   GLUTEN FREE

parsley

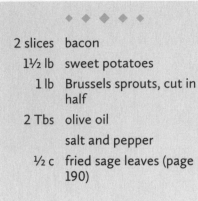

2 slices	bacon
1½ lb	sweet potatoes
1 lb	Brussels sprouts, cut in half
2 Tbs	olive oil
	salt and pepper
½ c	fried sage leaves (page 190)

Roasted Sweet Potatoes and Brussels Sprouts with Bacon and Sage

Served with a tossed green salad, this is a delicious and complete meal. The sage need not be fried if you are pressed for time; simply chop the raw sage and mix in.

1. Dice bacon. Put in an ovenproof dish and into a 425°F oven.

2. Meanwhile, peel and cube sweet potatoes.

3. Toss sweet potatoes with bacon, season with salt and pepper, and return to the oven. Roast until browned and soft, about 20 minutes.

4. In a separate pan, toss Brussels sprouts with olive oil, salt, and pepper. Roast in the oven for 15 minutes, or until tender and caramelized on the bottom.

5. Mix the two together. Garnish with fried sage.

Roasted Turnips I

This approach has a deep European history and has recently become a staple in many of the better restaurants here in the US. The dish particularly complements heavier meat dishes, from Thanksgiving turkey to chicken or calves' liver to roasted beef, lamb, or pork. The mellow complexity of the roasted roots also adds unmatched character to vegetarian pasta or rice dishes.

1. Cut any larger roots into pieces about 1½-inch long; leave smaller ones whole. Place in roasting pan; add salt, pepper, and oils, and toss around. Bake in a 350°F–375°F oven, stirring occasionally, until only the very centers of the larger roots are still hard.

2. Add garlic, onions, and herbs, and continue roasting until all roots are just soft. Many will have begun to caramelize (i.e., turn brown, shriveled, and sweet). The roots cool quickly, so serve soon or in a lidded bowl.

3–4 c	baby turnips and/or rutabagas, washed, trimmed, but unpeeled
3 Tbs	olive oil or neutral oil + olive oil blend
1 tsp	salt
½ tsp	black pepper
2 tsp	fresh chopped thyme or rosemary, or 1 tsp dry rosemary (whole leaf, not powder)
1 Tbs	chopped garlic
2 Tbs	chopped onion

Roasted Turnips II

◆ ◆ ◆ ◆ ◆

1	Macomber or other large turnip, to yield 2–3 cups diced
1–2 Tbs	butter
1 tsp	minced fresh ginger
1 tsp	minced fresh garlic
1	crisp apple
	salt and pepper to taste

Serve as a side dish to braised short ribs, salmon, or pork chops.

1. Preheat the oven to 375°F.

2. Peel turnip and cut into ¾-inch cubes.

3. Melt the butter in a skillet over medium heat. Add ginger and garlic, and cook for 2 minutes, just to soften.

4. Toss the butter with the turnips. Season with salt and pepper. Spread them in a single layer on a cookie sheet and put them in the oven.

5. Roast the turnips for 20 minutes.

6. While they're roasting, core the apple and cut it into a ½-inch dice. Do not peel it.

7. After 20 minutes, add the apple to the turnips. Toss them together to make sure the apples get a little butter coating. Roast for 5 minutes more.

Root Vegetable and Potato Gratin

*This is a rich casserole that can serve as a whole meal
if served with a good salad. No need to use
fresh new potatoes; anything will do.*

1. Butter a 9-inch × 13-inch Pyrex dish.

2. In a large bowl, mix all ingredients together (including optionals) and then place into the baking dish. With the back of a spatula, press down the potatoes and root vegetables so they lie flat and are submerged in the cream.

3. Bake at 340°F until tender all the way through, about 40 minutes. Test by inserting a butter knife into the middle of the dish. If it goes in easily, the potatoes are cooked.

4. Let cool for 10 minutes before slicing and serving.

◆ ◆ ◆ ◆ ◆

2 Tbs	butter
2 lb	potatoes, washed, not peeled, but sliced very thin
1 lb	parsnips or Jerusalem artichokes, not peeled, scrubbed, and sliced very thin
2 c	milk, half and half, or cream
5 cloves	garlic, medium-large, chopped
2 tsp	salt
¾ tsp	black pepper
1	onion, chopped
½ c	grated cheese: Cheddar, Gouda, Gruyère or Parmesan

————— Optional —————

1 bunch	arugula, chopped, and/or 1 apple, chopped

◆ ◆ ◆ ◆ ◆

2	medium spaghetti squash
½	onion, peeled and sliced
3 cloves	garlic, chopped
2 Tbs	olive oil
1 Tbs	capers
1 Tbs	butter
2 Tbs	white wine
	salt and pepper to taste

Sautéed Spaghetti Squash with Capers and Garlic

This is excellent alongside seafood, beef, or vegetarian beans.

1. Cut spaghetti squash in half and scoop out and discard the seeds and inner soft pulp with a large metal spoon.

2. Place face down on a plate and microwave about 2 minutes per half (multiple batches should be necessary) until BARELY soft. If you lack a microwave, steam for about 6 minutes until just soft. Let cool, then plunge a fork longitudinally through the inside flesh and work it from end to end to make the "spaghetti." Use a metal spoon to get out the last strands.

3. Meanwhile, sauté onions with garlic in olive oil until just soft. Add capers, stir around, and then add spaghetti squash, 1 Tbs butter, and ½ tsp each salt and pepper, or to taste. Sauté for about 3 minutes more at moderate heat, then finish with white wine.

Simple Garlic-Roasted Potatoes

This can be prepared using new potatoes or older ones, and are best using washed but not peeled spuds.

1. Mix the potatoes, salt, pepper, and oil; bake in a 350°F oven until just soft, stirring occasionally. Add garlic and bake until garlic starts to brown slightly. Add optional fresh herbs with the raw garlic.

2. A nice twist on this is to omit the other herbs but to squeeze half of a lemon, with some freshly chopped basil, when the garlic has just browned. Then roast 60 seconds more.

3. Leftovers are excellent served cold the next day, drizzled with vinaigrette.

2 lb	potatoes, cut into 1-inch to 1½-inch chunks if too big whole
½ tsp	salt
¼ tsp	black pepper
2 Tbs	olive oil
4 cloves	garlic, peeled and chopped

—————— Optional ——————

2 tsp	chopped fresh rosemary, sage, thyme, or oregano

Simple Simmered New Potatoes

◆ ◆ ◆ ◆ ◆

2 lb	new potatoes
1 tsp	salt
	cold water to cover potatoes
¼ tsp	black pepper
¼ c	butter

———— Optional ————

1 Tbs	chopped fresh parsley, chives, or fennel leaf

While these can be prepared with older spuds,
they are truly sublime with freshly dug new potatoes.
Be sure always to wash new potatoes gently, by immersing
in cold water then rubbing any soil off, as the skins
will too easily come off otherwise and are a required
part of the new potato flavors.

1. Put spuds, salt, and water in a pot. Bring to a simmer. When fully cooked, a slender fork or knife will encounter little resistance when used to pierce a few of the potatoes.

2. Drain off all but 2 Tbs of the water, add butter and pepper, and cooked another 2 minutes.

3. Stir in the herb(s), and taste again for salt and pepper.

Spiced Turnips

*This is a great side dish for hearty roasted meat dishes,
such as venison, beef, or pork. You could also use rutabagas
in place of the turnips.*

1. In a large skillet over medium-high heat, toast the mustard seeds until they start to pop. Add the coriander and allspice. Remove from the pan and set aside.

2. To the same hot pan, add half of the oil. Add the apples and cook until they begin to caramelize. Remove from the pan and add to the mustard seeds. To that same hot pan, add remaining oil and turnips. Cook, covered, for about 5 minutes or until tender.

3. To the turnip pan, add the maple syrup and cook for a few minutes more. Return all the other ingredients to the pan, and add the parsley.

4. Season to taste with salt and pepper.

2 Tbs	mustard seeds
½ tsp	allspice
½ tsp	coriander
3	apples, peeled and diced, to yield 4 cups
1–2	large turnips, peeled and diced to yield 4 cups
3 Tbs	plain oil
3 Tbs	maple syrup or honey
1 Tbs	parsley
	salt and pepper to taste

Squash Gnocchi

♦ ♦ ♦ ♦ ♦

1	butternut squash
1	acorn squash
1½ c	all-purpose flour
2	eggs
½ tsp	curry powder
1 tsp	salt
½ tsp	baking powder
1 c	chicken broth or 2 Tbs butter

*Puréed blue hubbard squash would also be delicious
in place of the butternut and/or acorn.*

1. Cut squash in half. Put on a baking sheet, cut side down. Add water to the pan, and bake at 350°F for 40 minutes or until squash are tender. It may be necessary to add more water to the pan if it all evaporates.

2. Let squash cool. Scoop out seeds and discard.

3. Scoop out pulp into a food processor and blend until smooth. Measure out one cup of purée (set aside the remainder for soup or another favorite recipe). Add flour, eggs, curry powder, salt, and baking powder. Blend in food processor minimally, just until smooth.

4. Bring a large pot of water to a boil. Season with salt.

5. Fill a piping bag with a large plain tip. Fill with gnocchi filling. Gently pipe out ¾-inch logs, and then cut off into the water with a butter knife. Boil for 2 minutes. Scoop out with a slotted spoon into a dish with either the butter or chicken broth (this will keep the dumplings from sticking together before serving).

6. It may be necessary to cook the dumplings in batches. Serve with Brussels sprouts, duck, or turkey.

Sumptuous Sweet Potato Salad

*This recipe comes courtesy of
The Good Earth Natural Food Co., in Leonardtown, MD.
This makes 8–16 servings, and is terrific as leftovers
the second day.*

1. For the dressing, whisk the ingredients together in a small bowl. Season to taste with salt and pepper.

2. Toss sweet potatoes with olive oil, salt, and pepper. Lay them on baking pans in a single layer and roast in a 425°F oven until tender, approximately 15 minutes. Let potatoes cool to room temperature.

3. Place sweet potatoes in a large bowl. Add scallions, parsley, pecans, and raisins. Pour dressing over and toss gently to blend. Adjust seasoning with salt and pepper.

◆ ◆ ◆ ◆ ◆

Dressing

½ c	extra virgin olive oil
2 Tbs	pure maple syrup
2 Tbs	orange juice
2 Tbs	sherry or balsamic vinegar
1	lime, juiced
2 tsp	minced fresh ginger
½ tsp	cinnamon
¼ tsp	nutmeg
¼ tsp	cardamom
	salt and pepper to taste

Salad

6 lb	Beauregard or other orange variety sweet potato, peeled and cut into ¾-inch cubes
¼ c	olive oil
1 c	chopped scallions
1 c	chopped fresh parsley
1 c	pecans, toasted and coarsely chopped
1 c	raisins, brown or golden, or mix of both
	salt and pepper to taste

Superb Sweet Potato Stuffing for Chicken or Turkey

This delicious stuffing accomplishes 3 things: it adds (if using Japanese purple-skinned sweet potatoes) great chestnut flavor to stuffing easily and affordably; it adds more nutrition than any bread-based stuffing; and it provides a wheat-free stuffing fit for more diners (many fewer people are allergic to sweet potatoes than wheat).

1½–2 lb	sweet potatoes, washed well but not peeled (Japanese purple-skinned is the preferred chestnut-flavored variety, but any high-quality sweets may be used)
1 Tbs	olive oil
1 tsp	salt
½ tsp	pepper
½–1 lb	high-quality pork sausage or 1 Tbs olive oil (optional)
1	onion, chopped
½ c	chopped celery (optional)
½ c	white wine or beer
2 Tbs	fresh chopped herbs, preferably with some rosemary and sage (other herbs can supplement)
	salt and pepper to taste

1. Cut the sweet potatoes into ½-inch chunks, place in a baking pan, toss with the olive oil, salt, and pepper, and bake in a 350°F oven until soft (approximately 30 minutes). Alternatively, you may microwave the chunks until just soft.

2. In a sauté pan, cook the crumbled sausage until fully cooked, then add the onions and celery and sauté until these are soft. If not using sausage, sauté the veggies in olive oil. Add the wine or beer and simmer another 30 seconds. Let cool, then add the fresh herbs and toss with the sweet potatoes. Taste for salt and pepper and adjust if needed.

3. A superior option is to mince the bird's liver and heart and add to the sautéing vegetables. This also substitutes for the pork sausage.

4. Generously salt and pepper the inside of a raw chicken or turkey and stuff it. Rub the outside as well with salt and pepper. Roast as per any other poultry recipe.

Sweet Potato Fries

These are really easy, and are just like French fries.
Assume 1—2 medium sweet potatoes per person.

1. Trim any bad spots from clean sweet potatoes but do not peel. Bake whole at 350°F until just soft (cooking too long will lead to hollow sweets that break apart upon frying). Let cool. At this point, the baked sweets can be refrigerated as is for up to six days before using.

2. To fry: slice each sweet potato into French fries, leaving the skin on. Deep-fry until they float and have gotten a bit brown.

3. Drain, sprinkle with salt (optional), and serve. Good condiments are Julia's hot sauce (see page 266) and ketchup (see page 265).

Tabouli

This Mediterranean salad is a refreshing side dish
to any grilled meat of fish.

½ c	fine-grain bulgur
¼ c	fresh lemon juice
2 c	finely diced tomatoes
½ c	thinly sliced scallions
2	pinches cinnamon
	salt and freshly ground pepper
⅓ c	extra virgin olive oil
2 c	finely chopped flat-leaf parsley
2 Tbs	slivered fresh mint leaves

1. Place the bulgur in a fine sieve, rinse under cold running water, squeeze dry, and soak in the lemon juice for 45 minutes. Use a fork to fluff the bulgur.

2. To the bulgur, add the tomatoes, scallions, cinnamon, and a few pinches of salt and pepper. Drizzle on the olive oil and toss. Mix in the parsley and mint. Refrigerate for 1 hour, stirring occasionally.

Tater Tots

◆ ◆ ◆ ◆ ◆

4	medium potatoes
½ c	grated Parmesan cheese
½ c	all-purpose flour
1–2 tsp	salt
1	egg
1 c	panko bread crumbs
1 c	clarified butter or canola oil

To make these tater tots gluten-free and vegan, omit the egg, cheese, and bread crumbs. Add instead 2 Tbs cornstarch, ¼ tsp of xanthan gum, and ¼ tsp sugar to the potato mix.

1. Put potatoes in a pot and cover with cold water. Bring to a boil and cook until tender, about 20 minutes.

2. When potatoes are cooked, drain them and put them through a potato ricer. The ricer will extract the skin from the potatoes. Alternatively, you can grate the potatoes using a food processor or hand grater. In any case, grate the potatoes while they're still warm.

3. Let potatoes cool to room temperature.

4. Mix potatoes with Parmesan cheese, flour, salt (to taste), and egg. Be careful not to over-mix.

5. Divide dough into 4 balls and roll potato dough into 4 logs. Cut each log into 1-inch pieces.

6. Roll each tot in panko bread crumbs. If you'd like, you can further reshape the tots to a round shape.

7. Heat a large skillet over medium-high heat. Add butter or oil. In batches, cook tots on all sides until evenly browned, about 5 minutes.

Serve with ketchup (see page 265).

Asparagus Relish

Pairs very well with chicken that has been marinated in soy sauce, coated in sesame seeds, and baked.

1. Bring a pot of salted water to a boil. Cook the asparagus for 2 minutes. Drain and run asparagus under cold water. Mix together all ingredients for relish. Season to taste with salt and pepper.

◆ ◆ ◆ ◆ ◆

1 lb	asparagus, trimmed and cut into ½-inch pieces
2 tsp	chopped garlic
4 tsp	chopped pickled ginger
1	tomato, chopped
1	yellow or red pepper, diced
1⅓ c	red wine vinegar
1 c	olive oil
2 tsp	sesame seeds
	salt and pepper to taste

Basic Italian Sautéed Greens

◆ ◆ ◆ ◆ ◆

1   large bunch pre-washed kale, collards, or mustard greens

    ¾-inch water to steam or 2 quarts salted water to boil

    ice bath (see "Shocking" (see page 43)

1½ tsp   olive oil

1½ tsp   neutral oil

2–4   cloves garlic, coarsely chopped

    salt and pepper to taste

This was an endless theme in Brett's childhood: his mother Roberta was and is a master of Italianate cooking, and superb ingredients and simple techniques resulted in perfect meals. Roberta might do any leaf green this way, including escarole, Swiss chard, spinach, or wild dandelion.

1. Barely wilt greens in steamer or by blanching; shock in ice bath if you'll not immediately sauté. Drain. Coarsely chop.

2. Sauté greens by heating garlic in oils until garlic edges have just started to brown, and IMMEDIATELY dump drained greens into the skillet. Stir around and sauté about 30 more seconds. Will cool quickly, so a lidded serving dish is apt.

Variations of the Basic Italian

a. Delete the garlic, and substitute for it slivered onions, half-moons of yellow summer squash or zucchini, and/or sweet red pepper pieces.

b. Keep garlic and onions, and add 1 Tbs butter or ½ cup heavy cream to the skillet when the greens are almost done. Serve with toasted chopped almonds, or whole toasted pine nuts, on top.

c. Add fresh sage or rosemary to the hot skillet the second before adding the greens.

Basic Chinese Sautéed Greens

*Use the same ingredients as the basic Italian,
but exchange the olive oil with toasted sesame oil
(e.g., Kadoya), substitute 1 Tbs soy sauce or tamari for the
last salt, and sauté 1 tsp fresh minced ginger with the garlic.
Proceed as per the basic Italian.*

Variations of the Basic Chinese:

1. Add more vegetables, especially 1½-inch pieces of scallion, sliced Brussels sprouts, sweet red pepper, etc.

2. Add precooked, drained udon, Asian vermicelli, or ramen noodles to the skillet when the greens are nearly done. Increase seasoning appropriately.

3. Add 2–3 beaten eggs to the sautéing greens; cook to scramble. Serve over steamed rice and re-season. Excellent boost for people just recovering from sickness.

Braised Celery

◆ ◆ ◆ ◆ ◆

8 stalks   celery, rinsed and trimmed, leaves chopped and reserved

1 Tbs   unsalted butter

1   small onion, peeled and sliced

pinch kosher salt

pinch freshly ground black pepper

½ c   chicken or beef broth

Often we buy a whole head of celery at the farmers market just to use one or two stalks. Celery languishes in the crisper drawer because we don't often think of serving it as a vegetable. This is a great way to use copious amounts.

1. Peel any of the fibrous outer stalks of celery with a vegetable peeler and slice into 1-inch pieces diagonally.

2. Heat the butter in a large skillet over medium heat. Once melted, add the onions and cook for 5 minutes until soft. Add the celery, salt, and pepper and cook for another 5 minutes until just beginning to soften slightly. Add the broth and stir to combine. Cover and reduce the heat to low. Cook until the celery is tender but not mushy, approximately 15 minutes.

3. Uncover and allow the celery to continue to cook for an additional 5 minutes or until the liquid has been reduced by half.

4. Transfer to a serving dish and garnish with chopped celery leaves.

Braised Green Cabbage with Apples

*This is one of those accidental recipes created
when Julia was cleaning her fridge after a party and
noticed a half-consumed bottle of sparkling cider.
It worked so well that it became a regular part of her repertoire.*

1. Cut the cabbage in half and cut out the core. Cut into 1-inch chunks.

2. Peel the apple if desired, core and chop. Peel and chop the onion. Chop the garlic clove.

3. In a large skillet, over medium heat, melt the butter. Add the onions and garlic and cook for 3 minutes, just until they soften.

4. Add the cabbage and apple. Cook for a few minutes, stirring to mix well. Add the cider and cover the pan.

5. Cook over medium-low heat for 20 minutes. Season to taste with salt and pepper.

◆ ◆ ◆ ◆ ◆

1	small green cabbage
1	apple
1	small onion
1 clove	garlic
2 Tbs	butter
¼ c	cider, still, sparkling or slightly spiked (5% alcohol content)
	salt and pepper to taste

Braised Red Cabbage

*Braised red cabbage is a classic fall dish
to serve with roasted game meats, turkey, or pork.*

2 slices	bacon (optional) or 2 Tbs butter
1	onion
¼ c	red wine
¼ c	red wine vinegar
1 Tbs	red currant or raspberry jelly
1 Tbs	sugar
1	small red cabbage, cut in half, core removed, and sliced thin
1	apple, cored and chopped
	salt and pepper to taste

1. In a medium pan, render bacon fat over medium heat for about 3 minutes. Add the onions and cook until onions are soft, about 5 minutes.

2. Add red wine, red wine vinegar, sugar, jelly, sugar, cabbage, and apple. Stir well to combine everything. Cover and cook for 20 minutes, or until cabbage is tender.

3. Remove cover and continue cooking until most of the liquid has evaporated.

4. Set aside in a warm place until ready to serve.

Broccoli Masala

*This is a variation on the Indian Cauliflower Masala.
It can also be prepared with cauliflower—
increase the cooking time to 15 minutes.*

1. Heat butter in a large skillet over medium heat, and fry mustard seeds until they start to pop. Add cumin, fenugreek, turmeric, ginger, garlic, and onions. Cook, stirring frequently, until onions are soft.

2. Add broccoli, and stir until well coated. Add tomato, chili, and salt, and cook until broccoli is bright green, about 3 minutes. If pan seems dry, add ¼ cup of water.

◆ ◆ ◆ ◆ ◆

3 Tbs	clarified butter or olive oil
½ tsp	brown mustard seed
½ tsp	cumin
	pinch fenugreek
½ tsp	turmeric
1 Tbs	minced fresh ginger
2 cloves	garlic, finely chopped
1	onion, finely sliced
1 lb	broccoli, separated into florets
1	small tomato, chopped
1	fresh green chili, sliced
½ tsp	salt

Broccoli Raab with Honey and Grapes

1 bunch	broccoli raab
2 tsp	olive oil
1 clove	garlic, minced
¼ tsp	chili flakes or Aleppo pepper
½ tsp	cumin
1 c	grapes, cut in half
2 Tbs	honey
	salt and pepper to taste

The sweetness of the grapes balances nicely with the bitterness of the raab. This is a wonderful side dish for grilled lamb or quail.

1. Trim the ends off the broccoli raab, and coarsely chop. Wash.

2. Heat a large skillet over high heat. Add the oil. Add the garlic and cook for 2 minutes or until aromatic. Add the spices and cook for 1 minute more to toast them before adding the raab.

3. Cook the raab, stirring frequently until it turns bright green. If the pan seems dry, add ¼ cup of water.

4. Stir in the grapes and honey. Season with salt and pepper.

Broccoli Raab with Toasted Sesame Seeds and Ginger

The ginger adds clean flavors; the sesame seeds contribute nuttiness and textural contrast. Fine served simply, over rice, or as a side dish.

1. In a dry skillet, over medium heat, toast sesame seeds until golden brown. Immediately add sesame oil and garlic. Sauté until garlic just starts to brown.

2. Add ginger, and cook for 10 seconds. Add the raab. Then add the sake and soy sauce. Cook until just barely wilted. Remove from heat. Stir in butter.

3. If weather conditions make the raab slightly bitter, adding a touch of honey or sugar with the greens can make the dish more balanced.

2 tsp	raw sesame seeds
1 tsp	sesame oil
1 clove	garlic, chopped
1 tsp	fresh chopped ginger
1 bunch	broccoli raab
1 Tbs	sake or mirin
1 tsp	soy sauce or tamari

— **Optional** —

1 tsp	butter

 VEGAN

 GLUTEN FREE

broccoli raab

Broccoli with Lemon Zest and Parmesan

*Broccoli does well with either an aged cheese
or with an acid like vinegar or lemon juice;
this recipe marries the three. Most traditional in spring.*

1 lb   broccoli
1 Tbs   olive oil
2 cloves garlic, chopped
1   lemon, zest
¼ c   grated Parmesan or Romano cheese
        salt and pepper to taste

1. Trim tough stalks off broccoli and cut into florets.

2. Heat a large skillet over high heat. Add oil and then garlic. Cook for 2 minutes.

3. Add broccoli and ¼ cup of water. Season with salt and pepper. Cook for 5 minutes, uncovered, stirring every so often, until broccoli is bright green.

4. Just before serving, toss with lemon zest and Parmesan cheese.

Buttered Leeks

*Leeks rarely get the proper showing they deserve.
This simple recipe lets their sweet onion flavor shine.*

3   large leeks
2 Tbs   butter
½ tsp   salt
1 Tbs   fresh lemon juice

1. Trim the leeks: cut off the dark green and set aside for another use. Cut the leeks in half lengthwise, then into ½-inch slices. Soak in cold water to remove the dirt. Lift the leeks out of the water.

2. Heat a large skillet over medium heat. Add the butter and let it melt. Then add the leeks and salt. Cook, stirring occasionally, until the leeks are soft, about 15 minutes. Add the lemon juice at the very end.

Button Mushrooms and Greens

This is excellent served with crusty bread, freshly boiled potatoes, or baked potatoes. It is also lovely served over pasta or alongside chicken or scallops. Generous addition of freshly ground black pepper can really highlight all the flavors.

1. Blanch and shock the greens: in a large pot of boiling salted water, cook greens until just wilted, approximately for 1 minute and drain. Shock in an ice bath, and drain well.

2. Coarsely chop greens if desired, or leave whole.

3. In a large skillet, add oil. Over medium-high heat, cook onions and garlic until barely translucent. Add the mushrooms and continue cooking for 1 minute more, stirring often.

4. Add white wine to mushroom pan and simmer for 2 minutes.

5. Add cream and continue cooking to reduce for 5 more minutes, until approximately 1 cup of liquid remains.

6. Add the greens, stir well, adjust seasoning with salt and freshly ground black pepper. Cook only until greens are heated through, about 30 seconds.

1	large bunch prewashed greens: kale, collards, mustard greens, or Swiss chard
2 tsp	olive oil
½	onion, sliced
2 cloves	garlic, chopped
¼ lb	button mushrooms (portobellos or crimini would also work well), sliced ¼ inch thick
¼ c	white wine
1 tsp	salt, plus salt and pepper to taste
1½ c	heavy cream

Caramelized Carrots with Honey

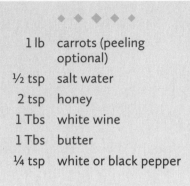

1 lb	carrots (peeling optional)
½ tsp	salt water
2 tsp	honey
1 Tbs	white wine
1 Tbs	butter
¼ tsp	white or black pepper

—————— Optional ——————

1 tsp	lemon juice

Carrots grown in uniformly cool weather are often so sweet that they need no honey. But even a short run of hot weather can cause carrots to have a slight astringency. The honey in this approach helps the carrots overcome challenged growing conditions.

1. Leave carrots whole if they are small, or cut into 1-inch pieces.

2. Put carrots in a pot with salt and add enough cold water to barely cover.

3. Cover pot and simmer carrots until just tender.

4. Drain all but ¼ cup of water from carrots, stir in honey until fully dissolved. Cook uncovered under very low heat until all the water has evaporated. Toss with butter and pepper.

5. Season to taste with white wine, more salt, and/or pepper. The lemon juice makes it lighter and more appropriate for serving alongside poultry, pork, or lamb.

Carrots in Butter

Fresh carrots done this way are so flavorful and indeed can be perfect; frozen, chunked carrots prepared just with butter are usually awful.

1. Leave carrots whole if they are small, or cut into 1-inch pieces.

2. Put carrots in a pot with salt and add enough cold water to barely cover.

3. Cover pot and simmer carrots until just tender. Drain water and toss carrots with butter and pepper.

4. Season to taste with white wine, more salt and/or pepper. Very good with snow peas or shelled English peas added in the last 30 seconds of cooking the carrots.

1 lb	carrots (peeling optional)
½ tsp	salt
1 Tbs	butter
¼ tsp	white or black pepper
	white wine

♦ ♦ ♦ ♦ ♦

2 Tbs	raisins
½ c	warm water
¼ tsp	saffron threads
2 Tbs	olive oil
1	small red onion, diced
2 cloves	garlic, minced
1	small tomato, chopped
1	anchovy (omit to keep the dish vegan/vegetarian)
	cauliflower, cut in half, core removed, and then cut into florets
1 Tbs	toasted pine nuts or chopped almonds
1 tsp	red wine vinegar
	salt and pepper, Romano cheese, parsley to taste

Cauliflower with Pine Nuts, Saffron, and Raisins

Serve as a side dish, or toss with pasta.

1. Soak raisins in ¼ cup of warm water. Steep saffron in remaining water.

2. Heat oil in a large skillet over medium heat. Add onions and garlic. Cook until soft, about 5 minutes.

3. Add tomatoes, anchovies, and cauliflower. Cook for 10 minutes, stirring occasionally. Add saffron and raisins, along with their liquid. Cook for 10 more minutes or until cauliflower is tender. Add nuts.

4. Season to taste with vinegar, salt, pepper, cheese, and parsley.

Chilled Spaghetti Squash and Tomato Salad

A really nice and unique salad created by Brett one late September, when cucumbers were over, spaghetti squash was just beginning to ripen, and cherry tomatoes were still producing great fruits. The tomatoes add a lot of valuable acidity to the salad.

1. Cut spaghetti squash in half and scoop out and discard the seeds and inner soft pulp with a large metal spoon.

2. Place squash face down on a plate and microwave about 2 minutes per half (multiple batches should be necessary) until BARELY soft. If you lack a microwave, steam for about 6 minutes until just soft. Let cool, then plunge a fork longitudinally through the inside flesh and work it from end to end to make the "spaghetti" (see page 24). Use a metal spoon to get out the last strands. Let cool to room temperature or cooler in the refrigerator.

3. Cut tomatoes into ½-inch chunks. Add tomatoes, onions and garlic to the cold squash strands. Mix in vinegar, olive oil, salt and pepper, soy sauce, and fresh basil.

4. Taste and adjust for vinegar, salt, and pepper.

◆ ◆ ◆ ◆ ◆

2	spaghetti squash, about 4 pounds
1 qt	tomatoes
3 cloves	garlic, minced
½	onion, peeled and sliced
1–3 Tbs	balsamic or cider vinegar
1 Tbs	olive oil
1 Tbs	soy sauce or tamari
3 Tbs	thinly sliced fresh basil
	salt and pepper to taste (about ½ tsp each)

Classic Southern-Style Greens

◆ ◆ ◆ ◆ ◆

¼–½ lb	bacon, ham, or sausage, raw but coarsely chopped
1	onion, sliced or chopped
1	large bunch prewashed collards, kale, mustards, etc., coarsely chopped
½ tsp	black pepper
	salt only after tasting
1 tsp	red wine or cider vinegar

This staple of the American South is still great comfort food. We advise seeking out the absolute best bacon or ham you can find; most commercial types such as Smithfield and Armour have lots of water and chemicals added.

1. Cook meat in heavy skillet at 350°F until crisping at edges. Pour off most of fat but retain at least 2 Tbs. Add onion and continue baking until onions and meat are fully cooked, about 15 minutes.

2. Carefully remove from the oven, add greens, and sauté on the stove-top until greens are just wilted or beyond. Season with salt to taste.

3. Splash 1 tsp red wine or cider vinegar into the skillet, loosen all the caramelized bits, and drizzle all over the greens. Particularly nice on blustery winter nights.

Nice served with sweet potato, herbed grits, or mashed potato. The first time we were served this dish properly prepared, we were encouraged to join our hosts in bourbon and soda, and that beverage still fits.

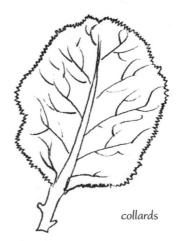

collards

Corn and Tomato Succotash

There's no "right" recipe for succotash:
use whatever summer vegetables you have on hand. Simply
seasoned with basil and lemon juice, there's nothing better!

1. Prepare vegetables: Chop tomato. Dice onion, chop garlic, dice zucchini and bell pepper. Cut corn kernels from cob.

2. In a heavy skillet, heat butter over medium-high heat. Add the corn in a single layer and sprinkle the onions and garlic on top. Do not stir for a few minutes until the corn develops a sweet, roasted aroma. Stir, and continue cooking for 1 minute.

3. Add the squash, pepper, and lima beans, stirring occasionally, until the squash is bright, about 3 minutes. Stir in tomato and basil and simmer, stirring occasionally, for 2 minutes, until everything is heated through.

4. Season with salt, pepper, and lemon juice to taste.

1	medium tomato
1	small onion
2 cloves	garlic
1	zucchini or yellow squash
1	small red bell pepper
2 ears	corn
1½ Tbs	olive oil or butter
	lima, fava, butter, or green beans cut into 1-inch pieces
1 Tbs	fresh basil
	salt, pepper, and lemon juice to taste

Creamed Braising Greens

◆ ◆ ◆ ◆ ◆

6 Tbs	butter
2 cloves	garlic, minced
1	shallot, peeled and thinly sliced
1 c	heavy cream
	pinch freshly grated nutmeg
	salt
¾ lb	young greens, like collards, kale, or mustard, stemmed and finely shredded (chiffonade)

This recipe comes courtesy of longtime Even' Star friend and CSA subscriber Sherry Jones.

1. In a saucepan, heat 2 Tbs of the butter over high heat until it foams. Add the garlic and shallots and cook over medium-low heat, stirring, until softened and golden, 5 minutes. Add the cream, bring to a simmer and cook until slightly thickened, 10 minutes. Add the nutmeg and salt to taste. Using a hand blender, purée until smooth.

2. In a large pot, heat the remaining 4 Tbs of butter over high heat until it foams. Add the greens and cook, stirring constantly, until tender but still bright green, about 5 minutes. Sprinkle with salt and add the cream mixture. Lower the heat, cover and let simmer until cooked through, 5 minutes more. Taste for nutmeg and salt, season to taste and serve hot.

Yield: 8 servings

Creamed Spinach

Creamed spinach is classic to 1950's American cuisine and steakhouses. This is an updated version that is a bit lighter.

1. In a large sauté pan, reduce wine with shallots and garlic until there is almost no liquid.

2. Add the cream, and reduce until it is very thick and about ¼ cup remains. Do not worry that it will be too thick as the liquid from the spinach will thin it.

3. Add spinach. Cook until it wilts. Season with salt, pepper, and lemon juice.

¼ c	white wine
1	small shallot or onion, diced
2 cloves	garlic, sliced
1 c	cream
2	large bunches spinach, washed, stemmed, and coarsely chopped (or 1 pound baby spinach)
	salt, pepper, and lemon juice to taste

Curried Greens

Sometimes we get lots of greens month after month, and are at a loss for something new. The cumin, curry powder, and yogurt bring on flavors that are so pleasantly powerful that we forget that it is greens on our plate. Nice served alongside brown or basmati rice, or with pan-fried potatoes.

1. Sauté onions, cumin seed, and curry powder together in oil until the onions are translucent, then add greens to cook until just wilted or beyond. Add yogurt if desired and reduce heat.

2 tsp	vegetable oil
1	onion, chopped
1 clove	garlic, chopped
¼ tsp	whole cumin seed
½–1 tsp	curry powder
1	large bunch prewashed greens
	salt and pepper to taste

——————— Optional ———————

¼ c	plain yogurt

Eggplant Caponata or Ratatouille

♦ ♦ ♦ ♦ ♦

3 lb	ripe eggplant, skin on, cut in ½-inch chunks
3	medium onions, chopped
½ bulb	garlic, chopped
¼ c	olive oil
1 c	red wine
2 tsp	salt
1–2 tsp	black pepper
4	large bell peppers, chopped
1 qt	ripe or very ripe tomatoes, puréed in a blender
1 large	(or 2 medium) summer squash
¾ c	stuffed green olives
¼ c	capers
	fresh oregano, thyme, basil (about ¼ cup total), and/or fennel seed

This is a great way to use up a lot of eggplant, squash, and very ripe tomatoes when the vegetable flood of summer is at peak. Caponata is wonderfully intense, and may be canned (see page 32) or even frozen to enjoy in autumn or winter, though a post-thaw re-seasoning is advised if freezing. Caponata is traditionally served with bread or crackers as an appetizer; as a vegetarian main course over rice, polenta, or pasta; on pizza, or in sandwiches (hot or cold). If you omit the olives and capers, this recipe produces a version of ratatouille.

1. Sauté eggplant, onions, and garlic in the oil in a large heavy stainless steel pot. Use moderate heat and a lid to minimize sticking, but add water if anything starts burning.

2. Add wine, salt, black pepper, and bell peppers once the eggplant has softened somewhat. Simmer 3 more minutes to slightly soften the peppers, and then add everything else but the herbs. Simmer until the squash has just softened, then remove from heat.

3. Stir in the herbs, and add more salt and/or pepper to taste.

Fennel with Raisins

*Fennel, raisins, and olive oil all originally hailed
from the regions surrounding the Mediterranean.
After all these millennia, they still play well together.*

1. Cut off tops of fennel. Discard or save for garnish.

2. Cut fennel lengthwise into quarters.

3. Heat olive oil over medium heat in a large ovenproof skillet.
   Add onions and cook until soft, about 3 minutes. Add cumin,
   and cook until fragrant, about 1 minute more.

4. Add fennel, raisins, and chicken broth to the pan, and season
   with salt and pepper. Cover and cook in a 350°F oven for
   20 minutes, or until fennel is tender.

5. Serve with roast meat, chicken, fish, or vegetarian pasta.

3	fennel bulbs
2 Tbs	olive oil
1	onion, diced
1 tsp	whole cumin seed
¼ c	raisins
¼ c	chicken broth or water

VEGAN   GLUTEN FREE

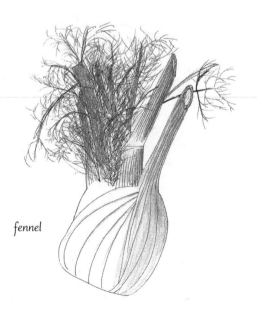

fennel

Ginger Sesame Bok Choy

* * * * *

3	large (or 6 small) heads bok choy
2 Tbs	dark roasted sesame oil (such as Kadoya brand)
3 cloves	garlic, peeled and chopped
1 tsp	minced fresh ginger
¼ tsp	black pepper, or to taste
¼ c	sake or white wine
2 Tbs	mild soy sauce or 1 Tbs dark soy sauce or 2 Tbs tamari
2 Tbs	butter
	salt and lemon juice to taste

This recipe also works well with tat soi, Swiss chard, and/or Napa cabbage, though these greens should be cut into 1-inch pieces, instead of being left whole.

1. Cut whole heads lengthwise in half and rinse thoroughly.

2. In a large skillet, heat sesame oil over medium heat. Add garlic and ginger, sauté for 2 minutes, or until garlic just begins to soften. Add bok choy halves, cut side down, and pepper.

3. Cover the greens and steam for 1 minute. Add sake or white wine and soy sauce. Flip bok choy.

4. When inner core is just soft (about 3 minutes, depending on size), add butter. Shake pan to incorporate.

5. Adjust seasoning with salt and lemon juice if necessary.

bok choy

Green Beans with Chilies and Lime

This dish is inspired by the small cafés in Bali.
Snow peas or snap peas would also work well in this dish,
but reduce the cooking time drastically.

1. Heat a large skillet, and add oil. Add garlic, ginger and chilies and cook until the mixture becomes aromatic, about 2 minutes.

2. Add green beans and cabbage and sauté, stirring frequently, until green beans are bright green. If the pan seems dry, add ¼ cup of water. If using sugar snap or snow peas, cook the cabbage first for 5 minutes before adding the peas.

3. Add sugar, lime zest and adjust seasoning to taste with salt, pepper, and lime juice.

4. Toss green beans with bean sprouts and fried shallots.

◆ ◆ ◆ ◆ ◆

1 Tbs	oil
2 Tbs	chopped garlic
1½ inch	ginger, chopped
2	chili peppers, seeded and diced (more or less to taste)
½ lb	green beans, snipped
½ head	green cabbage, shredded
½ tsp	sugar
1	lime, zested (or 3 lime leaves, finely chopped)
	salt, pepper, and lime juice to taste
1 c	bean sprouts
2 Tbs	fried shallots*

* Fried shallots can be purchased at Asian supermarkets. Or you can make your own by frying thin slices of peeled shallots in plenty of canola oil over medium heat for 12–15 minutes, or until golden brown. Drain on a paper towel. Oil can be reserved for other cooking uses.

Green Beans with Sesame Dressing

◆ ◆ ◆ ◆ ◆

8 Tbs	sesame seeds
2 Tbs	sake
2 tsp	sugar
2 Tbs	soy sauce or tamari
1 Tbs	rice vinegar
1 lb	green beans, snipped
1 tsp	salt

This dressing would also be delicious with asparagus and snow or snap peas.

1. Toast sesame seeds in a small skillet over medium heat, stirring continuously, until seeds turn lightly brown. Immediately remove seeds from the pan.

2. Combine sesame seeds with remaining ingredients, except green beans and salt, in a blender. Purée until smooth, adding up to ¼ cup of water as necessary to thin the dressing.

3. In a large skillet on the stovetop, bring to a boil 1 cup of water and salt. Add green beans, and cook for 5 minutes, or until bright green. If using snap or snow peas, cook for just 30 seconds.

4. Remove green beans from heat and toss with sesame dressing.

Green Beans with Tarragon

Simple and light, this is an early summer treat.
Add a bit more butter, and the dish can be tossed with gnocchi
or linguine for nearly a complete meal.

1 Tbs   olive oil or butter
1 lb   green beans, trimmed
2 Tbs   lemon juice
1 Tbs   fresh tarragon leaves
        salt and pepper to taste

1. In a large skillet, over medium-high heat, melt butter or olive oil. Add green beans and toss to coat. Add ¼ cup of water and continue cooking for 4 minutes until the water has evaporated and the green beans are bright green.

2. Remove from heat. Add lemon juice and tarragon. Season to taste with salt and fresh black pepper.

Kale Sautéed with Bacon, Scapes, and Lemon

Swiss chard would also work well in this recipe.

2 slices	bacon, diced
½ lb	kale, coarsely chopped
2–3	garlic scapes, chopped
¼ tsp	chili flakes (optional)
	juice of ½ lemon
	salt and pepper to taste

1. Heat a large skillet. Add the bacon and cook until the fat starts to render and the bacon begins to brown. Drain off excess fat.

2. To the bacon pan, add the scapes and chili flakes, and then the kale. Cook for 3 minutes, or until kale is wilted and tender.

3. Season to taste with salt and pepper. Squeeze lemon on top just before serving.

Tuscan kale

curly kale

Minted Peas with Cucumbers

Rarely do we cook cucumbers, but this is a delicious, light, and refreshing dish. Excellent for the short period when harvests of peas and cucumbers overlap.

1. In a large skillet, over medium heat, melt butter. Add cucumber slices and sauté for 2 minutes.

2. Add chicken broth and season with salt and pepper. Bring broth to a boil, and add peas. Cook just until peas turn bright green (approximately 2 minutes for shelled peas and 30 seconds for sugar snaps).

3. Remove from heat and stir in mint.

4. Serve as a side dish to lamb or grilled salmon.

1 Tbs	butter
2 lb	English peas, shelled, or 1 lb snap peas
2	small cucumbers, sliced
½ c	chicken broth or water
2 Tbs	fresh mint
	salt and pepper to taste

Miso-Rubbed Grilled Eggplant

3 cloves	garlic
3	Japanese eggplants, sliced in half lengthwise
3 Tbs	olive or canola oil
½ c	white miso paste
½ c	sugar
2 Tbs	mirin (sweet rice wine)
2 Tbs	sake

Japanese eggplants have no trace of bitterness, even without salting. They cook more quickly than the conventional varieties, and the flavor is sweeter.

1. Finely chop garlic. Toss eggplant with garlic and oil to marinate.

2. Combine remaining ingredients in a saucepan. Cook over medium heat, stirring constantly until completely combined and sugar has dissolved.

3. Prepare a charcoal grill. Grill eggplants, cut side down, for 3 minutes or until lightly charred. Flip over and brush with miso paste. Cook for 2 minutes more. If you'd like, flip again to char the miso paste onto the eggplants.

4. Serve with rice, shrimp, or grilled corn.

Peas with Caramelized Onions

Makes a perfect side dish for baked chicken or grilled meats or fish. Beware of overcooking the peas: brief is best.

1. Heat a large skillet over medium heat. Add butter and olive oil. Add the onions and cook, stirring frequently for 10 minutes, or until they start to brown.

2. Add peas and fresh thyme, and a few Tbs of water. Cook until water evaporates and peas are bright green.

3. Season to taste with salt, pepper, and lemon juice.

1 Tbs	butter
1 Tbs	olive oil
1	large onion, chopped
2 c	fresh shelled peas
1 tsp	fresh thyme, stems removed
	salt, pepper, and lemon juice to taste

♦ ♦ ♦ ♦ ♦

½ lb   (heaping) fresh tender okra

2–3 tsp   of any good vinaigrette (any in this book are good options)

Refreshing Chilled Okra

An excellent light appetizer to serve guests or yourself, especially when the heat of summer makes heavier foods less appealing.

1. Bring a pot of salted water to a boil. Steam or boil the okra until the color just changes from bright green to darker green, about 3 minutes. Immediately drain the okra and quickly shock them in an ice water bath.

2. Swirl okra until cold, and then drain again.

3. Place onto a serving platter or into a pretty bowl. Chill. Drizzle vinaigrette onto the okra about 5 to 20 minutes before serving.

2 Tbs   olive oil

1 Tbs   chopped garlic

¼ tsp   chili flakes (optional)

1 head   broccoli, cut into florets

1   squeeze lemon juice

1–2 Tbs   freshly grated Parmesan

salt and pepper to taste

Roasted Broccoli with Chili Flakes and Parmesan

This can be served as a side dish to roast chicken or tossed with buttered noodles for a simple supper.

1. Heat a large skillet over high heat. Add olive oil, then garlic and chili flakes. When garlic starts to brown, add broccoli. Stir to coat in olive oil and garlic.

2. Add ¼ cup of water to steam broccoli. When water evaporates and broccoli is bright green, season with salt, pepper, and lemon juice.

3. Sprinkle cheese on top just before serving.

Roasted Brussels Sprouts with Balsamic and Olive Oil

Very nice for brisk autumn weather. When the deep flavors of the Brussels and balsamic pair superbly with a vegetarian potato soup or roasted pork or poultry. This is another variant of the "brassica family likes vinegars" theme.

1. Preheat the oven to 400°F.

2. Trim ends off sprouts, and cut them in half.

3. Toss in a bowl with enough olive oil to coat evenly, then add balsamic vinegar, salt and pepper to taste.

4. Lightly oil a sheet pan. Spread out sprouts in a single layer, cut side down. Use two sheet pans if necessary; if the sprouts are crowded, they won't brown well. Roast in the oven for 15 minutes; flip sprouts to cut side up, and then roast for about 10 minutes more or until gently browned.

brussels sprouts on the stalk

1 lb	Brussels sprouts
¼ c	extra virgin olive oil
2 Tbs	balsamic vinegar
½ tsp	salt
	fresh cracked black pepper

Roasted Carrots

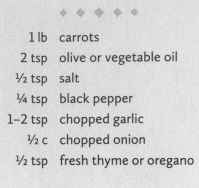

1 lb	carrots
2 tsp	olive or vegetable oil
½ tsp	salt
¼ tsp	black pepper
1–2 tsp	chopped garlic
½ c	chopped onion
½ tsp	fresh thyme or oregano

This classic approach to carrots also works really well with turnips, small potatoes, rutabagas, onions, or even radishes mixed into the same roasting pan. Best if roasted with a chicken or turkey on top of the carrots/veggies.

1. Cut carrots into 1-inch chunks. Drizzle oil on top, and then stir in salt and pepper.

2. Roast in a heavy pan at 400°F until the edges start to brown, about 15–20 minutes. Add garlic, onions, and herbs.

3. Lower heat to 350°F and continue roasting until garlic has slightly browned and carrots have somewhat softened, about 8–10 minutes more.

Roasted Cauliflower

*Perhaps the most simple and flavorful way to prepare cauliflower.
Once it's roasted, you can simply season it with lemon juice,
or toss it with pasta and cheese, capers, or bacon bits.*

1. Preheat the oven to 400°F.

2. Cut cauliflower in half. Cut out core and break the cauliflower apart into florets.

3. Toss cauliflower with olive oil, salt, and pepper.

4. Put florets on a cookie sheet in a single layer. If there's a cut side, put that down. Be sure to not crowd the pan. If necessary, use two cookie sheets.

5. Roast in the oven for 25 minutes or until the cauliflower's underside is dark brown.

♦ ♦ ♦ ♦ ♦

1 head	cauliflower
2 Tbs	extra virgin olive oil
	generous pinch of salt and pepper

◆ ◆ ◆ ◆ ◆

1 bunch	French breakfast radishes
1 Tbs	butter
1 Tbs	soy sauce or tamari
	lemon juice to taste

Roasted Radishes with Butter and Soy

Roasting radishes in butter is a great way to get the refreshing texture of radishes without the spicy bite.

1. Trim the fuzzy hair and leaves from radishes. Wash and cut into quarters.

2. Preheat the oven to 375°F.

3. Heat an ovenproof skillet on medium-high. Add the butter. When melted, add the radishes. Cook for 3 minutes. Add the soy sauce, toss, and put the pan in the oven.

4. Roast radishes for about 5 minutes. Just before serving, squeeze a little lemon juice on top.

2	large cucumbers
1 Tbs	butter
1 Tbs	fresh mint or dill
	salt, pepper, and lemon juice to taste

Sautéed Cucumbers

These cucumbers are a perfect dish for those occasional rainy summer nights.

1. Peel the cucumbers and slice in half lengthwise. Scoop out the seeds using a melon baller or teaspoon. Cut into ½-inch slices.

2. Heat a large skillet over medium heat. Add butter and melt. Add the cucumbers and cook for 4 minutes, stirring frequently. Season with salt and pepper.

3. Remove from heat and add fresh herbs and a squeeze of fresh lemon juice.

Sautéed Okra or Summer Squash with Tomato and Corn

A delicious meeting of some of the vegetable stars of summer. This is akin to a light succotash, and pairs really well with chicken, steamed shellfish, or sautéed white fish like flounder, croaker, or striped bass.

1. Cut squash or okra into ½-inch-thick slices. Chop tomato. Dice onion, chop garlic, and cut corn kernels from cob.

2. In a heavy skillet, heat 1 Tbs oil over moderately high heat until hot but not smoking and sauté okra or squash with salt to taste, stirring occasionally, until browned, about 3 minutes. With a slotted spoon, transfer okra to a bowl.

3. Add remaining tablespoon of oil to skillet and add corn, onions, and garlic. Sauté over high heat until it begins to brown, about 2 minutes. Stir and continue cooking for 2 minutes more until onions and garlic are soft. Stir in squash or okra, tomato, and basil. Simmer, stirring occasionally, for 2 minutes, until everything is heated through.

4. Season with salt, pepper, and lemon juice to taste.

◆ ◆ ◆ ◆ ◆	
2	medium summer squash or ½ pound fresh okra
1	medium beefsteak tomato
1	small onion
2 cloves	garlic
1 ear	corn
1½ Tbs	olive oil or butter
1 Tbs	fresh Genoa basil
	salt, pepper, and lemon juice to taste

Simple Fried Okra

◆ ◆ ◆ ◆ ◆

2 c	semolina, all-purpose flour, and/or cornmeal, in any proportions
1 tsp	salt
½ tsp	pepper
1 tsp	dried thyme
1	large egg, beaten with ¾ cup milk or buttermilk
2 qt	oil for frying: peanut, corn, or canola
½ lb	(heaping) fresh tender okra
	your favorite vegetable dip

Yes, deep-frying can intimidate many home cooks. But mastery and occasional use of the technique will add zing to your repertoire. Deep-fried okra is like tempura: it truly honors the vegetable's delicate flavor and is texturally perfect. If you're not a fryer yet, see Chapter 4, Key Techniques, to get started.

1. Whisk together the flour, salt, pepper, and thyme. Prepare a batter by mixing just enough of the dry ingredients with the egg and milk to make a mix of pancake batter consistency.

2. Heat the oil in a large pot carefully, until a tiny drop of water spatters when added to the oil. Lower the heat to medium. Roll the okra in the remaining dry dredge; dunk them into the batter, wiping off excess. Then redredge the wet okra in the dry dredge and place onto a plate. Fry about 8 or 10 at a time, raising the heat under the oil pot just before the frying begins. Okra is done about 15 seconds after they float.

3. Use a slotted spoon to remove the okra from the pot onto a drain rack or paper towels. Keep hot in the oven until all okra is cooked, about 8 minutes maximum.

4. Serve with any good dip; Brett's personal favorites are vinaigrette (see page 251) and agrodolce (see page 250). Julia prefers mayonnaise mixed with smoked paprika.

Simple Summer Squash with Garlic

A light and very Italianate side dish. The basil is highly recommended. Be aware that the ⅛" squash slices can easily overcook: don't walk away from the skillet, and you'll overcook less frequently if you remove the pan from the heat when about 25% of the slices are still a bit firm and brightly colored.

1. Slice squash into ⅛-inch-thick rounds.

2. In a large skillet, over medium heat, add olive oil. Sauté garlic until the edges are barely browning, about 3 minutes. Add squash slices, ¾ tsp salt, and ½ tsp black pepper and continue cooking and stirring until squash has just softened, approximately 5 minutes.

3. Stir in any or all optional ingredients. Remove from heat and serve.

5	small zucchini or summer squash
2 Tbs	olive oil
4 cloves	garlic, chopped
	salt and pepper to taste

———— Optional ————

¼ c	white wine
2 Tbs	butter
2 Tbs	fresh herbs, such as basil, parsley, or tarragon

◆ ◆ ◆ ◆ ◆

½ lb	bacon, chopped coarsely, or 1–2 Tbs vegetable oil
1	onion, sliced
2–3 lb	summer squash, preferably a yellow variety, cut into quarter-inch half-moons
¼ tsp	salt
½–1 tsp	black pepper

Southern-Style Summer Squash

We also often add some fresh thyme and a splash of white wine, and really go for an excess of pepper, but the thyme and wine aren't really part of the Deep South tradition.

1. If using bacon, cook in a heavy iron skillet or heavy-bottomed pot until browning at the edges. Add the onions and cook until they brown slightly. Otherwise, simply sauté the onions in the oil until browning.

2. Add squash, salt, and pepper; stir generously, reduce heat to low, and cook, lidded, until the squash is very mushy. Ideally the squash browns a bit and sticks slightly to the pan bottom, but does not burn. Taste for seasoning again, adding salt and pepper if needed. The flavor should be slightly smoky, dominated by the sweetness of the squash and with a lot of black pepper.

3. This would typically be served alone, atop crusty bread as an American take on bruschetta, but more traditionally alongside roasted chicken, burgers, or steak.

Sugar Snap Peas with Onions, Blue Cheese, and Walnuts

*Unlike many spring vegetable dishes,
this dish is excellent with red wine and red meats.*

1. In a large skillet, without any oil, toast the walnuts over medium heat, stirring constantly until they are fragrant. Remove from pan and reserve.

2. To the same pan, add the butter and olive oil. Sauté onions over medium heat until edges brown, stirring often. Add peas and sauté for 45 seconds (green beans should be cooked 1–2 minutes); add white wine, salt, and pepper. Stir to make sure nothing is sticking to the bottom. Remove from the heat.

3. Add blue cheese and walnuts; toss and serve.

¼ c	walnuts, coarsely chopped
1 tsp	butter
2 tsp	olive oil
1	medium onion, sliced thinly
3 c	sugar snap peas or green beans
2 Tbs	white wine
½ tsp	salt
¼ tsp	black pepper
¼ cup	blue cheese, crumbled

Zucchini Stewed with Tomatoes

◆ ◆ ◆ ◆ ◆

5	small zucchini
2 Tbs	olive oil
½	onion, sliced thin
4 cloves	garlic, chopped
	salt and pepper to taste
1–2 c	stewed tomatoes (see page 237)

——————— Optional ———————

¼ c	white wine
2 Tbs	butter
2 Tbs	fresh herbs, such as basil, parsley, or tarragon

If small zucchini aren't available, medium or tender large squash can also be used (many of the newer varieties stay tender even when large). Just cut into half moons or quarter moons. If you're serving folks who don't love squash, consider adding more garlic and basil.

1. Slice zucchini into ½-inch thick circles.

2. In a large skillet, over medium heat, add olive oil. Sauté onions and garlic, the edges barely browning, about 5 minutes. Add squash slices, ¾ tsp salt, and ½ tsp black pepper. Continue cooking and stirring until squash begins to soften, approximately 5 minutes.

3. Add the white wine and stewed tomatoes. Continue cooking as long or as briefly as you like; this is traditionally cooked until fully soft but need not be.

4. Stir in the butter and add the optional fresh herbs at the very end. This is very nice served over pasta or rice, with grated fontina cheese.

Pasta

Asparagus Primavera

◆ ◆ ◆ ◆ ◆

2 Tbs	olive oil
¾ lb	asparagus, trimmed of woody ends, and cut into 2-inch pieces (diagonally is prettiest)
3	garlic scapes, chopped into ¼-inch pieces; or 3 garlic cloves, minced
4	scallions or 2 baby leeks, greens and whites, chopped, 2 Tbs reserved for garnish
4 c	raw greens (spinach, chard, kale, collards, or arugula: anything except turnip greens)
1–2 c	snow or sugar snap peas, destringed
	Salt and black pepper
1 c	heavy cream or ¾ cup fresh ricotta; grated Parmesan or Romano cheese (optional)
1 lb	fettuccine or linguine, preferably homemade
1	beaten egg (optional)
¼ c	chopped parsley

Primavera means spring; this version of pasta primavera is geared toward what you will most easily find at many farmers markets from late April until June. What it lacks in color contrast, it more than makes up for in bursting spring flavors.

1. Bring a large pot of water to a boil. Season generously with salt.

2. Heat a very large skillet over medium heat. Add olive oil, garlic scapes, and scallions, and cook for 1 minute.

3. Add asparagus and cook for 30 seconds; add greens and cook until they are barely wilted.

4. Add cream if using, bring to a simmer and set aside. Season lightly with salt and pepper.

5. Cook pasta according to package directions. Drain. Return to pasta pot.

6. Bring veggie mix back to a simmer, add sugar snap or snow peas, and immediately mix with pasta, and stir in egg if using.

7. Lightly toss in ricotta.

When serving, garnish with parsley, reserved scallion, and Parmesan.

Bolognese Sauce for Pasta

Bolognese is one of the most deeply flavored meat pasta sauces and perhaps one of the best. It rises to near-perfect status when autumn nights start to cool down. Longer slow cooking adds great depth to the final array of flavors. The key concept: diverse meats, a supporting cast of vegetables, tomato and cream as the stage, and fresh herbs added late to lighten.

1. Heat olive oil over medium heat in a large saucepan. Add onions and garlic, stirring occasionally, until wilted and lightly browned. Add meat, breaking it up with the back of a spoon. Add celery, salt, and pepper and continue to cook for 5 minutes.

2. Add tomato purée and wine. Simmer for 20–40 minutes until thick. Stir in cream or yogurt. Simmer 3 more minutes.

3. Adjust seasoning with salt, pepper, and fresh herbs. Serve with pasta, or use for your favorite lasagna recipe.

♦ ♦ ♦ ♦ ♦

1 Tbs	olive oil
1 c	diced yellow onions
4 cloves	garlic, chopped
1 lb	ground beef, ground chicken, ground pork or pork sausage, or leftover cooked poultry or beef (or any combination)
½ c	diced celery
2 tsp	salt
1 tsp	black pepper
4 c	chopped tomatoes or whole cherry tomatoes, puréed raw in the blender
½ c	dry red wine
1 c	heavy cream or plain yogurt
½ c	fresh basil, parsley, or combination of both

——— Optional ———

mushrooms, eggplant, or sweet peppers

Broccoli Raab with Sausage and Pasta

1 bunch broccoli raab
1 Tbs olive oil
1 lb sweet Italian sausage, sliced
2 cloves garlic, chopped
½ tsp chili flakes
¾ lb pasta (penne or linguine or other favorite shape)
¼ c freshly grated Parmesan
salt, pepper, and lemon juice to taste

A traditional "pasta asciutta," i.e., a dish with no discernable sauce of tomato or cream. The slight bitterness of broccoli raab is nicely offset by the pork sausage. Vegetarians could succeed as well by substituting white beans, butter beans, or limas.

1. Wash broccoli raab and coarsely chop.

2. Heat a large skillet over high heat. Add half the olive oil and sausage. Cook sausage until it starts to brown. Remove from skillet and set aside.

3. To the same pan, add the remaining olive oil and garlic, and cook over medium heat until it starts to brown. Add the broccoli raab and chili flakes, and cook for 2 minutes more, or just until it turns bright green. Stir occasionally.

4. Meanwhile, bring a large pot of water to a boil. Season with salt and cook pasta according to package directions.

5. When pasta is done, strain the water, reserving about ¼ cup.

6. Toss pasta with sausage, raab, and cheese. If it seems dry, add some pasta water (or extra virgin olive oil).

7. Season to taste with salt, pepper, and lemon juice.

Brussels Sprouts "Carbonara"

This variation on the traditional Italian dish uses Brussels sprouts instead of spring peas. You can use bacon, pancetta, turkey bacon, or chicken to give a little meaty flavor to the dish.

1. Preheat the oven to 425°F. Bring a large pot of water to a boil. Season generously with salt.

2. Meanwhile, cut sprouts in half. Toss them with bacon (or olive oil, if using), salt, and pepper. Put them in the oven to roast for 15 minutes.

3. Boil pasta for 1 minute less than the package instructions.

4. After the sprouts have roasted 15 minutes, toss them with garlic and chili flakes. Return to the oven for an additional 5 minutes to toast the garlic.

5. Drain pasta. Toss with cream and Parmesan. Add chopped smoked chicken (if using) and sprouts. Adjust seasoning with salt, pepper, and lemon juice to taste.

1 lb	Brussels sprouts
2 slices	bacon, 2 boneless chicken thighs, smoked, or 2 Tbs olive oil
¾ lb	pasta
2 cloves	garlic, chopped
	pinch chili flakes
¼ c	cream
¼ c	freshly grated Parmesan cheese, or more to taste
	salt, pepper, and lemon juice to taste

Capellini with Chanterelles, Cream and Lobster

Delectable, absolutely delectable.
A wonderful dish for special romantic occasions.
Superb served with Champagne and crusty bread. Serves 2.

1 Tbs	butter
1 tsp	canola oil
½	onion or shallot, peeled and finely diced
1–2	cloves garlic, chopped
¼ lb	chanterelle mushrooms, washed and sliced ¼-inch thick
½ tsp	salt
¼ tsp	black pepper
¼ c	dry white wine or brandy
1 pt	heavy cream
½ lb	capellini or angel hair pasta
	meat from 1¼ pound lobster or ½ pound peeled shrimp or ½ pound scallops
3 sprigs	fresh thyme, or ¼ tsp dried thyme
2 Tbs	chopped parsley
	salt and pepper
	fresh lemon juice (optional)

1. In a heavy-bottomed skillet or saucepan, over moderate heat, melt butter with oil. Add the onion and garlic, and sauté until just transparent. Add chanterelles and sauté 2–3 minutes. Add white wine or brandy, simmer for another minute. Add cream and thyme, black pepper and salt. Reduce heat to low, and simmer until liquid is reduced by half its volume.

2. Meanwhile, bring a large pot of salted water to a boil.

3. While cream is reducing, cook pasta in boiling water according to package directions.

4. When cream is reduced, add the seafood, and cook 30 seconds more. Add thyme and parsley.

5. Drain pasta and immediately toss with cream/shellfish/ chanterelle mix. Adjust seasoning to taste with salt, pepper, and lemon juice.

Fettuccine with Bacon, Greens, and Sweet Corn

A sauceless pasta, light and full of flavor.
Traditionally one type of "Pasta Asciutta."

1. In a large skillet, over medium-high heat, add olive oil. Sauté onions, peppers, and garlic until the onions are just translucent, about 4 minutes. Add bacon (or black beans), corn, salt, and pepper. Cook 1 more minute. Set aside while cooking the pasta.

2. Cook the pasta in boiling salted water according to package directions.

3. Return the onion/veggie pan to heat, and add the greens. Cook just until the greens are wilted, 1–2 minutes. Remove from heat and toss basil, veggies, and pasta all together.

4. Sprinkle cheese on top when serving.

◆ ◆ ◆ ◆ ◆

2–3 Tbs	olive oil
1	onion, sliced thin
2	red bell peppers or 8 slender Italian seasoning peppers, sliced thin
3 cloves	garlic, chopped
½ lb	bacon, chopped, fully cooked, and drained; or 1 can black beans, drained and rinsed.
3 ears	corn, kernels removed
¾ lb	washed arugula, or 1 lb mustard greens, kale, Swiss chard, or collard greens
1 lb	penne, rigatoni, or fettuccine pasta
½ c	coarsely chopped fresh basil
4 oz	Romano or Parmesan cheese, grated
	salt and pepper to taste

Halushki

*This version of Eastern European comfort food
hails from Pittsburgh.*

◆ ◆ ◆ ◆ ◆

1	16-ounce package wide egg noodles
¼ c	bacon fat, chicken fat; or leftover ham or bacon + 1 Tbs butter
2	large onions, sliced
3 cloves	garlic, chopped
½ head	green cabbage, thinly sliced
1 tsp	salt
½ tsp	black pepper

1. Cook noodles according to package directions. Drain well.

2. Add fat and/or meat to a skillet over low heat. Add the onions and garlic. Sauté until soft.

3. Add cabbage, salt, and pepper. Stir often. Once the cabbage is soft, add noodles and stir until well mixed.

4. Reheated, this makes great leftovers.

   Vegetarian or Vegan Option: use 1 stick butter or 3 Tbs olive oil instead of bacon fat

   Greens substitutions: instead of cabbage, use 1–2 gallons washed kale, collards, or Swiss chard, coarsely chopped

Pasta Estivi

*This is another of the really light and healthy meals
that match hot summer evenings. Estivi celebrates really good
tomatoes and fresh basil or other herbs.*

1. Cook the pasta according to package directions and drain.
   While still very hot, add the olive oil, salt, pepper, and garlic;
   toss. Let cool.

2. When at about room temp, add the basil and tomatoes. Taste
   for final seasoning, and consider adding a splash of wine or
   balsamic vinegar.

3. Serve with grated cheese on the side for diners to add as
   they wish.

1 lb box	capellini, fettuccine, linguine, or other pasta of your choice
1–2 Tbs	olive oil
4 cloves	garlic, chopped
1 tsp	salt
½ tsp	black pepper
1 c	Genoa basil leaves or ½ cup fresh Provençal herbs mix, chopped
1 lb	rainbow cherry tomatoes, halved, or 3 4 cups cubed heirloom tomatoes
	salt, pepper, and balsamic vinegar to taste
	On the side: grated Romano, Parmesan, or Asiago cheeses

Pasta with Fried Sage and Parmesan

◆ ◆ ◆ ◆ ◆

¾ lb	pasta of choice
2–4 Tbs	butter (to taste)
1 bunch	sage, leaves picked
5 cloves	garlic, sliced
¼ c	grated Parmesan cheese
½ c	chicken broth or cream
	salt, pepper, and lemon juice to taste

Frying the sage leaves tames their flavor and gives a nice light texture. If you are hesitant to fry, then skip this recipe.

1. Cook pasta according to package instructions.

2. Meanwhile, melt butter over medium-high heat in a sauté pan. Add sage leaves. Cook until they begin to look translucent and a little spotty. Add garlic slices. Continue cooking until garlic is lightly browned, about 1–2 minutes. Remove from heat.

3. When pasta is done, drain. Toss with sage and butter mixture. Add chicken broth and Parmesan. Stir to coat pasta. Season to taste with salt, pepper, and lemon juice.

Pasta with Peas, Mushrooms, and Scallions

A light simple version of a primavera (spring) pasta. The earthy flavors of the mushrooms contrast well with the sweetness of fresh peas.

1. Trim the mushrooms (remove and discard shiitake stems, if using). Slice ¼-inch thick.

2. Heat a large skillet over medium-high heat. Add the butter and olive oil. Add the mushrooms, onions, and garlic. Cook for 5 minutes, stirring every so often, until mushrooms are tender. Season to taste with salt and pepper.

3. Bring a large pot of heavily salted water to a boil. Add the pasta and cook according to the package directions. Two minutes before the pasta is cooked, add the English peas, if using.

4. Drain pasta and add sugar snaps, if using. Toss with mushrooms, scallions, and parsley. Adjust the seasoning with salt and pepper.

◆ ◆ ◆ ◆ ◆

¼ lb	fresh button mushrooms, portobellos or shiitakes
1 Tbs	butter
2 Tbs	olive oil
1	medium onion, sliced thin
2 cloves	garlic, chopped
1 lb	linguine, fettuccine, or pasta of your choice
¾ lb	sugar snap or snow peas, or 1–2 cups of shelled English peas
1 bunch	scallions, chopped
¼ c	chopped parsley
	salt and pepper

Sherry's Spicy Fig Pasta

◆ ◆ ◆ ◆ ◆

8	medium-sized fresh figs, stem removed, and cut in half or quarters
4 cloves	garlic, chopped
6–8	scallions (could also use leeks, red onion, or yellow onions)
2 Tbs	olive oil
½–1 tsp	red pepper flakes, or ½ fresh jalapeño or diced Serrano pepper (more or less to taste)
½ lb	fettuccine or linguine
	salt and pepper to taste

———— Optional ————

chopped parsley and/or grated Parmesan cheese

This delectable dish is a favorite of Sherry Jones, longtime friend and Even' Star Farm supporter. This works well with underripe figs as the cooking brings out their sweetness. Serve as a meal on its own or a side to roast chicken.

1. Bring a large pot of water to boil. Salt heavily.

2. Cut the scallions to separate the white portion from the green portion. Dice each and reserve separately.

3. Heat large skillet over medium heat. Add olive oil and sauté white part of the scallion and garlic until soft and just starting to brown.

4. Add chilies and figs. Cook for just 1 minute more; be careful not to overcook as figs will melt into nothing. Set aside.

5. Cook pasta according to package instructions. Drain. Mix with figs. Sprinkle green scallions on top just before serving. Garnish with parsley and Parmesan, if using.

figs

Main Dishes

◆ ◆ ◆ ◆ ◆

½ c	chickpea flour
¼ c	all-purpose flour
1	egg yolk
¾ c	water (or a mix of cream and water)
1 Tbs	extra virgin olive oil, plus extra for cooking
1 bunch	kale or arugula, washed and coarsely chopped
2 cloves	garlic, chopped
2 Tbs	pine nuts
2 Tbs	currants or raisins
¼ tsp	curry powder
	salt and pepper to tase

Chickpea Crepes Stuffed with Wilted Greens

This recipe was inspired by the Southern France street-food socca: a chickpea crepe baked in a cast-iron skillet. Romesco Sauce (see page 270) is a wonderful addition to this dish.

1. Sift flours with salt and pepper. Make a well in the center. Add the egg and water. Whisk to incorporate. Add the olive oil. The batter should be the consistency of heavy cream. Let rest for 30 minutes.

2. Meanwhile, heat a large skillet over medium heat. Add olive oil, raisins, and garlic. When garlic starts to brown, add the curry powder and pine nuts. Cook for 1 minute more and add the greens. Cook until just wilted. Coarsely chop the greens. Season with salt and pepper.

3. Heat a non-stick skillet over medium heat. Brush the bottom of the pan with olive oil. Pour in a thin layer of batter, and cook until set. Flip over and cook for 30 seconds more. Remove from pan and repeat process until all the crepes are made.

4. Roll each crepe like a cigar, with about ½ cup of filling. Reheat just before serving, and slice in half.

Chinese Stir-Fried Eggplant

If your skillet isn't large enough,
you may need to fry the eggplant in several batches.

1. Cut eggplants into 1-inch cubes and salt.

2. Combine ingredients for sauce.

3. Return to the eggplant: brush off excess salt and toss eggplant in cornstarch.

4. Heat a large skillet over high heat. Add the oil. When oil is hot, add eggplant in a single layer.

5. Cook eggplant until it starts to brown, and toss. Add ginger and garlic and cook until fragrant.

6. Stir in sauce and scallions and cook until the sauce thickens.

7. Serve over rice.

2	large Italian eggplants or 4 small Asian eggplants
1 tsp	salt
2½ Tbs	cornstarch
2 Tbs	plain oil
1 Tbs	fresh chopped ginger
1 tsp	fresh chopped garlic
3	scallions, cut into rings

Sauce

2 Tbs	oyster sauce
2 tsp	dark soy sauce
1 tsp	sugar
2 tsp	gin
¾ c	chicken stock
1–2 tsp	chili paste or sriracha, depending on taste

Coconut Curried Vegetables

◆ ◆ ◆ ◆ ◆

1 Tbs	plain oil
2 cloves	garlic, chopped
½	onion, chopped
1 Tbs	Chinese chili-garlic paste (more or less to taste)
1	sweet potato, peeled and cubed into ¾–inch pieces
1	13-ounce can coconut milk
1 bunch	kale, washed and coarsely chopped
2	plum tomatoes, chopped
1 Tbs	fried shallots or onions*
	salt or fish sauce to taste

The perfect "shoulder season" recipe, it uses tomatoes from the summer and sweet potatoes and kale from the early autumn. We prefer this combination for the flavor, color, and textural contrasts, but you could use any veggies you like.

1. In a large skillet, heat oil over medium-high heat. Add garlic and onions and cook until they wilt and start to brown.

2. Add the chili paste and sweet potatoes and stir to evenly mix everything. Cook for 2 minutes to toast the chili paste and bring out its flavor.

3. Add the coconut milk and reduce heat to simmer. Season with salt or fish sauce. Cook, covered, until the sweet potatoes are just tender, about 15 minutes.

4. Add the kale and tomatoes and cook until the kale is wilted and tender, about 5 minutes more.

5. Sprinkle fried shallots on top. Serve over steamed rice.

*Fried shallots can be purchased at Asian supermarkets. Or you can make your own by frying thin slices of peeled shallots in plenty of canola oil over medium heat for 12–15 minutes, or until golden brown. Drain on a paper towel. Oil can be reserved for other cooking uses.

Easy White Pizza with Squash Blossoms

Buy raw (premade) pizza dough or make your own.

1. Bake crust as per directions or your own experience to the just-golden-brown stage. Remove from the oven and leave the oven on.

2. Arrange the toppings on the crust, with the cheeses placed on last.

3. Bake at 400°F or broil very carefully until golden brown.

4. Excellent served with a chilled white wine, a lager, or a pilsner.

♦ ♦ ♦ ♦ ♦

Toppings

4 cloves	garlic, chopped
½	onion, sliced thin
20–25	squash blossoms
2–3 c	grated mozzarella
¼–½ c	grated Romano or Parmesan cheeses
2 Tbs	olive oil
½ tsp	each salt and pepper

Optional

2 Tbs	fresh parsley or basil, or 1½ tsp dried basil or oregano
1 c	chopped tomatoes

Eggplant Curry

◆ ◆ ◆ ◆ ◆

1 Tbs	plain oil
4	small eggplants, cut in quarters lengthwise, and then into 1½-inch slices
1	small onion, chopped
3 cloves	garlic, chopped
1 tsp	salt
⅛ tsp	turmeric
½ tsp	coriander
¼ tsp	cumin
⅛ tsp	ground fennel seed
¼ tsp	mustard seed
	pinch (or more) cayenne pepper
1 c	unsweetened coconut milk
½ c	water
½	lime, juiced

Loosely adapted from Singapore Food *by Wendy Hutton.*

1. Heat a large skillet over high heat. Add oil and then eggplant in a single layer. Let eggplant sit so that it can brown on the bottom side for about 4 minutes, then flip.

2. Add onions and garlic to the pan and continue cooking, stirring occasionally, for about 3 minutes, until onions start to soften.

3. Add spices and salt, and stir to coat eggplant.

4. Add coconut milk and water and simmer for about 10 minutes or until eggplant is tender.

5. Season with lime juice just before serving.

Ginger Sautéed Tat Soi with Tofu

*A light approach to greens, perfect for late-season tat soi
(i.e., when cool spring evolves to hotter days).
The tofu adds both textural contrast and protein.*

1. Put tofu slices on a paper towel to dry them.

2. In a small bowl, combine the soy sauce, vinegar, sugar, and lime juice.

3. In a large skillet (preferably non-stick) over medium-high heat, add canola oil and a few drops of the sesame oil. Add tofu slices; cook for 5–7 minutes per side, or until golden brown. Remove from skillet. Add remaining sesame oil to skillet. Add ginger and garlic and cook for 1 minute, or until fragrant. Add the chili flakes and then the tat soi, and stir for a minute more. When the tat soi starts to wilt, add the sauce and cook for 3 minutes more, or until sauce begins to thicken.

4. Divide greens on plates. Top with half of the tofu. Drizzle with remaining sauce, and sprinkle with sesame seeds. Serve immediately.

6 oz	extra firm tofu, sliced ½ inch thick
2 Tbs	soy sauce or tamari
¼ tsp	rice vinegar
2 tsp	brown sugar
2 tsp	lime juice
1 Tbs	canola oil
1–2 tsp	toasted sesame seeds
2 tsp	minced fresh ginger
1 tsp	minced garlic
¼ tsp	chili flakes
2	small bunches tat soi or bok choy
1 tsp	sesame oil

Mediterranean Eggplant and Tomatoes

◆ ◆ ◆ ◆ ◆

¼ c	plain oil
3	medium eggplants, sliced in half lengthwise
2 Tbs	currants or raisins
2 Tbs	pine nuts
1 Tbs	butter or olive oil
1	shallot, peeled and diced
1 clove	garlic, chopped
¼ c	white wine
2 c	diced tomatoes
2 Tbs	fresh basil or 1 Tbs fresh dill
	salt and pepper to taste

Eggplant and tomato are a classic Mediterranean combination. With basil, this dish takes an Italian flair and pairs beautifully with grilled steak and potatoes. With dill, the Turkish inspiration takes over, making it perfect with mackerel and basmati rice.

1. In a large skillet, heat oil over high heat. Add eggplant, cut side down, and cook until a deep brown. Flip over and cook on the other side until the eggplant is soft, about 1 more minute. It's important to cook the eggplant in a single layer, so you may need to cook them in batches. Drain on a paper towel and season with salt.

2. When eggplants are cooked, pour off the oil from the pan. Return the pan to a medium heat. Add the pine nuts and raisins and cook for 2 minutes, stirring constantly, or just until the pine nuts start to brown. Remove from heat and drain on a paper towel.

3. Wipe the pan clean, return to medium-high heat, and add the butter. When the butter melts, add shallots and garlic. Cook for 5 minutes, or until soft. Add the wine and reduce. Add the tomatoes. Cook until the tomatoes have released their liquid and the sauce starts to thicken. Season to taste with salt and pepper.

4. Just before serving, stir in the fresh herbs. When serving, sprinkle toasted pine nuts and currants on top.

Potato and Cheese Gratin

This is a rich casserole that can serve as a whole meal if served with a good salad. No need to use fresh new potatoes; anything will do.

1. Mix all ingredients together in a large bowl, then place into a 9-inch × 13-inch baking pan. With the back of a spatula, press down the potatoes so they lie flat and are submerged in the cream.

2. Bake at 340°F until tender all the way through, about 40 minutes. Test by inserting a butter knife into the middle of the dish. If it goes in easily, the potatoes are cooked.

3. Let cool for 10 minutes before serving.

◆ ◆ ◆ ◆ ◆

3 lb	potatoes, washed, not peeled, and sliced very thinly
2 c	milk, half-and-half, or cream (your choice)
5 cloves	medium-large garlic, chopped
2 tsp	salt
¾ tsp	black pepper
1	onion, chopped
1 lb	coarsely grated cheese: Cheddar, Gouda, Gruyère, Colby, etc.

Pizza

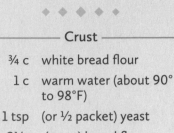

—— Crust ——

¾ c	white bread flour
1 c	warm water (about 90° to 98°F)
1 tsp	(or ½ packet) yeast
2¼–2½ c	(more) bread flour
1 tsp	salt
1 tsp	olive oil

— Great Topping Combinations —

White pizza:

Bell peppers and cooked new potatoes

Summer squash and fresh basil
Greens, black olives, and garlic
Sweet red pepper, hot pepper

Summer squash and garlic

Chopped raw tomatoes, Genoa basil, and onion

Baked garlic-infused butternut squash and basil

Arugula, garlic, and capers or anchovies

With tomato sauce:

Braised eggplant and any sausage or ground meat

Cooked new potatoes and green olives

Braised eggplant and fresh Ancho or other spicy peppers

Brett was taught to homemade pizza by his mother from age six onward. It was time-consuming but was one of the most welcome rituals of his entire youth, and he would still rather be in the kitchen with his Ma than almost anywhere else.

Creativity and "cleaning out the refrigerator" goals are best with this versatile dish. Any tomato sauce, or just olive oil, can be used. Cheese is a must: pizza without cheese is not pizza, it is focaccia. The cheeses can be mozzarella or Monterey Jack, plus Romano or Parmesan. We will also freely use odd bits of goat cheese, Asiago, Gouda, etc. The other ingredients can be extraordinarily diverse: zucchini, blanched greens, green or black olives, simmered new potatoes, fresh mushrooms, fresh basil, braised eggplant, meat or seafood of any type, fresh or roasted sweet peppers, even cooked sweet potatoes or butternut squash. We like each pizza to have a focus (with only one to three ingredients), but we never make fewer than three different pizzas per batch. This recipe makes three medium pizzas.

1. **Prepare a sponge:** mix the first three ingredients in a large bowl and let sit in a warm part of the room, stirring about twice in the first hour. The sponge is the baking term for a perfect environment for yeast to rapidly grow and multiply, and it is yeast that makes the dough light and flavorful. The sponge works best if you give it between 90 minutes and 12 hours to work. You can make this in the morning before work, stirring only twice or three times before departure, and then complete the dough when you get home. To complete, add the salt, oil, and bit by bit the flour. Add flour and knead until the dough doesn't leave many wet sticky bits on your worktable. Knead into a smooth ball, then cut this into 3 pieces. Lightly flour and let them rest while you get three pans ready by

sprinkling with cornmeal. Then use a rolling pin to roll out each piece of dough to the right size for your pans, often sprinkling more flour on your work surface to stop the dough from sticking. The dough will be fluffier if you press it out with your hands, omit the roller, and then work it out to the right size by gently stretching it with both hands and lots of flour.

2. Once the crusts are done, you must give them enough time to rise slightly, about 1½ to 2½ hours. Then bake as is in a 350°F oven until very lightly brown. This baking makes for a crispier crust. If you prefer a doughy crust, let the dough rise but omit this step.

3. These crusts may be made weeks ahead of time, baked, and then stored frozen.

Assembly

4. Choose a sauce: any good tomato sauce, or olive oil for a "white" pizza. For pizza of this size, use about ½ cup tomato sauce or 1 Tbs olive oil per crust. Sprinkle with salt and pepper to taste. Then add your other ingredients. We like to have all the other ingredients we're considering already chopped, in little piles, prepared while the crusts are rising. Beware of too much loading of ingredients per pizza: sometimes less is more, and pizza cannot cook properly if it is too thick with vegetables et al. For crusts of this size, we'd use a maximum of ¾ cup total fillings per pizza.

5. For three pizzas we recommend 1–1½ pounds coarsely grated mozzarella and 6 Tbs finely grated Parmesan or Romano. Substitute other cheeses appropriately, but keeping a little mozzarella or Monterey Jack in a blend of more diverse cheeses keeps the cheese layer cohesive. Sprinkle the cheeses over the pizzas, then bake in a hot oven (at least 375° F) until the tops are medium brown, about 25 minutes. Let cool at least a few minutes before cutting and serving. Outstanding the next day, either cold or reheated.

6. Adjust all these amounts to your own tastes when you want to make pizza again.

Quinoa with Feta, Dates, and Pea Shoots

♦ ♦ ♦ ♦ ♦

1 c	quinoa
¼ c	medjool dates
1 c	pea shoots
2 Tbs	olive oil
3 cloves	garlic, sliced thin or chopped
¼ c	feta, crumbled
1 Tbs	sherry vinegar
	salt and pepper to taste

VEGETARIAN **GLUTEN FREE**

It's very important to rinse quinoa before cooking as the grains often have a bitter residue on them that comes from processing.

1. Put quinoa in a fine mesh strainer and rinse under cold water. Put in a small saucepan and cover with water by 1 inch. Add 1 tsp salt. Cover the pot and cook over medium heat for 10 minutes, or until quinoa has popped and is cooked through. When quinoa is cooked, drain excess water; set aside to cool.

2. Meanwhile, pop the pits out of the dates and discard. Coarsely chop the dates.

3. Cut the pea shoots into 1-inch pieces.

4. Heat a large skillet over high heat. Add the olive oil, and heat for 1 minute. Add the garlic and cook for 3 minutes or until aromatic. Remove from heat, and add to the quinoa.

   When the quinoa is cool, mix in the dates, feta, pea shoots, and vinegar. Mix well. Adjust seasoning to taste with salt and pepper.

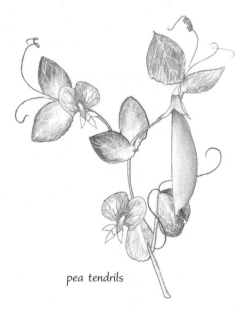

pea tendrils

Roasted Stuffed Cubanelles

*The basic recipe is a traditional stuffed pepper,
but the optionals enable you to tailor the dish to your own
tastes and to use up leftovers.*

1. Toss peppers in oil and lay out in a single layer on a cookie sheet. Roast peppers at 400°F for 15 minutes or until the skin starts to blister and turn light brown. Take them out of the oven and let cool.

2. Meanwhile, mix together the rice, corn, cheese, and any of the optional additions. Check seasoning for salt and pepper.

3. Cut the tops off the peppers and scoop out the seeds. Stuff the filling into the cavity of the pepper.

4. Return the stuffed peppers to the oven and bake at 375°F for 10–15 minutes.

5. Serve with tomato sauce (see page 271).

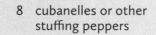

8	cubanelles or other stuffing peppers
1 Tbs	plain oil
½ c	(leftover) cooked rice
1 c	raw or cooked corn kernels
½ c	grated Monterey Jack cheese
	tomato sauce
	salt and pepper to taste

——— Optional ———

jalapeños, basil, scallions, black beans, leftover cooked chicken

Savory Vegetarian Greens and Potatoes

◆ ◆ ◆ ◆ ◆

3–4	average sized russet potatoes, washed but with skins on
1 bunch	any cooking greens (kale, collards, Swiss chard, or even arugula)
3–6 Tbs	mix of olive and neutral oils
3 cloves	garlic, chopped
1	large onion, chopped
1 tsp	black pepper
½–1 tsp	salt
½ bunch	scallions, chopped
	fresh basil or 1 tsp dried oregano, basil, or rosemary
	salt and pepper to taste

A complete meal: the potatoes with skins contribute protein and starch, and the greens vitamins and minerals. Equally important, this really savory dish and the toppings can please even carnivores.

1. Dice potatoes to yield about 3 cups. Toss with about ½ tsp of salt and let sit for about 5 minutes.

2. Coarsely chop the greens.

3. In a heavy skillet (works best in seasoned cast iron), sauté the potatoes for about 5 minutes, or until they start to brown. If the potatoes are still firm, add ½ c of water. Add the onion and garlic and continue cooking until barely soft. Add the greens, and cook 2 minutes more or until they are wilted. Stir in the herbs and chopped scallions. If needed, season further before serving: this should be hearty, not bland.

4. Can nicely be served with a dollop of sour cream, homemade guacamole, or with grated Cheddar or Monterey Jack on top. Also really good with 1 tsp whole cumin seed (added to skillet right before spuds go in) in lieu of or in addition to other herbs. Hot peppers complement the latter approach well.

Summer Squash Casserole I

*This recipe comes from Even' Star CSA subscribers
Don and Cindy Fletcher.*

1. Preheat the oven to 375°F. Heat butter in a large skillet over medium heat. Add the sliced squash, sprinkle with salt and pepper, and sauté, tossing frequently, until golden (about 5 minutes).

2. In a mixing bowl, stir together the sour cream, chives, paprika, and 2 Tbs grated cheese. Add the cooked squash, stirring to combine ingredients, and transfer the mixture to a buttered shallow baking dish, such as a 6-inch × 9-inch pan. Sprinkle the bread crumbs over the surface.

3. Bake 10 minutes; then scatter the remaining ¼ cup cheese on top and bake 5 minutes longer. Run briefly under the broiler till golden brown, about 1 minute. Serve immediately.

3 Tbs	unsalted butter
1 lb	summer squash, thinly sliced (about 4 cups)
	salt and freshly ground pepper
½ c	sour cream
1 Tbs	fresh chives or scallion greens
¼ tsp	paprika
¼ c	grated Swiss cheese plus 2 Tbs (or to taste)
3 Tbs	fresh bread crumbs

Summer Squash Casserole II

◆ ◆ ◆ ◆ ◆

3	large or 6 small summer squash
1¼ c	milk
2 Tbs	vegetable oil
1 Tbs	flour
1 tsp	salt
½ tsp	pepper
¼ tsp	cayenne pepper
4	eggs, well beaten
½ c	grated Gruyère or Swiss cheese

This recipe comes from Julia's grandmother Charlotte Weil, a native of Montgomery, Alabama.

1. Preheat the oven to 400°F.

2. Dice the squash into ½-inch dice.

3. Pour oil in a heavy saucepan and add the squash. Sprinkle with salt and pepper, cover, and cook over very low heat, stirring from time to time until squash is soft and mushy.

4. In a mixing bowl, combine eggs, milk, flour, and cayenne.

5. Drain squash and add to egg mixture. Beat well with a rotary beater or whisk.

6. Pour into a 2-quart buttered baking dish and sprinkle with cheese.

7. Bake 20 minutes or longer until top is brown and casserole is lightly puffed.

Swiss Chard and Ricotta Dumplings

*These dumplings can be made a day in advance,
through step 5, and heated with the melted butter or
sauce and cheese before serving.*

1. Wash the greens in a sinkful of warm water to clean. Dirty spinach may need more than one change of water. Lift the greens from the water and drain them in a colander. Remove any thick stems.

2. Heat a large skillet over high heat. Add olive oil and garlic. When garlic becomes fragrant, add greens. Cook for 3–5 minutes or until bright green and wilted. Remove the greens and place them in a colander. Let cool.

3. Divide the greens in three parts and squeeze to remove all excess water. Reserve the liquid to add to sauce.

4. Coarsely chop the greens with a knife and then put in the food processor. Add the ricotta, Parmesan, eggs, 1 tsp salt, lemon zest, and nutmeg. Process to form a smooth paste. Fold in flour.

5. Bring a large pot of water to a boil. Season generously with salt. Transfer the paste to a pastry bag with a large tip or a medium-sized plastic bag with a ½-inch corner cut off. Pipe out ½-inch dumplings. Alternatively, use two spoons to form dumplings and drop into the water.

6. Poach 8–9 dumplings at a time, for 2–3 minutes or until they float to the surface. Transfer with a slotted spoon to a large baking dish.

7. Preheat the oven to 400°F. Drizzle the dumplings with melted butter, or tomato or meat sauce, and sprinkle with grated cheese. Bake for 10–15 minutes or until lightly browned and cheese has melted, and serve.

◆ ◆ ◆ ◆ ◆

1 lb	Swiss chard or spinach to make 1⅓ cups squeezed cooked greens
1 Tbs	olive oil
2–3	cloves garlic, chopped
1 c	ricotta, drained in a sieve if watery
½ c	grated Parmesan
2	eggs
½ c	flour
1	lemon, zested
	pinch of nutmeg
	salt and pepper to taste

—————— Sauce ——————

¼ c	melted butter, ½ cup tomato sauce (mixed with pine nuts and raisins), or ½ cup homemade tomato-meat sauce
¼ c	grated Parmesan

Swiss Chard Quiche

◆ ◆ ◆ ◆ ◆

1	homemade or frozen pie crust, without sugar if possible
1 bunch	Swiss chard salted water to blanch
1 tsp	olive oil
1	medium onion, chopped
2 Tbs	white wine
2 c	milk, half and half, or light cream
3	large eggs (or 4 medium)
2 Tbs	chopped fresh herbs such as chervil, parsley, dill, tarragon, or thyme, or dry if need be (1 tsp)
¼–½ lb	Gruyère, Cheddar, Jack, mozzarella, or similar cheese, grated
1 tsp	salt
½ tsp	black pepper

——— Optional ———

pine nuts, almonds, garlic and fresh basil.

Very versatile: this quiche is delicious and can be enjoyed as brunch, lunch, or dinner. Quiche can be a great way to use a lot of greens. It's balanced nutritionally with starch (the crust), protein (the eggs and cheese), and calcium (the cheese and milk).

1. If making your own crust, consider adding ½ tsp dried thyme to the flour before cutting in the shortening. Bake crust until barely brown at edges. Remove crust and keep the oven at 350°F.

2. Meanwhile, blanch or steam the greens, shock, drain as thoroughly as possible, and chop medium or coarsely. Set aside. Sauté onion in olive oil until translucent, add white wine, and simmer 1 more minute. Let cool.

3. Beat together milk, eggs, salt and pepper, herbs, and onion-wine mix.

4. Place drained chopped greens into pie shell. Sprinkle grated cheese over greens, then pour batter over all. Bake about 50 minutes, until center of quiche doesn't jiggle when you poke the pie pan's edge. Center of quiche should also be slightly raised and golden brown at this point. Remove from the oven and let cool at least 10 and as many as 60 minutes before serving. This gives clean edges to the crust and filling upon cutting and plating.

5. For a particularly Italian variant of this, add 3 cloves garlic to the sautéing onions, use dry or fresh basil in lieu of other herbs, and sprinkle pine nuts atop the cheese before pouring in the batter.

Vegetarian Cuban Sandwiches

Cuban sandwiches traditionally are filled with roast pork, ham, pickles, and cheese. Here, roasted vegetables lend a meaty flavor, and the chipotle peppers give a hint of smokiness.

1. Mix mayonnaise, chipotle and its juice, cilantro, and 2 Tbs red onion. Set aside. Toss eggplant with ¼ tsp salt.

2. Heat a large sauté pan over high heat. Add 1 Tbs oil. Add remaining onion and garlic. Cook for about 2 minutes. When the onions brown, add carrots and squash. Cook for another 2–5 minutes, or until the carrots are tender (the time may vary depending on the size of the carrots). You may need to add a little bit more oil, or water, to keep the vegetables from scorching. Remove veggies from pan and return it to the burner.

3. To the same pan, add remaining oil and eggplant. Cook for 2–3 minutes, over high heat, until the eggplant is tender.

4. Meanwhile, slice bread in half and toast in the oven.

5. When vegetables are cooked, remove from heat. Mix in pickles.

6. To assemble: spread a spoon of mayonnaise mixture on each side of the toasted bread. Top one side with veggies, the other with cheese.

7. Bake in a 350°F oven until cheese melts, about 4 minutes. Put the cheese side on top of the veggie side and press together. Cut into sandwiches.

♦ ♦ ♦ ♦ ♦	
½ c	mayonnaise
1–2	chipotle peppers (canned and packed in adobo), chopped, + 1 tsp adobo juice
2 Tbs	chopped fresh cilantro
1	red onion, chopped
1	small eggplant, thinly sliced
2 Tbs	oil
2 cloves	garlic, chopped
1	carrot, peeled and sliced thin
1	yellow squash, sliced
1	zucchini, sliced
1	French baguette
1–2	dill pickles, diced
¼ lb	Swiss cheese, sliced

Vegetarian/Vegan Burgers

◆ ◆ ◆ ◆ ◆

2 Tbs	olive or canola oil
½ c	minced onions
3 cloves	garlic, peeled and chopped
2 c	cooked black beans, slightly mashed
¼ c	fresh oregano
1 tsp	salt
¼ tsp	cayenne
2 c	cooked sweet potatoes, mashed (preferably a mix of different varieties)
	salt and pepper to taste
	sour cream, cilantro and/or cheese for garnish

Too often vegetarian burgers lack flavor or nutritional balance. These burgers have deep stand-on-their-own flavors and are a complete meal. The only downside is they need to be flipped carefully: these don't hold together like ground meat.

1. In a large skillet over medium-high heat, add 1 Tbs of the oil. Sauté the onions and garlic until just cooked. Immediately remove from heat.

2. Add the beans and oregano to the onions and garlic.

3. Sprinkle cayenne and salt on top of the mashed sweet potatoes. This helps to better disperse the seasoning.

4. Mix all ingredients together and chill for at least 45 minutes. Season to taste with salt and pepper.

5. Once chilled, form patties approximately 1½-inch thick and 4 inches in diameter.

6. Heat a large skillet over high heat, add remaining oil. Fry patties until golden brown and crispy on both sides. Flip gently, as these burgers don't hold together as well as meat patties do.

7. Serve with sour cream mixed with fresh cilantro, any cheese, or any condiment that you would normally serve with a beef burger. Best to serve with toasted crusty bread such as baguette or kaiser roll.

Vietnamese Eggplant

This recipe comes from Even' Star CSA member Mai-Liem Slade. As she writes, "An ode to my mom who passed away almost 5 years ago. The only way I was introduced to eggplant as a kid was roasted in an oven, drenched in Vietnamese dipping sauce (nuoc mam) and served over warm jasmine rice."

1. Roast whole eggplants in a 375°F oven until soft. When cool, peel the skin and use a fork to spaghetti the eggplant, then cut stem away.

2. Put eggplant in a bowl. In a skillet, heat 2–3 Tbs of oil and sauté scallions. Pour it into the eggplant bowl.

3. Then make the fish sauce dressing as below (according to your taste, i.e., spicy or sour).

Nuoc Mam

1. Mash the garlic and peppers together (we use a mortar and pestle) to form a paste (use a little sugar so that the garlic won't jump around). Add the fish sauce, water, lime juice, and sugar. Adjust the ingredients according to taste.

2. Serve eggplants over rice or onto the side and pour the fish sauce over it.

Hopefully it's not too addicting. Enjoy!

2	medium eggplants
2–3 Tbs	neutral oil
2	scallions, cut into rounds
	nuoc mam

—— **Nuoc Mam** ——

2 cloves	garlic
1–2	chili peppers
3–4 Tbs	fish sauce
3–4 Tbs	water
	juice of half a lime
1 tsp	sugar to taste

GLUTEN FREE

Chicken Criollo

2½ c	cilantro (stems and all)
1 Tbs	cumin
1 Tbs	fresh oregano
2 tsp	salt
1 Tbs	ground black pepper
¾ c	coarsely chopped onion
⅓ c	coarsely chopped garlic
1⅓ c	vinegar
¼ c	oil
2	chickens, cut into pieces additional salt and pepper to taste

This recipe works best with bone-in, skin-on chicken pieces. The vinegar balances well with the richness of the skin and dark meat. If you prefer boneless, skinless chicken, then reduce the vinegar to ½ cup.

1. Combine all ingredients, except chicken, in a blender.

2. Season chicken with salt and pepper. Marinate chicken in above mixture for at least 30 minutes and up to 2 days (the longer the better).

3. Bake chicken in the marinade at 350°F for 20–30 minutes or until cooked through. Serve with rice.

Curried Greens Stuffing for Chicken

2 Tbs	butter or olive oil
3 cloves	garlic, sliced
1½ tsp	curry powder
1 bunch	mustard greens or other washed cooking greens, coarsely chopped
½ c	raisins
	salt and pepper to taste

Really simple and really tasty! Nearly any greens may be used, from kale or collards to dandelion to escarole to mustard greens or even watercress. These greens would also be lovely stuffed in a roasted acorn squash.

1. Melt butter in a sauté pan. Add garlic. Cook for 2 minutes over medium heat, and add the curry powder. Cook for 1 more minute and add the raisins.

2. Add the mustard greens, and cook until they wilt.

3. Cool before using stuffing. Stuff under skin of chicken breast before baking.

Friday Night Chicken

Growing up, Julia's family served roast chicken every Friday night with roasted potatoes and onions. Now, in her own home, she adds carrots and parsnips. Not much oil is needed: as the chicken renders its fat, it provides the perfect medium for roasting the vegetables. Serve with a green salad, and the meal is complete.

1	free-range roasting chicken
1 Tbs	plain oil
2–3	carrots
2–3	parsnips
2	onions or 4 shallots
1 tsp	olive oil
3 sprigs	fresh thyme or rosemary
	salt and pepper

1. Preheat the oven to 400°F.

2. Rub chicken with plain oil, which will help crisp the skin, and season generously with salt and pepper.

3. Peel potatoes, carrots, and parsnips; and cut into chunks.

4. Peel onion and cut into chunks.

5. Mix vegetables together with olive oil in a bowl. Season with salt and pepper. Put vegetables in a single layer in the bottom of a roasting pan. Place the chicken, breast side up, on top of the veggies.

6. Roast in the oven for 15 minutes. Remove and stir the vegetables with the now-rendered chicken juices.

7. Reduce the oven to 350°F. Continue roasting for 30 minutes or until the chicken is cooked through. To check for doneness, pierce the thigh just enough to release some juice; it should be clear with minimal pink color.

8. Let the chicken rest for 10 minutes before carving and serving. Pairs nicely with a red or white wine.

Thai Red Curry with Chicken and Vegetables

* * * * *

2 c	jasmine rice
2 Tbs	canola or other plain oil
1 ½ tsp	salt
2	boneless, skinless chicken breasts, sliced ¼ inch thick
	salt and pepper
½ c	chopped onion
2 Tbs	red curry paste (use heaping spoons for more spicy, scant spoons for delicate palates)
1	13 ounce can (unsweetened) coconut milk
2 Tbs	fish sauce

—————— Options ——————

1 tsp	brown sugar
3 c	chopped vegetables, summer or winter options (see below)
¼ c	fresh basil leaves
3–4	scallions, cut into long strips or rounds
	salt and pepper

Curries are incredibly versatile; you can use whatever vegetables you have in your CSA box or find fresh at the farmers market. The key is to add the vegetables to the sauce in order of how long they take to cook. For example, carrots cook more slowly than snap peas. Use this recipe as a guide and feel free to adapt to what you have on hand.

1. In a large saucepan, mix rice, 1 tsp oil, and 1½ tsp salt, ensuring to coat each grain of rice in oil. Add 3 cups of water. Bring to a boil over high heat, cover and reduce heat to low. Let cook for 10 minutes. Turn off heat and let stand for 5 more minutes, covered.

2. Meanwhile, season chicken with salt and pepper. Heat a large sauté pan over high heat. Add 1 Tbs oil, and then the chicken and onions. Stir-fry for 4 minutes, remove from pan and set aside.

3. In the same pan, heat remaining oil over high heat. Add red curry paste, and stir-fry for 1 minute. Add coconut milk, fish sauce, (plus 1 tsp brown sugar, if using) and any root vegetables (such as carrots, potatoes, or rutabagas). Let simmer for 3–5 minutes. Add green vegetables (broccoli, okra, cabbage, eggplant, and greens). Just when the greens turns bright green (after 1–2 minutes), add remaining vegetables (such as tomatoes, bell peppers, and summer squash) and chicken. Cook for 1 minute more until everything is heated through

4. Serve curry over rice. Garnish with scallions.

Summer Vegetable Options: (total 3 cups, chopped) tomatoes, bell peppers, okra, potatoes, squash, and/or eggplant

Winter Vegetables Options: (total 3 cups, chopped) sweet potatoes, turnips, carrots, radishes, broccoli, rutabagas, cabbage, and/or greens

Vegan Option: use tofu instead of chicken; and ¼–½ tsp of salt instead of the fish sauce

Trinidad Curried Potatoes and Chicken

*Mild and gentle; if you want more contrast,
add the chopped vegetables at the end.*

1. In a large sauté pan, heat oil. Sauté onions, garlic, and ginger until they are soft. Add chilies and curry powder. Add enough vinegar to make a paste. Let cool.

2. Marinate chicken in paste for at least 2 hours, though overnight is ideal.

3. Barely cover chicken with water (approximately 1 quart) in a pot or large sauté pan. Add potatoes. Season with salt and pepper. Bring water to a boil. Reduce heat, and simmer for 20 minutes, or until potatoes and chicken are tender.

4. Garnish with optional ingredients, if desired.

◆ ◆ ◆ ◆ ◆

1 tsp	plain oil
1	large onion, minced
3 cloves	garlic, chopped
2 tsp	minced fresh ginger
½ tsp	crushed red chilies
3 Tbs	Madras-style curry powder
½ c	(or more) vinegar
	3-pound chicken, cut into 8 pieces
2	large potatoes, peeled and chopped
	salt and pepper to taste

——— Garnish ———

Chopped raw scallions, raisins, red peppers, cilantro, and/or basil

Beef Roulade with Cilantro Mojo

The key to this recipe is seasoning the meat with oregano, lime and garlic (and of course, salt and pepper). It gives the meat a classic Latin flavor.

2	red bell peppers, quartered, seeds removed
2 stalks	thyme
5 cloves	garlic, smashed
1 tsp	cayenne or chili flakes
1 c	extra virgin olive oil
2 lb	flank steak
1 Tbs	fresh oregano
1	lime, juiced
2	carrots, peeled and thinly sliced
1	stick butter, cut into chunks
4	sweet potatoes, peeled and chunked
2 slices	ginger
¼ c	cream
1 Tbs	plain oil
1 bunch	watercress
	salt, pepper, and lemon juice to taste

Cilantro Mojo

½ c	olive oil
¼ c	chopped garlic
½ c	chopped onion
2 tsp	cumin
1 Tbs	fresh oregano
2 tsp	pepper
1 Tbs	salt
1 c	white vinegar
1½ c	cilantro, leaves and stems

1. Preheat oven to 375°F

2. To a large saucepan, add red peppers, thyme, garlic cloves, and cayenne. Cover with olive oil. Simmer over medium heat for 15 minutes, or until peppers are tender. Let cool.

3. Season steak with salt (1½ tsp), pepper (½ tsp), oregano, and lime juice. Rub meat with roasted garlic. Lay out steak, and place red peppers and carrots on top. Dot with butter. Roll steak with the grain, and tie with kitchen string.

4. Put sweet potatoes and ginger in a pot of salted water and bring to a boil. Reduce heat to a simmer and continue cooking until potatoes are tender. Drain water and purée potatoes with cream. Season with salt, pepper, and lemon juice. Set aside in a warm place until ready to serve.

5. Heat oil in a pan. Brown meat on all sides, and finish cooking in the oven for about 10 minutes for medium rare. Let meat rest for 10 minutes. Remove strings, and slice meat as thin as possible. Garnish with watercress, sweet potatoes, and cilantro mojo.

Cilantro Mojo

1. Heat olive oil over medium heat. Add garlic, onions, cumin, and oregano. Cook for 3 minutes, or until garlic becomes aromatic.

2. Strain olive oil and reserve. Purée garlic-onion mixture with remaining ingredients. Slowly whisk in olive oil. Adjust seasoning to taste.

Beef with Eggplant

Adapted from The Chinese Kitchen *by Eileen Yin-Fei Lo,
a must-have book for lovers of Chinese cooking.*

1. In a large bowl, combine the beef, 1 tsp of ginger, gin, ¼ tsp salt, 1 tsp oil and cornstarch. Let beef marinate for at least 30 minutes.

2. Cut eggplant into ½-inch slices. Toss with 1 tsp salt. Let sit for 5 minutes. Rinse off salt and pat dry eggplant.

3. Mix together ingredients for sauce and set aside.

4. In a large skillet, add ¼ inch of canola oil. Heat to 350°F. Add eggplant slices and cook until deep golden brown, about 10 minutes. Drain the eggplant and set aside. Drain oil from the pan except for one tablespoon. Return pan to heat. Add the garlic and remaining ginger, and cook for 1 minute or until aromatic. Add the beef and stir-fry until the meat loses its pink edges, about 3 minutes. Add the sauce and cook until it thickens. Stir in the eggplant to coat with sauce.

5. Garnish with scallions.

½ lb	sirloin steak, cut against the grain into ¼-inch-wide strips
3 tsp	fresh chopped ginger
½ tsp	gin
¼ tsp	salt
1 tsp	canola oil
1 Tbs	cornstarch
2	small eggplants
1 tsp	salt
2 tsp	fresh chopped garlic
	canola or other neutral oil for frying
	scallions for garnish

Sauce

1 Tbs	Chinese bean sauce
½ c	chicken stock
2 tsp	sugar
2 Tbs	oyster sauce
1 tsp	soy sauce

Chiles Rellenos Picadillo

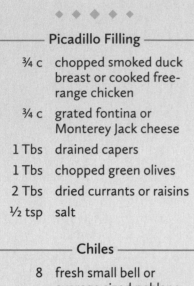

──── Picadillo Filling ────

¾ c	chopped smoked duck breast or cooked free-range chicken
¾ c	grated fontina or Monterey Jack cheese
1 Tbs	drained capers
1 Tbs	chopped green olives
2 Tbs	dried currants or raisins
½ tsp	salt

──────── Chiles ────────

8	fresh small bell or average sized poblano chilies
½ c	olive oil

GLUTEN FREE

Smoked duck is available at specialty food stores or through D'Artagnan.

1. Make Picadillo filling: mix together all ingredients except chilies and olive oil.

2. Toss chilies with oil. Roast in a 400°F oven until skin begins to turn light brown and blister, about 20 minutes.

3. When chilies are cool enough to handle, make a small incision (with a knife) along the side of the chili, in order to remove the seeds while still maintaining the shape of the chili. Gingerly remove the seeds with a spoon.

4. Stuff each chili with about ¼ cup of Picadillo filling and return to roasting pan, cut side up. Return to the oven to heat through before serving.

5. Serve with tomatillo salsa (see page 249) and/or roast chicken and rice.

Even' Star Gumbo

A deeply flavored stew of summer vegetables that requires okra. One of the West African names for okra is gumbo and the seeds were carried to this continent by slaves. Once made, the thick base can be frozen, to be thawed in deep winter, and simmered with poultry, seafood, sausage, or with only vegetables.

1. Sauté the garlic, onion, and peppers until soft in 1 Tbs of the oil, in a large stainless steel or cast-iron pot.

2. Add the puréed tomatoes and water or stock; simmer 10 more minutes.

3. Add the okra, herbs, salt, and pepper. Simmer 2 more minutes, then taste and adjust seasonings to taste.

4. If you want a thicker gumbo, make a roux by cooking the remaining two Tbs oil with 2 Tbs flour in a separate pan on moderate heat, stirring all the time. One minute after it starts bubbling, add into the larger pot of gumbo, beating vigorously with a whisk to prevent lumps. Simmer another 5 minutes, and again adjust seasonings to taste. This base may be frozen or used immediately.

5. To complete the gumbo, add whatever omnivore or vegetarian options you want, but be sure to add long-cooking items like chicken or sausage way before foods like shrimp or scallops that need only the briefest of cooking. Simmer all together until the brief-cookers are just tender.

6. Gumbo is nearly always served with cooked white rice, a spoonful in the center of each diner's bowl. This may be the best and only use for a converted rice like Uncle Ben's. Alternatively, a crusty French or Italian bread does well. Sprinkle each bowl with the chopped parsley or scallion at table-side. Excellent with a chilled white wine, any beer except stout or porter, or even a red wine (Portuguese or Spanish) or a moderately chilled Pinot Noir.

◆ ◆ ◆ ◆ ◆

3 Tbs	canola or other neutral oil
4 cloves	garlic, chopped
½	onion, chopped
2	mild green peppers, chopped
2 c	ripe or overripe tomatoes, puréed
4 c	water, chicken or vegetable stock
½ lb	okra, cut into ¼-inch rounds
2 tsp	dried thyme or oregano
2 tsp	gumbo file powder (optional, but very good)
2 Tbs	flour
	salt, pepper, and hot pepper to taste
	chopped scallions or parsley as final garnish

—— **Omnivore Options** ——

shrimp, chicken, game, scallops, crab, oysters, andouille or other sausage, or pork chunks

—— **Vegetarian Options** ——

sweet corn kernels, tempeh, eggplant, vegetarian sausage, and/or fresh mushrooms

Great Stuffed Peppers

◆ ◆ ◆ ◆ ◆

6	medium-large peppers: cubanelle, Italian, or red or green bell
1 tsp	olive oil
½ lb	sausage or ground beef
¼	onion, chopped
2 cloves	garlic, chopped
3 ears	corn, kernels cut off
½ tsp	salt
½ tsp	black pepper, unless the peppers are spicy
1 tsp	whole cumin seed
½ lb	(or more) grated Cheddar or Monterey Jack
½ bunch	cilantro, chopped

This diverges from typical stuffed pepper recipes in the lack of rice or bread. The sweet corn, cheese, and meat instead are more equal players that support each other beautifully.

1. Cut the shoulders off the peppers and remove the seeds and white tissue inside. Set the now ready-for-stuffing peppers aside.

2. Chop the white tissue and the meat from the pepper shoulders. Sauté this and the meat in a skillet with oil. When nearly cooked, add the onion and garlic and cook 2 more minutes. Add corn, salt, pepper, and cumin seed, and cook only 30 seconds more. Put into a large bowl and let fully cool. Then add the cheese and cilantro and mix well.

3. Stuff this into the peppers, and stand them up in a small roasting pan (with sides). Bake for about 35 minutes in a 350°F oven, until the peppers are soft throughout.

Excellent served with sour cream and more cilantro on the side, and a beer in the hand.

Moussaka

Moussaka is a layered casserole dish with origins in Greece. It reminds us of lasagna with fried eggplant slices instead of pasta, and uses besamel, the Greek version of béchamel.

1. Cut the eggplant into ½-inch slices. Sprinkle them with salt and let sit for 20 minutes.

2. Meanwhile, start the sauce: Heat olive oil in a large pot. Add onions and garlic, and cook until they start to soften, about 3 minutes. Add the lamb, salt, and pepper. With a spoon, break up the lamb. Add the cinnamon, oregano, and tomatoes. Continue cooking until the sauce is thick, about 20 minutes. Set aside and stir in the mint.

3. Make the besamel sauce: in a pot, heat 1½ cups of milk. In a bowl, whisk eggs with remaining milk. Knead together the flour and butter. Slowly pour hot milk into egg/milk mixture while whisking vigorously. Return pot to medium heat. Stir in flour/butter mix and continue cooking until it thickens. Season with salt and remove from heat.

4. Fry eggplant: Brush off excess salt and moisture. Dust slices with flour. Heat a large skillet over high heat. Add the oil. When the oil starts to shimmer, fry the eggplant slices until golden brown on both sides. It may be necessary to cook in several batches. Drain on a paper towel.

5. Assemble the moussaka: in a 9-inch × 9-inch Pyrex dish, layer half of the eggplant slices on the bottom of the pan. Sprinkle about ⅓ of the cheese on top. Pour sauce on top and spread evenly in the pan. Layer the remaining eggplant on top. Sprinkle another third of the cheese on top of the eggplant. Pour the besamel sauce on top and sprinkle remaining cheese on top of that.

6. Bake at 375°F for 30 minutes or until top is golden brown.

◆ ◆ ◆ ◆ ◆

Eggplant

3	medium-sized eggplant
1 Tbs	salt
½ c	flour
½ c	olive oil
½ c	grated Asiago cheese

Sauce

1 Tbs	olive oil
1	onion, peeled and chopped
3 cloves	garlic, peeled and chopped
1 lb	pound ground lamb
1 tsp	cinnamon
½ tsp	dried Greek or regular oregano
2 c	puréed tomato
	salt and pepper
2 Tbs	chopped fresh mint

Besamel Sauce

2 c	milk
2 Tbs	butter, room temperature
¼ c	flour
3	eggs
½ tsp	salt

Rhubarb Meat Stew

Common in Iran, this stew is sweet and savory.

◆ ◆ ◆ ◆ ◆

1½ lb	of cubed stew meat, either beef or lamb
4 Tbs	olive oil
8 stalks	rhubarb cut into small bite-sized pieces
1	large onion, peeled, finely chopped
1 bunch	parsley, chopped, to yield 2 cups
1 bunch	mint, chopped, to yield 1 cup
½ tsp	turmeric
1 tsp	coriander
¼ tsp	saffron
	salt and pepper to taste
2–3 Tbs	sugar, or to taste
2 c	chicken stock, broth or water

1. Season the meat generously with salt and pepper. In a large skillet, heat 2 Tbs of oil and brown meat on all sides. Remove meat from pan, put in an oven proof dish, and set aside. To the meat pan, add the chopped onions and cook until soft. Add turmeric, coriander, and saffron. Add chicken stock and bring to a boil. Pour this broth over the meat. Add additional water to cover the meat. Cover the dish and bake at 350°F.

2. After 1 hour, add the parsley, mint, and rhubarb. If the pan seems dry, add more water or chicken stock. Continue cooking for another 45 minutes or until the meat is tender.

3. Taste and add 2–3 tablespoons of sugar or to taste. Gently stir and cook for an additional 5 minutes.

4. Serve warm with basmati rice and (optional) sour cream or plain yogurt.

Summer Meatloaf (or Meatballs) with Spaghetti or Summer Squash

This quickly made dish is very low-fat. The vegetables and herbs lighten the dish enough for enjoying even in summer, and flavorful free-range meat adds substantially to its healthiness. Serves at least six, with nice leftovers. Fifty minutes total to prepare and cook.

1. Mix meatloaf together. Form into two loaves or many meatballs. Place in a roasting pan or cast-iron skillet, and drizzle olive oil over top. Broil on low broil setting until tops brown.

2. While meatloaf is broiling, quickly make the sauce by mixing the sauce ingredients in a bowl.

3. Once meat has browned, pour off most of the pan juices. Add the tomato sauce and broil until it too browns or slightly chars.

♦ ♦ ♦ ♦ ♦

Meatloaf

2 lb	lean, free-range ground beef or lamb
1 c	raw grated winter squash, summer squash or "forked" spaghetti squash
1 bunch	mint, coarsely chopped
2 tsp	salt
¾ tsp	black pepper
3 cloves	garlic, chopped
2 Tbs	olive oil

Tomato Sauce

4 c	fresh diced beefsteak or cherry tomatoes
1 Tbs	balsamic or red wine vinegar
2 cloves	garlic, chopped
½	onion, chopped
¾ tsp	salt
½ tsp	black pepper
2	medium-sized bunches fresh basil, coarsely chopped

Vietnamese Meatballs with Crispy Salad

♦ ♦ ♦ ♦ ♦

1 head	Boston lettuce or large tender Asian greens
1 bunch	mint and/or cilantro
1	large shallot, peeled and diced
2 stalks	lemongrass
2 cloves	garlic
1	small red chili
1 lb	ground pork
2 Tbs	honey
2 Tbs	canola oil
1 Tbs	fish sauce
2 Tbs	brown sugar
1 tsp	salt
1 tsp	freshly ground black pepper

—— Carrot–Daikon Salad ——

1	small daikon
2	small carrots, peeled
1 tsp	salt
¼ c	water
2 Tbs	fish sauce
1 Tbs	rice vinegar
1 Tbs	lime juice
3 tsp	sugar

—————— Optional ——————

1	small chili, seeds removed and sliced

These meatballs also go well with the Kohlrabi Salad (see page 99). To make a complete meal, serve with steamed rice.

1. Wash lettuce, mint, and/or cilantro. Soak in salt water for 5 minutes. Drain and set aside on a serving plate.

2. Finely chop lemongrass, garlic, shallots, and chilies (or grind with a food processor). Mix with ground pork. Add remaining ingredients and mix to combine. Let marinate for 10 minutes.

3. Form meat into meatballs about 1 inch in diameter. Put on a grill rack.

4. Cook meatballs over a charcoal fire (or under a broiler) until caramelized on the outside and cooked through, about 10 minutes, depending on the fire. Serve on a bed of lettuce with mint and/or cilantro, and the carrot-daikon salad.

5. To best enjoy the meatballs, wrap them in whole lettuce leaves with some fresh herbs and the salad.

Carrot–Daikon Salad

1. Thinly slice daikon and carrots. Toss with salt and let stand for 5 minutes. Rinse.

2. Heat water to a boil. Add garlic, chilies, fish sauce, vinegar, and sugar. Stir until sugar dissolves. Remove from heat and add carrots, daikon, and lime juice.

Carrot and Seafood Salad

*If serving a large crowd, you can also add
quartered hard-boiled eggs to this salad.*

1. Put shellfish in a pot with just enough water to cover. Add lemon rind, salt, and white wine. Turn on low heat and do not walk away. Cook until scallops are just white (or the shrimp is just pink), not simmering, not boiling. This keeps the shellfish at its most tender. Immediately drain water, put shellfish in a colander and mix with ample ice to stop the cooking process.

2. Drain shellfish from ice.

3. Meanwhile, in a large bowl, mix together olive oil, vinegar, and the juice from the lemon. Mix in well black pepper and cayenne.

4. Add remaining ingredients and shellfish to dressing. Toss well.

5. Fine to serve at room temperature, but refrigerate if you won't be serving the salad within 2 hours.

♦ ♦ ♦ ♦ ♦

1 lb	shelled, raw shrimp or sea scallops
½	lemon, juiced and rind reserved
1 tsp	salt
¼ c	white wine
	ice
2 Tbs	olive oil
1 Tbs	rice vinegar or cider vinegar, or to taste
	pinch cayenne or dash of Tabasco
1 lb	peeled carrots, cut into really thin, 1½ inch long strips
4	scallions, chopped
4	radishes, cut in half and then sliced thin
2 Tbs	fresh minced basil or dill; or ¼ cup chopped parsley or sorrel
¼ tsp	black pepper

——— Optional ———

¼	red onion, sliced thin, and 1 small cucumber, cut into 1½-inch slices

Eggplant Parmesan with Shrimp

◆ ◆ ◆ ◆ ◆

1	large eggplant, sliced into ½-inch slices
½ tsp	salt
½ c	all-purpose flour
1	egg
1 c	bread crumbs
2 Tbs	olive oil
1 Tbs	canola oil
1 ball	fresh mozzarella (about 4 ounces), sliced ¼-inch
3 cloves	garlic, minced
1	small chili, minced
1 lb	shrimp, peeled and deveined
¼ c	white wine
2 c	stewed tomatoes (see page 237)
	basil, salt, and pepper to taste

"Parmesan" dishes derive their name not from the namesake cheese but from the region where the dish originated: Parma. In fact, the traditional dish has a layer of Parma ham (prosciutto) and is made with veal.

1. Toss eggplant with ½ tsp salt and let sit for five minutes. Brush off excess salt. Preheat the oven to 375°F.

2. Prepare the breading: in 3 separate bowls, put the flour, egg and bread crumbs. Beat the egg with 2 Tbs of water until well mixed.

3. Dip each eggplant slice first into the flour. Shake off any excess. Then dip into the egg to completely coat, and finally coat the eggplant in the bread crumbs. Lay breaded slices on a cookie sheet. Repeat this process with remaining slices.

4. Heat a large skillet over medium-high heat. Add 1 Tbs olive oil and canola oil. Fry the eggplant slices until brown on both sides. Don't worry if they are not cooked all the way through. Remove eggplant from skillet and put on a cookie sheet.

5. Top each eggplant slice with a slice of mozzarella. Bake in the oven until the cheese is melted and bubbly, about 10 minutes.

6. Meanwhile, wipe out the eggplant pan. Add the remaining olive oil, garlic, and chili and return to heat. Add the shrimp and cook until they begin to turn pink. Add the wine, and then the tomatoes. Remove the shrimp from the pan as they are cooked through, but continue cooking the tomatoes until they reduce until thick. Season to taste with salt, pepper, and basil.

7. To serve, spoon the tomato sauce onto a serving platter and lay shrimp and eggplant slices on top.

Roasted Salmon with Sorrel Sauce

The bright acidity of sorrel makes it the perfect complement to the rich, buttery salmon. The sorrel loses its bright color quickly. You can purée the sauce with parsley or spinach leaves to bring green colors back.

1. Season salmon with salt and pepper. Refrigerate until just before cooking.

2. Meanwhile, make the sauce. Coarsely chop the sorrel. Heat a medium-sized skillet over medium heat. Add the butter. When melted, add the shallots. Cook the shallots until soft, but not brown. Add the wine and cook until most of the liquid has evaporated (about 1–2 Tbs remain). Add the sorrel leaves and stir until they wilt, about 3 minutes. Stir in the cream. Season to taste with salt and pepper. Set aside in a warm place until the salmon is ready.

3. Put salmon on a sheet tray, skin side down. Place under broiler for 10 minutes or until it the salmon begins to brown. Switch the oven to bake (375°F) and cook for 5 minutes more.

4. Serve salmon with sorrel underneath. Simple simmered potatoes would be an excellent accompaniment.

4	6-ounce salmon fillets
2 Tbs	butter
1	small shallot or onion, peeled and diced
¼ c	white wine
8 oz	sorrel (approximately 3–4 cups, loosely packed)
¼ c	cream
	salt and pepper to taste

Seared Sea Scallops with Asparagus Purée and Sautéed Morels

Morels are one of the few mushrooms that cannot be cultivated, and it's one of the treasures of spring. Asparagus and scallops are a classic pairing.

1 Tbs	olive oil
1	small leek, chopped
¼ c	diced potatoes
24	asparagus stalks, woody ends trimmed and discarded, tips cut and reserved
2 sprigs	parsley
1 c	chicken broth (more if needed)
1 c	spinach
1 lb	large scallops (small scallops overcook quickly, becoming rubbery)
2 Tbs	chopped parsley
	salt and pepper to taste
½ lb	morels or other mushrooms, sliced
2 tsp	fresh thyme
2 tsp	chopped shallots
6 cloves	garlic, sliced
¼ c	dry sherry
2 tsp	plain oil
1 bunch	chives, finely diced
1	lemon, juiced

1. Heat olive oil in large pot. Sweat leeks and potatoes. Add asparagus, parsley, and chicken broth. Simmer for 15 minutes or until asparagus is tender.

2. Put ¼ cup spinach in the bottom of a blender. Ladle asparagus mix into blender and purée. Add chicken broth as necessary to thin to sauce consistency. Season to taste with salt and pepper. Repeat process until all the asparagus is puréed.

3. Meanwhile, heat a large sauté pan on high heat with 1 Tbs plain oil. Add morels. Sprinkle with thyme, half of shallots, garlic, salt and pepper to taste. Deglaze with sherry, and cook until the morels absorb the liquid, about 3 minutes.

4. Season scallops with salt and pepper to taste.

5. Heat a large skillet over a high heat. Add plain oil. Sear scallops for 3 minutes, or deeply browned, flip and cook for 1 minute more for rare, or 2–3 minutes for cooked through.

Serve scallops with asparagus purée. Top with morels and chives. Sprinkle lemon juice over everything.

seared sea scallops with asparagus and morels

Striped Bass with Radish Salad, Soybeans, and Orange Glaze

This is adapted from
Thomas Keller's The French Laundry Cookbook.

1. Place orange juice in a pot, and cook over high heat until reduced to about ½ cup. Remove from heat and whisk in 3 Tbs butter. Season with soy sauce. Set aside in a warm place.

2. Combine scallions, carrots, and radishes in a bowl. Season with lemon, olive oil, salt, and pepper.

3. Melt 2 Tbs butter over medium heat. Add carrot dice, celery, and leek. Cook until soft, about 3 minutes. Add soybeans and tomatoes. Season to taste with salt and pepper.

4. Season fish with salt and pepper. Heat skillet over high heat, add plain oil. Cook fish on first side until brown and crispy, flip and cook for just a minute more on the second side.

5. Serve fish with orange reduction, small dice of vegetables, and the julienne salad.

2 c	orange juice
5 Tbs	butter
1 Tbs	soy sauce or tamari
2	scallions, julienned
1	carrot, julienned
3	radishes or ¼ daikon, julienned
1 tsp	lemon juice
1 Tbs	olive oil
½	carrot, finely diced
¼	celery stalk, finely diced
¼	leek, finely diced
1	tomato, finely diced
½ c	fresh shelled soybeans (edamame), blanched
2 lb	striped bass, arctic char, trout, or salmon fillets
	salt and pepper to taste
	plain oil for cooking

Condiments
and Sauces

Applesauce

3 apples, peeled, cored, and coarsely chopped

¼ c sugar

½ c water

a few drops of lemon juice

When making apple sauce, it's important to use baking apples such as Stayman or Ginger Gold. Empire apples also lend a lovely pink hue to the sauce when cooked with the skin on. When apples are mushy, pick out the skin and discard.

1. Cook apples, sugar, and water in a saucepan over medium heat, stirring until the sugar dissolves. Continue cooking over medium-low heat, covered, until apples turn mushy.

2. Remove from heat. Press sauce through a food mill, potato ricer, or colander. Add a few drops of lemon juice.

Cucumber Relish

¼ c white or rice vinegar

2 Tbs sugar

1 small chili diced or ¼ tsp chili flakes (optional)

½ tsp salt

2 cucumbers, peeled (optional), seeded, and diced

1 tsp sesame oil

—— Garnishes ——

1 Tbs scallions, chopped

1 tsp toasted sesame seeds

Waiting until the last minute to add the cucumbers to the vinegar/sugar mix ensures they stay crunchy and the dressing doesn't get watery.

1. In a small stainless steel, non-reactive pot, combine the vinegar, sugar, chilies (if using), and salt. Cook over medium heat, stirring constantly until the sugar dissolves. Let cool.

2. Toss cucumbers in seasoned vinegar and sesame oil; mix in garnishes.

Basic Stewed Tomatoes

*These tomatoes are the basis for many recipes in this book,
and an excellent way to cope with a flood of ripe tomatoes. They
also freeze exceedingly well as a way to extend the summer harvest.*

1. Remove any blemishes or rotten spots from fully ripe
   tomatoes. Wash, then chunk coarsely (you can leave cherry
   tomatoes whole, and should feel very free to mix many
   different kinds of tomatoes).

2. In a stainless steel pot, put tomatoes, 3 Tbs water, and about
   ½ tsp salt per 2¼ lb of tomatoes. Bring to a gentle boil, stirring
   often, then reduce to a simmer and cook 3 more minutes.
   Let cool.

3. Using a colander, strain out but reserve the juice. This makes
   an outstanding tomato juice for pure drinking or a Bloody
   Mary. Freeze juice within 4 days; it keeps poorly.

4. The pulp remaining in the colander is rich in seeds, skins,
   vitamins, and tomato meat. If this amount of roughage is not
   to your taste, blend until smooth. Puréed or not, this forms
   the base for outstanding tomato sauces or tomato soups.

Cantaloupe Salsa I

◆ ◆ ◆ ◆ ◆

¾ c	coarsely chopped cantaloupe
¼ c	chopped onion
2 Tbs	chopped fresh cilantro
2 tsp	olive oil
1 Tbs	fresh lime juice
1 tsp	minced seeded jalapeño chili

This salsa is a wonderful accompaniment to grilled fish, such as tuna or mahi-mahi. Couscous would be a good side dish. The recipe also works well with honeydew melons (or a combination).

Mix everything together. Season with salt, if desired.

Cantaloupe Salsa II

½	cantaloupe
1	cucumber
1	small onion
1 Tbs	fresh mint or cilantro (or combination of the two)
1 tsp	fresh chopped ginger
1	lime, juiced
	salt and pepper to taste
½ tsp	sriracha, or 1 small chili, minced

The ginger gives this salsa bite; the cucumber, a refreshing clean contrast that offsets well any overwhelming cantaloupe sweetness. Can also accompany chicken breast or pork or chicken kebabs.

1. Peel and seed cantaloupe, and finely dice. If using a large cucumber with tough skin (or a commercial, waxed cucumber), peel cucumber. Scoop out the seeds. Chop fine. Dice the onion and finely chop the herbs.

2. Mix cantaloupe, onion, cucumber, ginger, and herbs together. Season with lime juice, salt, pepper, and chili paste if desired.

3. Serve with grilled tuna or salmon.

Easy Pickled Green Tomatoes

*This is an "icebox" pickle, designed to be easy
and require no canning. It's a great way to use up
all the end-of-season tomatoes that won't have a chance
to ripen on the vine.*

1. Put tomatoes in a large plastic, glass, or steel container.

2. Fully dissolve salt in water, stirring if necessary. Pour over the tomatoes. Rrefrigerate.

3. Place chilies in a clean jar, and cover with vinegar. Refrigerate. Leave both vessels alone for 7–14 days.

4. Pour salt water off the tomatoes. Mix these, the chilies, and all other ingredients in a large bowl; return to the tomato container or to a quart Mason jar, and cover with new vinegar (more mild pickle) or the chili vinegar (more spicy pickle). Lid the pickle jar and return to the refrigerator. Leave pickle at least a week before eating.

5. These pickles keep about 2 months before getting soft.

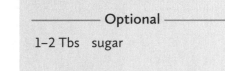

10 lb	tomatoes, whole cherry toms or 1-inch cubes of heirloom types, all green and underripe
½ c	kosher or sea salt (not iodized salt)
8 c	water
1–2	chilies, to your taste, cut into 1-inch chunks
	cider, red wine, or rice wine vinegar to cover (about 4 cups should be on hand, but likely won't all be used)
10 cloves	garlic, sliced
1 Tbs	pickling spice or a mix of coriander, fennel, and cumin seeds

——————— Optional ———————

1–2 Tbs	sugar

Fresh Kimchi

1 head	napa or green cabbage
2	large bunches bok choy or tat soi, coarsely chopped
1	daikon, peeled and shredded
1 bunch	scallions, chopped
1½ Tbs	sugar
1 c	chicken or beef broth
1 Tbs	chopped garlic
3 Tbs	ground Korean or regular chilies
	salt

Kimchi is typically fermented for several days or weeks, giving it a pungent aroma. This version can be prepared in only a few hours and has a milder flavor.

1. Mix the cabbage with about 2 Tbs salt, and put in a stainless steel bowl. Put a plate on top and weigh it down to extract the excess liquid. Let sit for at least 1 hour, or as long as 24.

2. Rinse the cabbage, and mix with remaining ingredients.

3. Refrigerate at least 2 hours before serving.

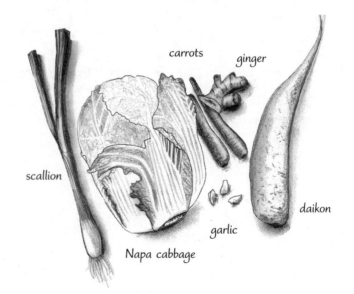

carrots

ginger

scallion

garlic

daikon

Napa cabbage

Fruit Salsa

This is a raw fruit relish that goes very well with broiled, steamed, or fried fish; with chicken breasts; with barbecue; or alongside vegetable salads. Let sit for an hour before serving to let the flavors develop. Does not keep, even refrigerated, for longer than 36 hours.

The salsa is designed to have as much sour flavor as sweet, so really sweet fruits like watermelon have to be supplemented with lime juice or a touch of vinegar.

Mix all ingredients, cover tightly, and refrigerate. Then taste 1 hour later for final seasoning. Typical serving size over fish is 2–3 tablespoons.

3 c	chopped fruit: any combination of cantaloupe, watermelon, apples, nectarines, or honeydew, seeded and cut into ¼–½-inch pieces
2 cloves	garlic, chopped
3 Tbs	finely chopped onion
1–2 Tbs	finely chopped cilantro
1 tsp	salt
1–2	dashes of hot sauce (see page 266)
	lime juice or vinegar to taste

— Optional —

1	chili pepper, finely chopped

Herb Butter

◆ ◆ ◆ ◆ ◆

1 Tbs	fresh tarragon
1 Tbs	fresh chives or scallions
1 Tbs	fresh parsley
1 Tbs	fresh basil
½ tsp	whole fennel seeds
1 stick	butter, room temperature
	salt and pepper to taste

We usually make a large batch of herb butter and store it in the freezer. You can put a pat under the skin of chicken before roasting. You can also use it as a finishing touch for grilled salmon or steak; or toss steamed broccoli or asparagus with it.

1. Chop herbs and fennel seed.

2. With a wooden spoon, mix herbs with butter. Season to taste with salt and pepper.

3. On a large piece of plastic wrap, roll into a log, wrap well, and store in the freezer until ready to use.

Japanese Nuka Bran Pickles

Adapted from Wild Fermentation, *by Sandor Ellix Katz. This is a very traditional Japanese ongoing pickling technique, suitable for any and all root vegetables as well as larger collard, kale, mustard greens, or cabbage leaves. They should be part of the repertoire of every pickle lover, and are served in the finest Japanese restaurants.*

After fully immersing the fresh vegetables into the fermenting grains (the medium), push a piece of plastic wrap into full contact with the surface of the medium. This prevents unwanted fungi from colonizing the surface of the pickle. Once the pickles are at desired crispness and sourness, remove them from the liquid and rinse off the medium very, very well. Only then are they ready to eat.

1. Toast the bran in a skillet until it slightly browns and smells nice, stirring often. Add to the cooled and cooked brown rice, and then mix all but the extra salt and water together. The vegetables should be immersed in the bran mixture and preferably not touching each other. If the blend is not as moist as prepared oatmeal, prepare a simple brine by dissolving 2 Tbs of the salt in two cups of tepid water; mix enough of this into the crock to bring the medium to that "wet oatmeal" stage.

2. Place the plate atop the mix, and then weigh this down with a jar filled with water or a Ziploc filled with brine. Cover with the Tupperware lid or (if a crock) a cloth. The mix should have a brine layer float to the top by the next day, partially immersing the plate. After 2 more days, remove the vegetables, clean and rinse as in the introduction, and taste them for sourness. If you like the whole package, add more vegetables and continue ad infinitum. You should sprinkle the medium with kosher or sea salt about every 8th or 10th batch, and consider adding more ginger and seaweed periodically as well. This culture is much easier to maintain in the winter months: summer vegetables and temperatures make it easier for microbes that are not *Lactobacillus* to invade.

Equipment

ceramic crock or 2-gallon (minimum) Tupperware-type container

dinner or dessert plate that fits inside above crock or Tupperware jar or Ziploc to fill with salted water to act as a weight

cloth cover

Ingredients

4 c	boiled brown rice (start with approximately 2 cups raw rice and 4 cups water)
1½ c	rice bran (health food stores will carry this)
3	4-inch strips dried kelp (sushi type is fine)
⅜ c	sea salt
½ c	miso
8 oz	beer or saké
1 inch	piece of fresh ginger, cut into slices
10	small turnips, 6 large radishes, or 3 carrots, approximately
	sea or kosher salt and water, as needed

◆ ◆ ◆ ◆ ◆

1 c	plain, non-fat yogurt
1 Tbs	fresh chopped mint
½	cucumber, peeled, seeded and chopped
¼	lemon, juiced
1 clove	garlic, chopped
¼ tsp	salt and pepper to taste

2 cloves	garlic, sliced
3–4	sprigs thyme
½ tsp	dried Greek oregano
1	bay leaf
2 tsp	coriander seeds
2 tsp	turmeric
1 tsp	fennel seeds
½ tsp	red pepper flakes
2 Tbs	salt
2 c	water
½ c	cider vinegar
1 Tbs	olive oil
1 lb	small turnips, unpeeled, cut into wedges

Mint and Cucumber Raita

This makes a wonderful condiment to grilled beef, lamb kebobs, or grilled vegetables.

Mix everything together.

Pickled Turnips

This recipe comes courtesy of longtime Even' Star CSA subscriber Sherry Jones. A great hors d'oeuvre for busy parties, or when heavier foods will later be served.

1. Combine all ingredients, except turnips, in a bowl. Stir to dissolve salt.

2. Pack turnip wedges into a jar; pour in brine mixture. Screw on lid. Put the jar on a shelf and turn it over every day for a week.

3. After a week, refrigerate.

Pickles

Bread and Butter

*These pickles have a sweet and sour flavor.
They are great in sandwiches or chopped up in tuna
or egg salad. Properly stored in the refrigerator,
they will keep up to six months.*

Put everything (including cucumber slices) in a stainless
steel (or non-reactive) pot. Bring to a boil, stirring frequently
to dissolve the sugar. Reduce heat to low and simmer for
20 minutes. Store pickles in this liquid in the refrigerator.

Half-Sour Dill Pickles

*Leaving the pickles at room temperature for a day
gives them the "sour" flavor.*

1. Slice cucumbers into sixths, lengthwise, to yield long spears.

2. Put them in a stainless steel bowl. Cover with cold water. Pour
   water out into a big bowl, and measure. For every 2 cups of
   water, add 1 Tbs of salt. Stir until salt dissolves.

3. Pour salted water back over cucumber spears. Add crushed
   garlic, fresh dill, and black pepper. Stir to distribute all the
   seasoning.

4. Use a plate to weigh down the cucumbers so that they are
   completely submerged in the liquid.

5. Let sit for at least 24 hours at room temperature to ferment
   before storing in the refrigerator or canning (see page 32).

◆ ◆ ◆ ◆ ◆

— Bread and Butter Pickles —

4	small firm cucumbers, sliced into ½-inch wheels
4 c	water
¼ c	salt
1½ c	cider vinegar
1¼ c	sugar
1 Tbs	mustard seeds
1	celery stalk
¼ tsp	turmeric
⅛ tsp	ground cloves
⅛ tsp	ground ginger
	black pepper, freshly ground

—— Half-sour Dill Pickles ——

6	medium cucumbers
1 bunch	dill
10	fresh garlic cloves, crushed
	salt
	black pepper

Plum (or Peach) Preserves

♦ ♦ ♦ ♦ ♦

2 lb	ripe plums, halved and pitted
¼–½ c	sugar
½ c	water
1	(3-inch) cinnamon stick

──── Optional ────

1 inch	piece of ginger (optional)

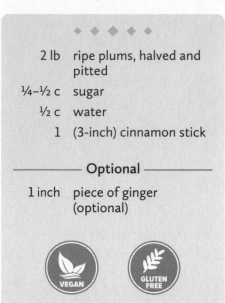

The lovely flavors of fresh peaches and plums are brief joys of deep summer. But many of those flavors can be captured, concentrated, and stored. Can or freeze these to enjoy in the depths of winter, atop toast, pancakes, waffles, or bagels with cream cheese. And remember summer.

1. Coarsely chop plums and stir together with sugar, water, cinnamon stick, and ginger (if using) in a 2-quart heavy saucepan. Simmer, uncovered, stirring occasionally (with a wooden spoon) until thickened and reduced to approximately 2½ cups, about 1 hour.

2. Discard cinnamon stick and ginger; and cool. Transfer to an airtight container and chill, covered.

Roasted Green Chili Salsa

*This is excellent as a dip, or with rice, beans,
eggs, chicken, mild fish, or pork.*

1. In an ovenproof skillet, mix green tomatoes (or husked
   tomatillos), 1 Tbs oil, garlic, and salt. Roast in a 400°F oven
   until soft and lightly browned. In a separate ovenproof dish,
   roast the chilies. This will allow you to adjust the spice level
   before committing the whole salsa to being too spicy. Let cool.

2. In a food processor, add the roasted green tomatoes/
   tomatillos and the desired quantity of roasted chilies, and
   process coarsely. You may also use a blender, but you may have
   to add some water or tomato juice to get the blending to start.

3. In a large skillet, over medium-high heat, add remaining oil.
   Add the onion, cumin, coriander, and optional corn and/or
   ripe tomatoes. Cook for 3 minutes, and then add the puréed
   green tomatoes and chilies. Simmer 1 minute, then let cool.
   Add cilantro and vinegar to taste.

4. Packed into a clean glass jar and lidded, this keeps only 5 to
   14 days in the refrigerator. The salsa can also be canned, but
   freezing in plastic is the easiest long-term storage. If canning
   (see page 32) or freezing, you may have to add more
   cilantro upon opening.

1–2 lb	green tomatoes or tomatillos
2 Tbs	olive or vegetable oil
4 cloves	garlic, coarsely chopped
1 tsp	salt
1–3	large mild green or red chilies (to taste)
1	onion, chopped
½ tsp	cumin
¼ tsp	coriander
2 Tbs	chopped fresh cilantro
1–3 Tbs	cider or red wine vinegar

——————— Optional ———————

½–1 c	fresh, sweet corn kernels, and/or ¼ cup chopped red tomatoes)

Smoked Tomatoes

♦ ♦ ♦ ♦ ♦

2 c   wood chips (hickory or apple is great, mesquite is okay) soaked in 4 cups of water or cheap white wine, for 1 hour

plenty of Roma or other plum tomatoes, cut in half.

Every summer, Julia smokes and cans 25 pounds of tomatoes to preserve through the winter. One or two tomatoes added to a sauce, stew or salad adds a nice meaty flavor. Puréed smoked tomatoes are a wonderful sauce for pastas or grilled meats.

1. Prepare a charcoal fire as you normally would on one side of the grill.

2. Drain the wood chips.

3. When the fire is on its last legs (there are still some red embers), get ready to move quickly: toss the wood chips on the fire. Put the grate on top, and place the tomatoes on the grate, ideally on the cool side of the grill and skin side down (should the skins burn, you can remove them; if the flesh burns, then cut it away). Cover the grill with the lid, open the vents only halfway. Let the tomatoes smoke for 30 minutes or longer.

4. Purée the tomatoes for a sauce for lamb or steak, or add them to your favorite recipe for a little zip. They can be stored in the freezer or canned for long-term preserving.

For a gas grill

Follow the directions as above, but put the drained wood chips in a disposable aluminum tray, and place it directly on top of the gas flame.

Tomatillo Salsa

This salsa can be tailored to your own tastes: reduce the chilies if you don't like that much heat, omit the sugar, cinnamon, and/or cloves if you prefer more simple sauces, or even return the purée to a stainless steel saucepan and simmer with chunks of firm tomato, green tomato, or bell peppers if you want textural contrasts.

1. Toss tomatillos, jalapeños, onion, and garlic with oil.

2. Roast in a 425°F oven until lightly browned and soft.

3. Purée in a food processor with remaining ingredients and approximately ½ cup of water.

4. Season to taste with salt.

1 lb	tomatillos, husked and washed
2–3	jalapeños
1	medium onion, roughly chopped
4 cloves	garlic, roughly chopped
1 Tbs	vegetable oil
¼ c	cilantro
⅛ tsp	cumin
½ tsp	cinnamon
⅛ tsp	cloves
½ tsp	sugar
	salt to taste

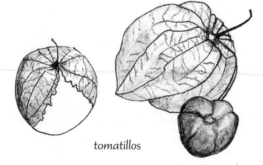

tomatillos

Agrodolce

◆ ◆ ◆ ◆ ◆

1	onion, minced
3 cloves	garlic, chopped
2 tsp	olive oil
2–3 Tbs	brown sugar
4 c	good beef or chicken stock
½ c	red wine
	pinch allspice
¼ tsp	ground black pepper
½ Tbs	finely chopped fresh thyme, oregano, and/or marjoram
	salt, red wine or balsamic vinegar, to taste

—————— Optional ——————

1-inch square of fresh
orange or tangerine zest

*An ancient Italian sweet and sour sauce.
Especially fitting for many vegetables, meat, and poultry;
not recommended for most seafood.*

1. In a stainless steel pot, sauté garlic and onion in the olive oil until just soft, about 3 minutes. Add brown sugar; once this bubbles, add stock, red wine, allspice, pepper, and zest, if using.

2. Let simmer until reduced in volume; approximately 1 cup should remain.

3. Add fresh herbs. Simmer 4 more minutes.

4. Add vinegar taste and approximately 1 Tbs salt to taste (if using canned broth, salt is likely not necessary). Traditionally served warm or hot; great as a dip for fried vegetables.

Reduced-Calorie Balsamic Vinaigrette

A typical vinaigrette tames the acidity of vinegar with plenty of oil. The roasted shallots offer the same effect of the oil, thus reducing the amount of fat for a well-balanced dressing.

1. Peel shallots. In a small ovenproof pan or dish, mix with ¼ cup olive oil. Cover with aluminum foil. Bake for 20–30 minutes or until soft, and nicely roasted.

2. In a blender, purée shallots, thyme, and vinegar together. Slowly drizzle in remaining olive oil. Add 1–2 Tbs of water if it seems too thick. Season to taste with salt, pepper, and sugar.

2	shallots or 1 onion
½ c	olive oil
1 Tbs	thyme
½ c	balsamic vinegar
½ tsp	salt
¼ tsp	pepper
½ tsp	sugar

Basic Stewed Rhubarb

◆ ◆ ◆ ◆ ◆

4 c   chopped rhubarb (be sure to remove and discard the leaves)

¾ c   sugar (more or less to taste)

½ c   water

This is the perfect base for sweet desserts or savory sauces. Adjust the sugar according to its use and your desired preference for sweetness.

1. In a heavy non-reactive pot (enamelware or stainless steel), combine rhubarb, sugar, and water.

2. Cover and simmer until very soft, stirring occasionally to dissolve sugar and stop from sticking to the bottom of the pan. Add more water if it becomes too dry.

Basil or Arugula Pesto

Pesto is a great way to use up vast quantities of basil or arugula, and freezes superbly. Arugula pesto, tossed with pasta and served with seared scallops, makes a great springtime dinner. Basil pesto brightens any summer meal.

1. Sauté the garlic in the ¼ cup olive oil until soft but not very brown. Immediately add salt, pepper, and wine and simmer until the wine volume has reduced by one half. Let cool.

2. Process all this in a Cuisinart until the garlic is fully puréed. Add the nuts and process until nearly smooth. Add the basil and plenty of olive or vegetable oil. Process further, until the basil is just barely smooth (no leaf pieces bigger than ⅛"), always adding more oil if the surface of the basil appears exposed to air. Add the cheese and process 15 seconds more. Taste for salt and pepper.

3. Place in Tupperware or a glass jar and immediately be sure that there is at least ¼-inch of oil floating over the basil.

4. The extra oil is intense and can be used for dressing salads. The surplus of oil in all stages keeps the basil from oxidizing to an unattractive black color.

5. Keeps 6 weeks in the refrigerator or 2 years in a freezer.

¼ c	olive oil
8 cloves	garlic, coarsely chopped
½ tsp	salt
¼ tsp	black pepper
¼ c	white wine
¼ c	almonds or pine nuts, toasted and then cooled
4 c	arugula or basil leaves
½ c	more olive oil or vegetable oil
¼ c	grated Romano cheese
	more salt and pepper to taste

VEGETARIAN   GLUTEN FREE

Beet Vinaigrette

◆ ◆ ◆ ◆ ◆

1   small beet, cooked until exceedingly tender

½ c   pomegranate juice

1   small shallot, peeled and coarsely chopped

¼ c   extra virgin olive oil

leaves from 1 spring of thyme

½   lime, juiced

salt and pepper to taste

This vinaigrette can be used for a salad or as a sauce for roast lamb or salmon. Sautéed portobellos served alongside would complement the vinaigrette, bringing out the sweet earthy flavors.

1. Peel and chop cooked beet. Put in a blender with the pomegranate juice and shallot.

2. Being careful about splatters, pour in olive oil. Add thyme and purée for 10 seconds more.

3. Season with lime juice, salt, and pepper.

Berry Vinaigrette

Extra strawberry, blackberry, or raspberry jam can be used to make a superb salad dressing.

1. In a heavy pan, carefully cook the jam until half-evaporated.

2. At the same time, sauté (in a separate pan and with the 2 Tbs oil) coarsely chopped onions and a garlic clove.

3. Blend all until smooth with the vinegar of your choice, ⅔ cup oil, and herb(s) and seasoning.

This dressing is suitable for all full-flavored salad greens and puts to shame the commercial raspberry dressings that are cloyingly sweet and weirdly thickened. A salad made with this dressing goes really well with a deep red wine like a syrah, petite syrah, shiraz, zinfandel, or cabernet franc or cabernet sauvignon. Quite appropriate when the winter winds howl.

1 c	high-quality berry jam
2 Tbs	oil
1	large onion, coarsely chopped
1 clove	garlic
1 c	sherry, rice, red wine, or balsamic vinegar
⅔ c	olive oil or oil blend
1 Tbs	fresh thyme or 2 Tbs fresh chervil
1 tsp	each salt and pepper

VEGAN   GLUTEN FREE

Blackberry-Sage Chutney

♦ ♦ ♦ ♦ ♦

2 Tbs	finely chopped bacon
¾ c	chopped shallots
4 Tbs	blackberry or raspberry liqueur
¾ c	blackberries
1 Tbs	chopped fresh sage
2 Tbs	brown sugar
4 Tbs	red wine vinegar

——— Spice Blend Rub ———

1 tsp	black pepper
⅛ tsp	ground star anise
1 tsp	salt
½ tsp	cumin
1 Tbs	chamomile (if you can't find it loose, just use chamomile from a tea bag)
1 tsp	orange zest, grated

Serve this chutney alongside grilled polenta, steak or tuna.

1. Add bacon to a dry skillet and cook over medium heat until lightly brown, about 5 minutes. Drain off excess fat, and add shallots. Cook for 5 minutes more or until shallots are soft.

2. Add liqueur and all remaining ingredients. Cook for 2–3 minutes, just to soften blackberries.

That Extra Loving Touch
While this chutney is great with plain grilled steak or tuna, you can enhance the meat by rubbing it before grilling with the spice blend.

Caramelized Cherry Tomato Sauce

This recipe was originally created for Restaurant Nora in Washington, DC.

1. Mix together tomatoes, sugar, orange zest, half the fresh herbs, salt, pepper, garlic, and onions.

2. Attentively broil, not bake, in an oven until the skins of the top tomatoes have just blackened. Remove from broiler, and stir in remaining chopped herbs, or fresh herbs of your choice (not dill). Add balsamic vinegar, and taste for any further need for salt or pepper.

3. The sauce is outstanding served atop otherwise mundane chicken, fish, shrimp, or vegetarian rice dishes. It freezes well, but taste after thawing for additional herb, vinegar, or salt needs.

3 pt (6 c)	ripe or over-ripe cherry tomatoes and/or cubed bigger heirloom tomatoes
2 Tbs	brown sugar
½–1 tsp	fresh orange zest
2 tsp	hardy herbs such as fresh thyme, rosemary and/or sage; *or*
3 Tbs	soft herbs such as basil, parsley and/or chervil, minced
1 Tbs	minced garlic
2 Tbs	minced onion
1 Tbs	balsamic vinegar
½ tsp	Kosher or sea salt
½ tsp	black pepper

Cilantro-Lemon Marinade

½ bunch	cilantro
2 Tbs	fresh lime or lemon juice
1½ tsp	chopped garlic
3 Tbs	chopped Egyptian onions or scallions
1 tsp	salt
1 tsp	black pepper
2 Tbs	olive oil
2 Tbs	white wine or beer
1 Tbs	soy sauce or tamari

For grilling rockfish/striped bass, grouper, shrimp, chicken or turkey breast, or, for vegetarians, zucchini, Chinese thick-stem mustard, tat soi or other heads of Asian mustards, boiled potatoes or firm tofu. Marinates enough to serve four.

1. Mix ingredients together in a bowl.

2. Marinate seafood or poultry for at least 2 hours. Vegetables should marinate for 45–60 minutes.

3. While the food is grilling, occasionally spoon some of the marinade onto it. Serve with freshly made salsa (mango, tomato, etc.) whenever possible.

Variation
Substitute a Provençal herb blend for the cilantro, 1 tsp red wine or balsamic vinegar for the citrus juice, and 3 Tbs red wine for the white wine or beer. Use same marinating times as above.

Dips for Raw Radishes

*For snacking, thinly sliced (but not peeled) radishes,
turnips, and rutabagas are excellent dipped into soy sauce,
hummus, or one of the following dips.*

Curry Dip

Mix thoroughly. Keeps 14 days in the refrigerator if covered.

Sesame–Soy Sauce Dip

Mix thoroughly. Keeps 14 days in the refrigerator if covered.

Spicy Salsa Dip

Mix thoroughly. Keeps 8 days in the refrigerator if covered.

◆ ◆ ◆ ◆ ◆

Curry Dip

¼ c	plain yogurt or sour cream
1 tsp	curry powder
1 Tbs	minced onion
¼ tsp	sea or kosher salt
1 Tbs	freshly squeezed lemon juice (optional)
	cayenne and/or cumin to taste

Sesame–Soy Sauce Dip

¼ c	mayonnaise
1 Tbs	sesame seeds, toasted and cooled
1–2 Tbs	tamari or soy sauce

Spicy Salsa Dip

¼ c	plain yogurt or sour cream
2 Tbs	good salsa
	Tabasco or hot sauce (see page 266) to taste
	salt to taste
1 Tbs	chopped cilantro

Dreamy Green Goddess

◆ ◆ ◆ ◆ ◆

¼ c fresh tarragon leaves

4 Tbs chopped garlic chives, scallions, and/or baby leeks

½ c arugula leaves or ¼ cup parsley leaves

½ c mayonnaise

2 Tbs sour cream

1 tsp capers

½ tsp white wine vinegar

salt and pepper to taste

This all-purpose sauce is excellent for rockfish/striped bass, grilled chicken, or grilled or blanched vegetables. It is also fabulous as a dipping sauce for fried okra, zucchini, or eggplant; or as a spread on burgers and sandwiches.

1. Combine herbs and greens in a food processor and process until coarsely chopped.

2. Add mayonnaise, sour cream, and capers. Pulse machine until the mixture in just smooth.

3. Season with vinegar, salt, and pepper.

Garlic Scape-Basil Pesto

*Scapes offer all the flavor of garlic without the
overpowering lingering taste of raw garlic.*

1. Put garlic scapes, basil, and lemon juice into a food processor
   with a steel blade, and process until scapes are very finely
   chopped. With food processor running, add oil through the
   feed tube and process 2–3 minutes.

2. Remove the lid, add half of Parmesan cheese and process
   2 minutes, then add the rest of cheese and salt and process
   2–3 minutes more.

3. Serve with pasta, as a spread for crostini, or as a condiment for
   grilled meat or fish.

¼ c	chopped garlic scapes
¼ c	fresh basil
4 Tbs	fresh lemon juice
½ c	olive oil
1 c	grated Parmesan cheese
	salt to taste

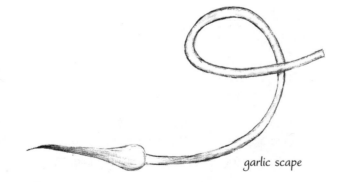

garlic scape

Great Caesar Salad Dressing

♦ ♦ ♦ ♦ ♦

2 Tbs	peanut or corn oil
½ bulb	(i.e., many cloves) garlic, chopped
½ c	white wine (not sweet)
1	really fresh egg, large or extra-large, at room temperature
1	additional cup peanut or corn oil
1 c	olive oil
1	2-ounce can flat anchovy fillets, packed in oil, or ½ tube anchovy paste (vegetarians could substitute ¼–⅓ cup capers)
¾ tsp	black pepper
1 tsp	kosher or sea salt
2 tsp	Worcestershire or soy sauce
	juice of 1½ large or 3 small lemons
¾ c	freshly grated Romano, Parmesan, or aged Asiago cheese
¼ tsp	Tabasco sauce
2 tsp	dried basil or ¼ cup chopped fresh basil or parsley

This recipe evolved to keep restaurant patrons really hungry for Caesar salads. Generally Caesar dressings are too bland, too fishy, too oily, too heavy, or too stale to enjoy. As a chef, Brett created this version and countless customers praised the bright, well-balanced flavors. Each ingredient listed is a necessary component.
Yield: approximately 3 cups dressing

1. Sauté the garlic in the 2 Tbs oil in a heavy skillet. When garlic edges just begin to brown, add the white wine. Simmer about 4 minutes more, until wine has reduced volume by about half. Let cool.

2. Meanwhile make a simple mayonnaise: crack the egg into a Cuisinart or food processor and run at high speed with the steel blade for 45 seconds, or until it is a pale yellow. Keep machine running, and very slowly pour in the two cups of oils in a thin stream (⅛"–¼" wide). It should take about 45 seconds for the oils to be all added to the egg. You've now made unseasoned super-fresh mayonnaise.

3. Add the anchovies (plus their packing juices) to the mayonnaise; pulse 15 seconds. Add all other ingredients except the cooked garlic and the lemon juice; pulse until all are incorporated (about 30 seconds). Then keep the machine running while slowly streaming in the lemon juice and garlic fluids, followed by a fast addition of the chopped garlic.

4. Store in a glass jar or plastic container (never in metal).

5. Dress salad greens, especially more robust varieties such as romaine, watercress, tat soi, or pac choi. A salad for four people would be about ½ pound of greens, 1½–2 Tbs dressing, about ½ cup seasoned croutons, and (optional) additional grated cheese, lemon wedges, 90-second soft-boiled eggs, or anchovy fillets.

This dressing keeps usually keeps 4 months refrigerated, and is best after the first day.

Green Tomato Jam

*As is, this is a great accompaniment to grilled fish.
Substitute apples and raisins for the green tomatoes for
a Major Grey chutney that's great with lamb.*

1. Put sugar and vinegar in sauce pan. Bring to a boil, stirring until sugar has dissolved. Add tomatoes and remaining ingredients.

2. Simmer over low heat until chutney is reduced and thick, stirring occasionally, about 1 hour.

2 c	brown sugar
2 c	cider vinegar
6 c	chopped green tomatoes
1	small onion, diced
1 inch	piece fresh ginger, peeled and chopped
6 cloves	garlic, chopped
1–2	jalapeños, chopped
1 tsp	cinnamon

Homemade Hoisin (aka Plum Sauce)

◆ ◆ ◆ ◆ ◆

2½ lb	very ripe plums, or 6 very ripe peaches, well washed
1	large onion, coarsely chopped
4 cloves	garlic, whole
2 inch	piece fresh ginger, coarsely chopped
¼ c	soy sauce or tamari
1 Tbs	dark sesame oil
dash	sriracha or other hot sauce (see page 266)
	cider vinegar to taste

This is a superb way to use up very ripe (and blemished) peaches or plums; underripe fruit will not work. As such, it should be made during August. It will keep for many months, especially frozen, so make plenty to use throughout the year.

1. Do not peel or pit fruit. Put in a deep non-reactive baking pan. Add onion, garlic, ginger, and sesame oil. Mix together.

2. Bake plums or peaches at 350°F for 40 minutes, or until fully soft.

3. Add soy sauce and bake an additional 5 minutes. Remove from the oven.

4. Once cool, remove pits. You may also remove the skins, but this is not necessary.

5. Purée in a blender or food processor until smooth. Starting with 1 Tbs increments of cider vinegar, add vinegar to achieve a brightly balanced flavor. Add sriracha to taste. Consider adding freshly minced ginger, as well.

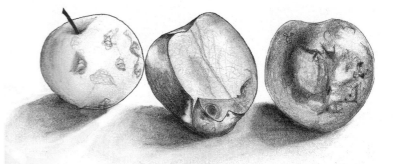

bruised and blemished plums are perfect for Hoisin sauce

Homemade Ketchup

*During peak tomato season, we suggest making a large batch
of ketchup to use throughout the year.*

1. Purée tomatoes with juice in a blender until smooth.

2. Heat a stainless steel saucepan (do not use aluminum because
   of the high acidity) over medium heat. Add oil, onions, and
   garlic. Cook for about 5 minutes, stirring occasionally, until
   soft and lightly gold. Add spices and cook for 1 minute just
   to help them release their fragrance. Add the remaining
   ingredients. Turn heat to low and simmer for 1 hour, stirring
   occasionally, until the ketchup is very thick. Let cool.

3. Purée ketchup in a blender until smooth.

   Will keep for several months in the refrigerator.

6 c	diced tomatoes
1 Tbs	plain oil
1	medium onion, chopped
4 cloves	garlic, chopped
2 Tbs	vegetable oil
¼ tsp	cinnamon
¼ tsp	allspice
½ cup	brown sugar
½ c	cider vinegar
1 tsp	salt
	pinch cayenne

Julia's Hot Sauce

♦ ♦ ♦ ♦ ♦

8	fresh red chilies (any variety available in the farmers market)
1	onion
1 bulb	garlic
½	red bell pepper
1	large tomato
1–2 Tbs	canola oil
¼–½ c	vinegar
	salt
	latex or nitrile gloves

Even if hot sauces aren't your passion, they are really convenient to have available to spoon little amounts into many dishes. If the chilies you chose are really hot or if you are particularly sensitive to capsaicin (the chemical that makes the hot in hot peppers), consider keeping the exhaust fan on or briefly leaving the house while the peppers are in the oven. Letting the vegetable mélange cool before blending also reduces capsaicin discomfort.

1. Put on gloves before handling chilies. Remove the stems from the chilies. Peel the onion and cut into chunks. Peel the garlic. Cut the red pepper into quarters. Remove the stem from the tomato and cut into large chunks.

2. Toss the vegetables in oil and roast in a 375°F oven for 20–30 minutes or until the chilies are blistered and lightly browned.

3. Put everything in the blender and add just enough vinegar so that you can purée into a smooth paste/sauce. Season with salt.

4. Refrigerate, can, or freeze.

Lemon–Garlic–Herb Dressing

This is especially good with cucumbers and summer squash.

Place all these in a blender and process until just smooth.
Refrigerate.

Also very nice with chilled boiled potatoes.

¼ c	freshly squeezed lemon juice (bottled juice won't work, so don't consider it)
¼ c	rice wine, cider or red wine vinegar
¼ c	extra virgin olive oil
¼ c	peanut or other neutral oil
1 c	loosely packed Provençal herb mix or Genoa basil
2 Tbs	minced sweet onion or fresh scallion
2 large	(or 5 small) cloves garlic, peeled
1 tsp	salt
½ tsp	black pepper
3 Tbs	Dijon or French country-style mustard

Marinade for Porcini and Puffball Mushrooms

½ c   red wine

2 Tbs   olive oil

2 tsp   chopped fresh herbs, such as Provençal blend, thyme, parsley, oregano, or any mix of the above

2 Tbs   minced onions

½ tsp   salt

¼   freshly ground black pepper

1 Tbs   balsamic or red wine vinegar

Porcinis and puffballs must be marinated before grilling. This all-purpose marinade works for shiitake and wild mushrooms, squash, eggplant, and bell peppers.

1. Combine all ingredients to make the marinade.

2. Toss ½-inch slices of porcini mushrooms, puffballs, summer squash, eggplant, or quarters of bell peppers with marinade. Let sit 20 minutes for mushrooms or 40 minutes for other vegetables.

3. Attentively grill or broil over high heat until slightly softened.

Marinara Sauce

4 cloves   garlic, chopped

1   onion, chopped

1 Tbs   olive oil

    salt and pepper to taste

4–6 c   stewed tomatoes (see page 237)

¼ c   red wine

¼ c   coarsely chopped fresh basil

———— Optional ————

½–1 lb   Italian sausage

1 c   bell peppers

1 c   coarsely chopped button mushrooms

Brett learned this from his mother, Roberta, who used marinara as a way to clean out the fridge of small amounts of leftover mushrooms, peppers, meat, or poultry. Be creative, but remember that the key concept of a marinara is tomato, garlic, onions, and herbs. Anything else you add is supporting cast.

1. Sauté the onions and garlic in the oil until just soft. If using any of the optional ingredients, add them now.

2. Continue cooking and add the tomatoes. Simmer about 20 more minutes, then taste for salt and pepper, add the red wine, and resume cooking for 5 minutes. Remove from heat.

3. Let cool slightly, and then stir in the basil or any other herbs of your choice.

Mint Mojo for Lamb or Salmon

Mint and lamb are a classic pairing.
This sauce is a fresh alternative to the classic mint jelly.
It also works well with salmon.

Purée mint, oil, sugar, and vinegar in a blender. Season to taste with salt and pepper. This will keep for several days in the refrigerator.

½ c	coarsely chopped fresh mint
½ c	extra virgin olive oil
⅓ c	red wine vinegar
1 Tbs	sugar
	salt and pepper

One Simple Salad Dressing

We prefer this dressing for tomatoes or mesclun.

1. Remove the tougher stems from the herbs, peel the garlic, and coarsely chop the onions or scallions.

2. Put everything in a blender and blend until smooth (less than 45 seconds). Pour into an old wine bottle, cork, and refrigerate.

Keeps practically forever. Shake well before using.

1 bunch	Provençal herb mix or basil
5 cloves	garlic
¼ c	chopped sweet onion or 2 scallions
1 c	balsamic, red wine, or rice vinegar
¾ c	peanut oil or corn oil
¾ c	extra virgin olive oil
2 tsp	salt or ⅓ cup soy sauce
1 tsp	ground black pepper

◆ ◆ ◆ ◆ ◆

½ c	fresh raspberries
½ c	extra virgin olive oil
3 Tbs	raspberry, sherry, or red wine vinegar
½ tsp	fresh thyme
1 tsp	sugar or honey
	salt and pepper to taste

Raspberry Vinaigrette

It is a true luxury to have satisfied one's need for fresh raspberries enough to blend more of that great fruit into a vinaigrette. But once you've enjoyed a real raspberry vinaigrette (not the chemically challenged super-sweet ones from a supermarket), you might choose to make this more often. Excellent with green salads, watercress, chilled cooked beets, parsnips, or leeks, or soft mild cheeses like chèvre or Gouda.

Combine ingredients in a blender. Purée until smooth. Adjust seasoning to taste with either more salt, sugar, oil, or vinegar. Will keep up to a month in the refrigerator.

1	red bell pepper
1	hot pepper
1	plum tomato
1	small onion or 2 shallots, quartered
4 cloves	garlic
¼ c	olive oil
¼ c	sliced almonds
1–2 Tbs	balsamic or red wine vinegar, to taste
	salt and pepper to taste

Romesco

Romesco is a versatile sauce for crudité, or served alongside beef, salmon, chicken, or polenta.

1. Seed peppers and cut into quarters. Cut tomato into quarters.

2. Put all ingredients, except vinegar, in a shallow pot. Roast in a 400°F oven until peppers begin to brown and almonds are toasted.

3. Pour off oil and reserve. Purée roasted veggies in a food processor. Drizzle in reserved oil. Adjust seasoning with vinegar, salt, and pepper.

Slow-Roasted Tomato Sauce

This is an easy recipe that tastes like a long-simmered sauce.

1. Toss tomatoes with shallots, garlic, thyme, and oil.

2. Roast the tomatoes in the oven for 30 minutes at 400°F or until tomatoes are tender and the garlic is lightly browned.

3. Purée the tomatoes, shallots, and garlic in a food processor. Adjust seasoning with balsamic vinegar, salt, and pepper.

10	plum tomatoes, cut in half, lengthwise
2	shallots or 1 onion, peeled and coarsely chopped
6 cloves	garlic, peeled and left whole
2–3	stalks fresh thyme
¼ c	olive oil
2–3 Tbs	balsamic vinegar
	salt and pepper to taste

Sublime Salad Dressing

Great with cucumbers, and also good for a lunch salad of greens, broccoli, chickpeas, and sunflower seeds. Also great with sliced ripe tomatillos, or slices of avocado and onion.

1. Toast sesame seeds in a skillet until golden brown; cool 5 minutes.

2. Put all ingredients in a blender; blend 30–60 seconds, until smooth. Taste; add salt and pepper as desired.

   Keeps indefinitely if refrigerated.

¼ c	sesame seeds
1 c	cider or rice vinegar
2 c	roasted (dark) sesame oil
½ c	peanut oil
½ c	soy sauce or tamari
2 Tbs	chopped ginger
4 cloves	garlic, chopped
½	onion, chopped
½ c	fresh mint
½ bunch	scallions
2 Tbs	honey
2 Tbs	white wine
1	medium egg

Tomato Coconut Sauce

◆ ◆ ◆ ◆ ◆

1 Tbs   plain oil

1–2   garlic scapes or cloves, chopped

1   jalapeño, chopped

3   large tomatoes, chopped

½ can   coconut milk

salt, pepper, and lime juice to taste

Serve this with a firm white fish.
Before cooking the fish, season it with salt, fresh oregano,
and a big squeeze of fresh lime juice.

1. In a saucepan, over medium heat, add oil, then garlic and jalapeño. Cook for 2–3 minutes or until aromatic and lightly browned.

2. Add the tomatoes and coconut milk. Bring to a boil, reduce to a simmer, and continue cooking for just 1 minute. Adjust seasoning with salt, pepper, and lime juice.

Desserts and
Sweet Treats

◆ ◆ ◆ ◆ ◆

8	apples, preferably Gala or Granny Smith
½ stick	butter
1 c	sugar
½	lemon, juiced
	pie dough
	crème anglaise (or whipped cream or vanilla ice cream)

Apple Tarte Tatin

Tarte tatin is a traditional French dessert that is cooked on the stove until the apples caramelize. This recipe simplifies the process without sacrificing the flavor.

1. Peel and core apples. Cut into ⅛-inch slices. Line a 9-inch pie dish with apples. Squeeze lemon juice over apples and put pats of butter on top.

2. Add sugar to a pan with ¼ cup water. Bring to a boil, stirring until sugar dissolves. Continue cooking without stirring until the sugar turns a deep amber and caramelizes. Pour sugar over apples.

3. Drape pie dough over apples. Bake at 350°F until pie top is golden brown. Flip tart over onto a platter. Serve with crème anglaise.

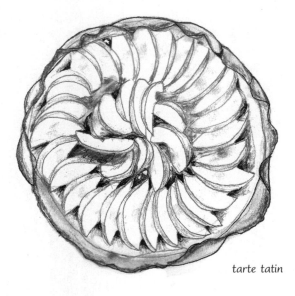

tarte tatin

Pie Dough

1. In a large bowl, combine flour, salt, and sugar.

2. Cut butter into 1 Tbs sized pieces, and add to the flour. With your fingers or a fork, combine the flour and the butter until the chunks are the size of peas.

3. Add just enough water to form dough. Do not over mix. Form into a ball that can stick together with only a few crumbs.

4. Let dough rest for 30 minutes in the refrigerator.

5. Roll dough ball out to ⅛-inch thickness. Chill again until ready to bake the apples.

Crème Anglaise

1. In a small pot, heat the half -n- half with vanilla bean (if using) just until small bubbles form around the side of the pot.

2. In a bowl, whisk eggs and sugar. Slowly pour hot half -n-half into eggs, whisking constantly and vigorously. Return mixture to heat and continue cooking over low heat until the custard thickens. This curdles easily so it is important to stir constantly and be attentive. Immediately remove from heat. If using vanilla extract, stir in.

♦ ♦ ♦ ♦ ♦

Pie Dough

2 c	flour
½ tsp	salt
1½ tsp	sugar
1½	sticks butter, very cold
¼ c	ice water, approximately

Crème Anglaise

1 c	half and half
½	vanilla bean split or 1 tsp vanilla extract
3	egg yolks
¼ c	sugar

◆ ◆ ◆ ◆ ◆

½ c	sugar
¼ c	balsamic vinegar
2 qt	strawberries
½ c	heavy cream, whipped to stiff peaks

───────── Biscuits ─────────

½ tsp	yeast
⅔ c	milk
1¾ c	all-purpose flour
1 tsp	salt
1 Tbs	sugar
2 tsp	baking powder
4 Tbs	cold butter

Balsamic-Glazed Strawberry Shortcake

The balsamic sauce for the berries provides a bright flavor contrast to the rich shortcakes and cream. (And if you reverse the ratio—2 parts vinegar to 1 part sugar, and add garlic—you'll have a wonderful sauce for pork or scallops.)

1. Put sugar in a sauce pan. Add ¼ cup water. Over high heat, stir sugar to dissolve. Continue cooking without stirring for about 7 minutes or until sugar turns amber brown.

2. Immediately add the balsamic vinegar (the sugar will harden). Continue cooking, stirring occasionally to help redissolve the sugar, until liquid is reduced by half. Remove from heat.

3. Just before serving, add strawberries. Serve biscuits with strawberries and cream.

Biscuits

1. Dissolve the yeast in milk.

2. Combine dry ingredients. With a knife or fingers, cut the butter into dry mix. Mix in milk.

3. Roll out to ¼-inch thickness. Cut into desired shapes, e.g., 2-inch rounds.

4. Bake for 12 minutes at 450°F.

Blueberry Bread Pudding

*Bread pudding is one of Julia's favorite desserts.
You can serve it with vanilla ice cream or
crème anglaise (see recipe on page 275).*

1. In a large saucepan, combine milk, vanilla, mint, lemon zest, and salt. Bring to a low simmer. Remove from heat and let stand for 15 minutes. Remove and discard vanilla bean (if using), mint, and zest.

2. Meanwhile, in a large bowl, whisk together eggs and sugars. Whisk in the milk. Stir in remaining ingredients.

3. Grease a 9-inch × 13-inch Pyrex dish with butter. Pour in bread pudding batter. Bake at 350°F for 45 minutes.

4. Let cool for 10 minutes before serving. Garnish with powdered sugar, mint, and blueberries.

◆ ◆ ◆ ◆ ◆

3 c	whole milk
½	vanilla bean, split, or 1 tsp vanilla
5	mint leaves
3	eggs
	zest from one lemon
⅓ c	brown sugar
⅓ c	white sugar
3 c	stale bread, cut into cubes
1 tsp	cinnamon
1 c	fresh blueberries
¼ tsp	salt
	butter
	powdered sugar, blueberry, and mint for garnish

Blueberry Crisp

This recipe works with most fruit: apples, peaches, plums, or blackberries.

1. Combine filling ingredients, and spoon into an 8-inch square casserole dish.

2. Combine topping ingredients and spoon over filling.

3. Bake for 45 minutes at 375°F, or until top is brown.

♦ ♦ ♦ ♦ ♦

——— Filling ———

½ c	brown sugar
3 Tbs	all-purpose flour
1 tsp	grated lemon zest
5 c	blueberries
½ tsp	cinnamon

——— Topping ———

⅔ c	rolled oats
⅓ c	brown sugar
¼ c	whole wheat flour
1 tsp	cinnamon
3 Tbs	melted butter

Blue Moon Carrot Cake

This recipe is adapted from the Blue Moon Restaurant in Montgomery, Alabama. It's by far the easiest and best-tasting carrot cake we've come across.

1. Mix oil and sugar and beat well. Add eggs and mix well to combine.

2. Sift together dry ingredients twice and then add pecans (or raisins). Combine with egg mixture.

3. Grease and flour two 9-inch cake pans. Fill pans and bake at 350°F for about 20 minutes. Cool.

4. Remove from pans and frost with icing.

Icing
Mix everything together with a wooden spoon or rubber spatula until well-combined. Spread evenly on cooled cake with a pastry knife or rubber spatula.

◆ ◆ ◆ ◆ ◆

1½ c	neutral oil such as canola or grapeseed
2 c	sugar
4	eggs, well-beaten
2 c	flour
½ tsp	salt
2 tsp	cinnamon
2 tsp	baking soda
2 tsp	baking powder
1 c	chopped pecans (or raisins or combination of the two)
3 c	peeled and grated carrots

--- Icing ---

1	8-ounce package cream cheese, room temperature
1 stick	(4 ounces) butter, room temperature
1	one-pound box confectioners' sugar
1 tsp	vanilla

Fruit Salad

◆ ◆ ◆ ◆ ◆

4 c	mixed fruit: seeded watermelon, cantaloupe, honeydew, apples, peaches, pears, (you name it) cut into bite-sized pieces
1 c	mixed berries, or more cut fruit.
1	lime, juiced
1	orange, juiced
1	lemon, juiced
2–4 Tbs	sugar, or 1 Tbs honey (depending on sweetness of fruit and your taste)
2 Tbs	amber or dark rum, or triple sec

VEGAN   GLUTEN FREE

This salad is designed to clean out your refrigerator of a lot of fruit. Almost any ripe fruit can be used. Berries add an especially nice color contrast. Increase lemon juice, sugar, and rum if a large portion of the fruit is underripe. If all of the fruit is very ripe, then omit the sugar. The alcohol helps ripen the underripe fruit.

Mix everything together. Chill well. Keeps refrigerated for 3–5 days.

Ginger Poached Peaches

Poached fruit is a simple, healthy dessert.
It keeps in the refrigerator for up to two weeks.

1. Combine water, sugar, lemon, spices, and ginger in a pot. Bring to a boil.

2. Meanwhile, slice peaches in half.

3. Add peaches, and turn heat down to a simmer. After 2 minutes, remove skin from peaches. Cook for 15 minutes more, or until tender. Let peaches sit in poaching liquid until ready to serve.

4. Whip cream to stiff peaks.

5. Serve peaches with cream and a drizzle of chocolate.

That Extra Loving Touch
Make a crisp topping: Combine 1 cup oats, ¼ cup flour, 3 Tbs sugar, ½ tsp vanilla, ½ tsp cinnamon, and ½ cup melted butter. Spread out on a baking pan and bake at 375°F for 15 minutes or until crispy. Sprinkle on top of poached peaches just before serving and then finish with the whipped cream and chocolate.

1 qt	water
2 c	sugar
½	lemon
1 tsp	vanilla extract or one vanilla bean, split
6	whole cloves
1	cinnamon stick
4	slices ginger
8	peaches or nectarines
½ c	heavy cream
¼ lb	chocolate, melted

Minted Berries

Serve this over chocolate mousse or ice cream.

1. Wash and hull the strawberries. Cut into quarters.

2. Cut the mint into thin strips.

3. Toss the strawberries with mint, sugar, and vanilla. Let sit for 30 minutes (or as long as overnight) to let the flavors blend.

1 pt	(¾ lb) strawberries, raspberries, or combination
5	large mint leaves
1– 2 Tbs	sugar (depending on the sweetness of the berries and your taste)
1 tsp	vanilla or ¼ vanilla bean

Nectarine Plum Crisp

Fruit crisp is one of those desserts that can be made with just about any fruit. Use whatever you have available: peaches, apples, pears, berries, etc.

1. Combine filling ingredients and spoon into a 9-inch square casserole dish.

2. Combine topping ingredients and spoon over filling.

3. Bake for 45 minutes at 375°F, or until topping is brown.

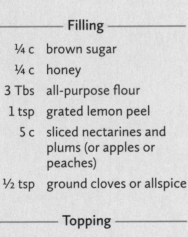

--------- **Filling** ---------

¼ c	brown sugar
¼ c	honey
3 Tbs	all-purpose flour
1 tsp	grated lemon peel
5 c	sliced nectarines and plums (or apples or peaches)
½ tsp	ground cloves or allspice

--------- **Topping** ---------

⅔ c	rolled oats
⅓ c	brown sugar
¼ c	flour
	pinch nutmeg
3 Tbs	melted butter

Peach Pie

You may substitute store-bought pie crust for this recipe. This recipe also works well with blueberries or strawberry/rhubarb.

1. Make pie dough: Cut butter into 1 Tbs sized pieces. Put in a large bowl with the flour, salt and sugar. With your fingers, combine the flour and the butter until the chunks are the size of peas. Add just enough water to form dough. Do not overmix. Form into a ball that can stick together with only a few crumbs.

2. Let dough rest for 30 minutes in the refrigerator.

3. Roll dough out to ⅛-inch thickness. Line a 9-inch pie pan with dough.

4. Make the filling: in a large bowl, mix all filling ingredients together.

5. Preheat the oven to 375°F.

6. Spoon filling into prepared pie dough.

7. Place pie on a cookie sheet lined with foil or parchment paper (this will catch any drippings and keep them from burning on the bottom of the oven).

8. Bake pie for 40 minutes. Let pie cool for 15 minutes before serving.

◆ ◆ ◆ ◆ ◆

Pie Crust

1½	sticks butter, very cold
2 c	flour
½ tsp	salt
1½ tsp	sugar
¼ c	ice water, approximately

Filling

¼ c	brown sugar
¼ c	white sugar
6 c	peach slices (peel peaches before slicing)
1 Tbs	cornstarch
1 Tbs	lemon juice
1 tsp	vanilla
	pinch salt

VEGETARIAN

Pumpkin Crème Brulée

Tired of dense traditional pumpkin pies?
This dessert highlights pumpkin's flavors but takes
them in a lighter direction. You can also substitute
cooked puréed butternut squash or sweet potato.
Yield: 8 custard ramekins

4	egg yolks
2	eggs
1 c	pumpkin purée (see page 20)
3 oz	brown or white sugar
1 pt	heavy cream
¼ tsp	salt
1	vanilla bean, split, or 2 tsp vanilla extract
	pinch of allspice
8	scant Tbs white sugar

1. Mix, do not whip, the egg yolks, eggs, pumpkin, and brown sugar.

2. Heat cream with vanilla bean to scalding point (bubbles will form on edges). Gradually pour it into egg mixture, while whisking vigorously.

3. Add salt. Scrape seeds out of vanilla bean and add back to custard.

4. Pour mix into 6-ounce ramekins. Put ramekins in a water bath (2-inch high, 9-inch × 13-inch pan with 1-inch of hot water in it). Cover with foil.

5. Bake at 325°F for about 25 minutes, or until just set. (It's not a bad idea to check them after 20 minutes.) When shaking the brulées, they should look slightly loose in the center.

6. Cool.

7. Sprinkle about 1 Tbs of white sugar on top of each custard. Blowtorch the top until sugar is amber brown. Alternatively, place custards under the broiler and attentively watch until golden brown.

Rhubarb Cake

*This recipe also works well with blueberries
or strawberry/rhubarb.*

1. Preheat the oven to 350°F. Coat a 9-inch × 13-inch pan with plain oil. Use a paper towel to wipe out the excess. Add 1 Tbs of flour and shake around the pan to get into all the corners. Discard any flour.

2. In a mixing bowl, combine the flour, baking soda, salt, and cinnamon. Whisk together to combine, remove lumps, and aerate.

3. With an electric mixer, cream butter and sugar on medium speed until light and fluffy. Add the egg and combine well. Add the buttermilk and combine well. Add the dry ingredients and mix until just combined.

4. Add the rhubarb and fold in with a rubber spatula. Transfer to the baking pan.

5. Bake for 30–35 minutes until the cake begins to pull away from the pan's edges and a knife inserted in the center comes out clean.

   Let cool until ready to serve.

½ c	(1 stick) salted butter, room temperature
1 c	white sugar
¾ c	brown sugar
2 c	all-purpose flour
1 tsp	baking soda
¼ tsp	salt
2 tsp	cinnamon (optional)
1	large egg
1 tsp	vanilla
1 c	low-fat buttermilk (or 1 cup milk mixed with 1 Tbs lemon juice)
3 c	rhubarb, cut in half-inch pieces
	plain oil and flour for greasing the pan

Summer Pudding

◆ ◆ ◆ ◆ ◆

6 c	assorted berries
¾ c	water
¾ c	sugar
1½ Tbs	fresh lemon juice
16–20	¼-inch-thick firm white bread slices
¾ c	chilled whipping cream

Essentially an uncooked bread pudding, laden with berries. You can use any berries you like—depending on what's available at your farmers market or in your CSA share. Strawberries, blueberries, and raspberries all work well in any combination.

1. Combine berries, water, sugar, and lemon juice in heavy large saucepan. Bring to simmer, and cook for 5 minutes, stirring occasionally. Strain berry mixture, reserving juices.

2. Line a 2-quart casserole dish with plastic, overlapping the sides. Trim crusts off bread, making both squares and rounds (to better line the dish). Dip each slice into fruit juices. Place in the bottom of the dish. Dip 5 bread slices, 1 at a time, into juices; place around sides of dish. Spoon ½ cup berries into the dish. Dip 3 more bread slices into juices. Place atop berries. Repeat process with bread rounds and squares, juices and berries to create another layer. Cover.

3. Place pudding on a rimmed baking sheet (to catch juices). Top with another baking sheet. Place heavy object on sheet to press down the pudding and help it set. Chill overnight.

4. Combine remaining berries and juices in bowl; cover and chill.

5. Beat whipping cream to soft peaks. Season if desired with 1 Tbs powdered sugar and ½ tsp vanilla. Unwrap pudding. Turn out onto a serving platter; remove plastic. Serve with berry-juice mixture, with whipped cream on top.

Sweet Potato-Chocolate Cake

Incredibly moist, excellent shelf life, freezes superbly.
A great way to add a healthy component to your dessert course.
Serve with whipped cream.

1. In a Kitchen Aid, with the paddle attachment, cream oil and sugar. Add beaten eggs and vanilla.

2. Sift dry ingredients and add all at once to the mixture. Continue mixing until just combined; the mixture will be somewhat crumbly. Add sweet potatoes, nuts, and chocolate, and combine with a rubber spatula. Do not mix too long.

3. Grease and flour a 9 × 13 inch pan, pour in batter, and bake at 350°F for 45–60 minutes.

½ c	Crisco oil (or neutral oil)
1½ c	sugar
2	eggs, beaten
4 c	peeled and diced sweet potatoes, cooked
2 tsp	vanilla
2 tsp	cinnamon
1 tsp	salt
2 tsp	baking soda
2 c	all-purpose flour
1 c	chopped white chocolate

Optional

1 c	walnuts, chopped

Sweet Potato Ice Cream

◆ ◆ ◆ ◆ ◆

1 lb	peeled sweet potatoes
	1 cup + 2 Tbs whole milk
⅔ c	light brown sugar
¼ tsp	vanilla extract
	pinch of salt
	a few drops of fresh lemon juice
	ice cream machine
	maple-glazed pecans

—— **Maple-Glazed Pecans** ——

½ lb	unsalted pecans
2 Tbs	unsalted butter, melted
2 Tbs	pure maple syrup
½ Tbs	light brown sugar

1. Dice sweet potatoes into 1-inch cubes. Put in a pot and cover with water; boil for 20 minutes or until tender. Drain and cool.

2. Put sweet potatoes, milk, sugar, vanilla, salt, and lemon juice in a blender. Purée until smooth. For extra-silky ice cream, you can push the mixture through a strainer, but it's not necessary.

3. Freeze the puréed mixture in your ice cream machine according to the manufacturer's instructions.

4. About 5 minutes before the ice cream is finished churning, add maple-glazed pecans.

Maple-Glazed Pecans

1. Preheat the oven to 375°F. Place all ingredients in a large bowl and toss to combine. Spread nut mixture in a single layer on a baking sheet lined with parchment paper or silpat.

2. Bake, stirring frequently, until browned, about 12–15 minutes; let cool. Pecans can be stored at room temperature in an airtight container up to one week.

Sweet Potato Pie

This recipe is adapted from that classic American kitchen aid,
The Joy of Cooking by Irma Rombauer and Marion Becker,
and we urge any of you that lack a copy to get one.
Countless years of working in restaurant kitchens have left us
still extremely appreciative of this simple but always useful text.

1. Bake a pie shell, homemade or store-bought, at 375°F until barely tan or brown.

2. Combine remaining ingredients with an electric mixer or by hand with a whisk. Pour into the pie shell and bake in a 325°F to 340°F oven until it sets, about 50 minutes. A slight shake should cause minimal waves in the filling. Let cool and serve.

Variation: An even lighter, more frothy pie can be had by separating the eggs into yolks and whites, whipping the yolks into all else, and whipping the whites separately to the soft-peak stage. Then carefully fold the whites carefully into the rest of the filling and bake as above.

1	9-inch pie shell
1½ c	cooked sweet potato, skinned and mashed
1½ c	heavy cream or canned evaporated milk
½ c	brown sugar
¼ c	white sugar
½ tsp	salt (omit if salt was added to sweet potatoes before baking)
1 tsp	cinnamon
½ tsp	dried ginger
⅛ tsp	ground cloves
4	slightly beaten eggs

Drinks

Bloody Mary

6 oz	stewed tomato juice, chilled
¼ tsp	salt
¼ tsp	black pepper or dash of Tabasco
1 stalk	fresh celery, cut into 8-inch x ½-inch strips (or ¼ tsp celery seed)
1½ oz	gin, vodka, or whiskey
	ice cubes
2 leaves	fresh basil, lemon or Genoa

*See Basic Stewed Tomato recipe (see page 237);
the juice that is strained out of the stewed tomatoes makes this
an amazing beverage. Makes one drink, though the recipe
easily scales up if serving a crowd.*

Assemble cocktail: put ice in a glass. Add everything else and stir with the celery stalk.

One of the healthiest cocktails imaginable.

Peach Sangria

1½ lb	peaches, peeled (optional) and sliced
⅔ c	sugar
2 c	apple juice
1 bottle	dry white wine
3 Tbs	Curaçao or other orange-flavored liqueur

——— Optional ———

2 c	soda water

*On hot summer days, we love Peach Sangria. It's light and
refreshing. And because it's diluted with juice and soda, it makes
for easy quaffing with minimal impairment (especially important
when drinking in the sun).*

1. Combine fruit, sugar, and apple juice in a pitcher. Stir to dissolve sugar and let sit for 1 hour.

2. Add wine and liqueur. Refrigerate.

3. Add soda water just before serving. Serve over ice.

peach sangria

Watermelon Purée

Good watermelon is not just for eating as a cut fruit. It is also excellent (after seeding) processed in a blender to make a purée for daiquiris, for homemade popsicles, or as the base for a sorbet. The purée freezes really well to enjoy in winter, when great watermelons are just a dream. Just pour it into a clean Tupperware container, freeze fully, and then press 2 layers of plastic wrap over the exposed purée before tightly lidding.

1. Take rind off the watermelon. Remove any seeds. Don't worry about the white low-mass seeds.

2. Cut flesh into chunks that will fit into your blender.

3. Blend until just smooth.

   For sorbet: use 3 cups of purée. Add 3 Tbs corn syrup or no sugar at all, the juice of 1 lime, and (optionally) 1 Tbs vodka. Put through an ice cream machine; refreeze if necessary. Superbly healthy and refreshing!

   Mixed drinks: not so healthy but delicious nonetheless. Blend 4 ice cubes and 1 cup purée with lime juice, pineapple juice, and a shot of rum or tequila. Serve over ice. For a lighter cocktail, mix 2 parts chilled Prosecco to 1 part chilled watermelon purée; serve in a champagne flute.

   Freeze pops: Pour purée and nothing else into paper cups, leaving ½-inch of space at the top of each cup. Place the cups in a baking dish, cover tightly with a layer of plastic wrap, then poke a small hole in the plastic right over the center of each cup. Into each hole put a wooden popsicle stick (available at craft stores). The plastic wrap holds these sticks straight up. Freeze at least 24 hours. To serve, peel away the paper cup. Much healthier for kids and adults than factory popsicles.

1   large watermelon

Recipe Index by Ingredients

Recipe Index by Course

About the Authors

Julia Shanks—chef and serial entrepreneur—developed a passion for cooking when she was 12 years old, cooking her way through the Time-Life Cookbooks. As a chef, she worked in restaurants around the country including Restaurant Nora in Washington DC and Chez Henri in Cambridge, developing a taste for fresh, local, and seasonal foods.

Julia received her professional training as a chef at the California Culinary Academy in San Francisco. She also earned her BA from Hampshire College and MBA from Babson College.

Today, Julia consults with restaurants, farms, and food producers, helping them maximize profits and streamline revenues. She lectures on sustainable food systems and is the regional leader of Slow Money Boston.

In her tiny urban garden in Cambridge, MA, she harvests vegetables seven months out of the year.

Brett Grohsgal has been the chef in nine establishments and cooked in seven others, from New England to Louisiana to California and at sea, and over a twenty-year period. Brett earned a bachelor's degree in botany

from Berkeley and a master's in soil science from North Carolina State University. As Brett's passion for cooking great foods evolved, he began to grow his own produce, and in 1996 he and his wife, Dr. Christine Bergmark, bought 100 acres of prime land in Lexington Park, Maryland.

Brett manages Even' Star Organic Farm for great foods, reliable harvests, and for respectful environmental stewardship. Brett and his treasured crew harvest crops year-round for restaurants, grocery stores, universities, and farmers markets. The driving force of the farm since 2004 has been its CSA, which serves 200 families in the winter months and 350 families in the summer. Even' Star remains committed to the ideal that life is too short, and farm life too arduous to ever grow or eat boring foods.

The Farmer's Market Kitchen is their first book and has received critical praise from the *Boston Globe*, the *Boston Herald* and *Taste of the Seacoast*. It was cited as a reference in Michelle Obama's book *American Grown*.

If you have enjoyed *The Farmers Market Cookbook*, you might also enjoy other

BOOKS TO BUILD A NEW SOCIETY

Our books provide positive solutions for people who
want to make a difference. We specialize in:

**Climate Change ◆ Conscious Community
Conservation & Ecology ◆ Cultural Critique
Education & Parenting ◆ Energy ◆ Food & Gardening
Health & Wellness ◆ Modern Homesteading & Farming
New Economies ◆ Progressive Leadership ◆ Resilience
Social Responsibility ◆ Sustainable Building & Design**

New Society Publishers
ENVIRONMENTAL BENEFITS STATEMENT

New Society Publishers has chosen to produce this book on recycled paper made
with 100% post consumer waste, processed chlorine free, and old growth free.

For every 5,000 books printed, New Society saves the following resources:[1]

44	Trees
3,976	Pounds of Solid Waste
4,375	Gallons of Water
5,706	Kilowatt Hours of Electricity
7,228	Pounds of Greenhouse Gases
31	Pounds of HAPs, VOCs, and AOX Combined
11	Cubic Yards of Landfill Space

[1]Environmental benefits are calculated based on research done by the Environmental Defense Fund and
other members of the Paper Task Force who study the environmental impacts of the paper industry.

For a full list of NSP's titles, please call 1-800-567-6772 or check out our web site at:

www.newsociety.com